Terms and Truth

Terms and Truth

Reference Direct and Anaphoric

Alan Berger

A Bradford Book

The MIT Press
Cambridge, Massachusetts
London, England

This book was set in Sabon by Graphic Composition, Inc., Athens, Georgia, and printed in the United States of America.

Library of Congress Cataloging-in-Publication Data

Berger, Alan.
    Terms and truth : reference direct and anaphoric / Alan Berger.
        p. cm.
    Includes bibliographical references and index.
    ISBN 0-262-02519-1 (alk. paper)
    1. Reference (Philosophy) 2. Anaphora (Linguistics) 3. Language and languages—Philosophy. I. Title.

B105.R25 B47 2002
121'.68—dc21

                                                                    2002023058

To Natalie, to my mother, and to the memory of my father

Contents

Preface

A central problem in the philosophy of language is to explain how terms refer. According to the traditional descriptivist view of Gottlob Frege and Bertrand Russell, the answer to this problem is clear for ordinary proper names and general terms. A name is an abbreviated definite description, and thus the referent of a name is the object that satisfies the description associated with the name. The associated description is the "meaning," or what Frege called the "sense," of the name or general term.

During the past thirty years or more, certain philosophers, notably Saul Kripke and Hilary Putnam, have raised objections to the descriptivist view. In particular, they have rejected the notion that proper names and certain general terms have Fregean senses that alone determine their reference. Instead, they advance a "new theory of direct reference" (of at least thirty years) according to which the reference of these terms are determined directly without the mediation of a Fregean sense. For them, the reference of such a term is passed on from speaker to speaker, along a causal chain (of speakers' intentions to corefer) initiated when a name was first bestowed on the object that is its referent.

This book takes the new theory of reference as a point of departure and further develops it. One central notion that I develop and apply to other philosophical problems throughout most of the book is my semantics for anaphora. Expressions the reference of which in a particular use is determined by *prior reference,* that is, by certain semantical information contained in prior (or sometimes, later) sentences in a given discourse are called *anaphoric expressions.* It is my contention that many uses of designating expressions—many more, indeed, than is commonly held—are anaphoric. Thus in my view, the study of anaphoric links within a linguistic community and the semantics for sentences containing anaphoric expressions is crucial in the theory of reference.

The book is divided into three parts. Part I begins by introducing an important distinction between two styles of rigid designation. The first style of rigid designation involves the epistemic relation of *focusing*. The second involves the semantic relation of *satisfying* a given condition and belongs to my theory of anaphora. With the aid of these styles of rigid designation, in chapter 2 I develop a theory of reference *transmission* and reference *change* for rigid designator terms. This theory seeks to preserve the historical-chain view of reference determination without, however, requiring that rigid designator terms must in all cases refer to what they referred to at the initial baptismal step. I use this theory to examine whether the term 'mass' has a different reference in Newtonian physics and in relativistic physics.

In chapter 3, I show that the semantics due to Kaplan regarding directly referential terms cannot capture anaphoric reference and our second style of rigid designation. The notion of the role of an anaphoric chain is missing. In connection with my discussion of Kaplan, I develop a new puzzle concerning identity statements and point out how the distinction between the two styles of rigid designation sheds light on this puzzle.

In part II, I address the problem of specifying the truth conditions and the basis for making belief reports (and more generally reports of an agent's propositional attitude), especially in cases where a vacuous name occurs within the belief context.

In his paper "A Puzzle About Belief," Kripke has introduced customarily accepted principles of belief attribution. The de dicto reading of a belief report, generally taken to be a relation between an agent and a proposition denoted by 'that-P', is supposed to express the *way* the agent thinks of or represents the content of the reported belief. The report supposedly captures the "point of view" of the agent. Thus any principle of de dicto belief attribution must capture the agent's point of view or perspective. Kripke's principles, by connecting an agent's verbal behavior with a belief ascription, appear to capture this point of view. Although I accept these principles as capturing central cases of belief attribution, I question the correctness of requiring them for all cases. The first problem, then, is describing under what conditions it is appropriate to make belief attributions for which Kripke's principles fail, and, second, explaining in what sense such belief reports for which these principles fail still capture an agent's perspective or point of view. These problems are addressed in chapter 4 and further discussed in chapters 5 and 6.

In cases in which a vacuous name occurs within the belief context, namely, 'that-P' contains a vacuous proper name, what, if anything, can this proposition be? Thus one question is what, if anything, is the object of belief expressed in belief reports of the form 'A believes that P', where P contains a nondenoting proper name or pronoun that fails to refer; another is under what conditions is it appropriate to make such a belief report. In chapter 5, I present a solution to these problems that is based upon my notion of anaphoric background conditions.

Chapter 6 confronts directly the problem of explaining an agent's perspective in a way that captures the agent's view of the world, and explicates what it means for an agent to have rational and semantic commitments. In order to explicate the notion of an agent's perspective, I further develop Hilary Putnam's view of members of a linguistic community appealing to linguistic experts in certain domains and apply this view to the notion of a rational agent. I then apply these notions to the philosophical problem of intentional identity statements. This problem arises when a pronoun occurring in a sentence within an intentional context is anaphoric upon an expression within a different intentional context. We generally know when different people intend to refer to one and the same object, even though we may not be able to identify that object or even to know whether the intended reference succeeds. We may, for example, understand two astronomers who speak of the planet Vulcan's being near the sun, without ourselves agreeing that Vulcan exists. Finally, for sentences involving a purported reference to the *same nonexistent* entity, I offer conditions under which we may correctly use these sentences, which do not require that such an entity exist. The chapter ends with my treatment of true singular negative existential statements, again based on the notions developed earlier in the chapter.

Part III is devoted to both philosophic and linguistic literature, primarily regarding anaphorically used pronouns. I argue in chapter 7, contrary to purported examples, that pronouns (as a type) are, indeed, rigid designators, for they may be represented as a variable relative to an assignment. Further, I argue that *occurrences* of anaphoric pronouns may be analyzed as bound variables, even when their anaphoric antecedents are expressions contained in different sentences than these pronouns. I also discuss and criticize several analyses of such pronouns, including those due to Geach, Evans, Neale, Kamp, Heim, and Kratzer. In the cases of Kamp and Heim, I discuss Discourse Representation Theory, a theory that accounts for anaphorically used pronouns the anaphoric antecedents of which are in prior sentences of the discourse by binding the entire discourse to the relevant quantifier and treating the entire discourse as expressing one proposition. One of my central objections to this view is that it cannot assign truth values to individual sentences in the discourse. I also argue that Dynamic Predicate Logic (due to Groenendijk and Stokhof) suffers from the same problem and is thus no better off.

In chapter 8, I present a formal semantics for sentences containing anaphoric expressions in a discourse and for intersentential binding. This system is then used to formalize various examples of discourse containing sentences involving complex pronominalizations, plural pronouns, and the like. This semantics provides, in particular, an account of the contributions that such terms make to the truth conditions for sentences in which they occur and assigns a truth value to individual sentences of the discourse. One example involving plural quantification formalizable within the system is the Geach-Kaplan sentence, "Some critics admire only one another," which is non-first-order-formalizable.

This book was deliberately written so that each part would be independent of the others (and by and large each chapter is independent of the others). Philosophers primarily interested in various philosophical problems about reference and who have little or no interest in technical matters may skip part III of the book. Linguists and logicians of a philosophical bent with an interest in anaphoric pronouns and the formalization of plural quantification or intersentential binding, and having no general interest in rigid designation, direct reference, and philosophical problems, especially regarding reference, may skip parts I and II.

Acknowledgments

I wish to thank my former teacher, George Kryzwicki-Herburt, for introducing me to the joys of studying philosophy. He has certainly influenced me in his general approach and outlook on the subject. I hope that I have succeeded in emulating him in philosophy.

I wish to express my indebtedness to the philosophy department of the University of North Carolina at Chapel Hill, where I began my research on this project, for their generous hospitality in offering me their research facilities. I especially wish to thank William Lycan, Stanley Munsat, and Jay Rosenberg for their useful comments on earlier drafts of this manuscript. I also wish to thank the contributors to the June 1998 Haifa conference—Naming, Necessity, and More, in Honor of Saul Kripke—especially Nathan Salmon.

I wish to thank Lynne Baker for valuable comments on various portions of this manuscript; George Berger for important comments on earlier versions of chapter 8; the late George Boolos for his discussion of my formalization and formal semantics of plural quantification; Ed Erwin for many general comments on portions of this manuscript; James Higginbotham, who stressed the importance to me of writing what eventually became chapter 7; Eli Hirsch, whose comments on an earlier version of chapter 1, which is now part of chapters 6 and 7, were quite useful; Elliot Mendelson, who has read and commented on much of what has become chapter 8; Scott Soames, who made general comments on several chapters, especially 3 and 7; and Fred Sommers for many enjoyable hours of walks and late-night discussions of the early stages of the book. Fred helped to bring my attention to different kinds of terms and how they designate, which plays an important role in part I (though I have a different view than his on these issues) and on the various rules for English discussed in chapter 7. I wish to give special thanks to my former student and good friend, Glenn Branch, who copyedited and indexed the manuscript and consistently made good philosophical comments along the way.

There are six people to whom I wish to express special indebtedness. I wish to thank Saul Kripke, whose seminal work *Naming and Necessity* made it necessarily possible to pursue these topics in the manner I have, and who, as my thesis adviser and long-time friend, has taught me much on this topic. His influence on my work and, indeed, on all philosophy of language has been inestimable. I further wish to thank him for access to his unpublished John Locke Lectures on reference and existence, which have strongly influenced part II of this book. I also wish to thank Hilary Putnam, my teacher and long-time friend, whose seminal papers on reference have influenced me throughout the book, especially in chapters 1, 2, and 6. His work and insights on reference, especially regarding scientific terms and the role of the linguistic community and environment in determining reference, have contributed profoundly to this discipline. I wish to thank Sidney Morgenbesser for many enjoyable afternoons discussing philosophy in general and many topics in this book in particular. Sidney has probably been the most influential person regarding the details of part II of the book. I especially owe to him much of the idea of what is implicitly assumed in an idealized rational agent and how that applies to the notion of an agent's perspective. I am deeply greatful to Nathan Salmon for many hours of conversation on various portions of the book throughout and especially for his reading and detailed comments on chapters 4, 5, and 7. To Gilbert Harman I owe a truly great debt of gratitude for comments on several portions of this manuscript. He has always made himself available to me, going back to the days of my doctoral dissertation, and has been supportive and encouraging ever since. Finally, I wish to express my special indebtedness to the late Albert E. Blumberg, who read every early version of this manuscript and whose wisdom and personal touch appears on every page. In addition to my appreciation of his philosophical comments, I owe much to his editorial wisdom.

Much of the material in "A Theory of Reference Transmission and Reference Change," *Midwest Studies in Philosophy* 14 (1989): 180–198, has been incorporated and expanded in chapter 2. Much of the material in "A

Formal Semantics for Plural Quantification, Intersentential Binding and Anaphoric Pronouns as Rigid Designators," *Noûs* 36, 1 (2002): 49–73, has been incorporated and expanded in chapter 8. I give thanks to the publishers for permission to use this material.

Finally, I wish to thank Natalie Sandler, who, even while working on her plays, has profoundly influenced me in nonphilosophical but more important ways.

I

A Distinction between Two Styles of Rigid Designation and Its Applications

1

A Distinction between Two Styles of Rigid Designation

In *Naming and Necessity,* Saul Kripke introduces the notion of a rigid designator. A rigid designator is a term that denotes the same object in every possible world, or else fails to denote. Contemporary philosophers such as Donnellan, Kaplan, Kripke, and Putnam defend a "new theory of direct reference" for proper names and certain sorts of scientific and natural kind terms. They reject the view that these terms have senses or, in some cases, senses that alone determine their referents. In their view, the referents of names and certain other sorts of terms are determined directly without the mediation of a "sense." Kripke includes such terms among those he calls "rigid designators," since they may be said to "rigidly" pick out the same object as their referents in every possible world in which the object exists.

In this chapter, I first introduce a distinction between two ways in which referents of rigid designator terms are determined. I show that one way rests on the intentional notion that I call "focusing"; the other rests on the semantic notion I call "satisfying-a-given-condition."

The "causal" view, following Kripke, breaks down the process of reference determination into an initial baptism or "dubbing," which provides the term with a reference, and the subsequent transmission of that reference. Transmission takes place by means of a historical chain of speakers' intentions to use a term to refer to what some previous speaker in the chain referred to by using that term. If we trace back the reference of a term, we arrive eventually at the baptismal step, where the rigid designator term first came to be used to refer to the particular object. The object baptized, or dubbed, at this initial step is the referent of the term.

This chapter has been highly influenced by Frederic Sommers, *The Logic of Natural Language* (New York: Oxford University Press, 1982), chapter 5.

1.1   F-Style Rigid Designation

In *Naming and Necessity,* Kripke mentions two ways in which an object may be initially baptized. "[T]he object may be named by ostension, or the reference of the name may be fixed by a description."[1] Kripke adds (in a footnote): "[u]sually a baptizer is *acquainted* in some sense with the object he names and is able to name it ostensively" (my emphasis).

Let us consider, first, the fixing of the referent of a name by ostension. For example, we may name an object by pointing to the heavens and uttering "let that star be called 'Hesperus'" or by pointing to a baby and uttering "let this baby be called 'Cicero'."[2]

Now in my view, ostension itself typically involves two aspects. First, the baptizer attends to or, as I say, *focuses* on a particular thing (or things). Second, the baptizer generally at the same time employs a description— but a description used *referentially,* or *ascriptively*—not attributively. That is, to use a description ascriptively is to attribute to an object a description that may not apply to it. The baptizer *ascribes* a certain property to that object, or *takes* the object to have that property even if the baptizer is mistaken, and the description does not apply to the object.

This is not to say that the act of baptizing an object by means of focusing necessarily requires perceptual access (or informational linkage[3]) during the act of dubbing. It is compatible with my notion of *dubbing an object by means of focusing* that a speaker may do so—even in the absence of the object—provided the speaker had *previously* focused on the object and is now offering a description (used ascriptively) of the object. What is central about this means of fixing the reference of a term is that its referent is in one way or another being determined by perceptual encounters with the referent.

It should be noted that in using a description ascriptively, the baptizer may of course be mistaken. Nevertheless, the name the reference of which

1. Saul Kripke, *Naming and Necessity* (Cambridge, MA: Harvard University Press, 1980), 96.

2. Of course, I am not claiming that the planet Venus was named 'Hesperus' that way or that the person who denounced Cataline was named 'Cicero' that way. These are only meant as illustrations of how demonstrative pronouns are required to fix the reference of a proper name by ostension.

3. For an interesting discussion on informational linkage, see Gareth Evans, *The Varieties of Reference* (New York: Oxford University Press, 1982).

becomes fixed by ostension refers to the particular thing (or things) that is (or are) taken to have that property. Thus when we say "There is a very bright star out tonight. Let that star be called 'Hesperus'," the term 'Hesperus' refers to the thing taken to be a star whether the thing in question is or is not a star.

Now it is the *focusing* on an object, as distinguished from *taking some thing as having a certain property*, that generally plays the principal role in fixing reference by ostension. The ascribing of some property to the thing usually serves only to indicate or draw attention to the thing the speaker wishes to focus on.[4]

A speaker may be aware of several descriptions that are taken to apply to the thing focused on, any one of which may serve to draw attention to the thing. Later speakers may never be aware of what properties were previously ascribed to the referent; yet as long as they know which object was focused on in fixing the reference of this term, they know which object the term refers to. They may not know whether, at the time the planet Venus was baptized with the name 'Hesperus', the property ascribed to it was the property of being the star first seen in the evening or that of being the star that can be seen at the latest time of the morning, or whether what occurred was merely a pointing to a certain region of the sky and the uttering of "that star." As long as they know that Venus is the object the community focused on in fixing the reference of the term, they know the term refers to venus.

According to the historical chain view, then, for any term the referent of which was *focused* on when the object was dubbed with the term, we can determine the reference by means of a historical chain. The chain goes back to the initial dubbing of the referent focused on. And the links in the chain are speakers' intentions, when using the term, to corefer, that is, to use the term with the same reference as the person from whom the speaker acquired the term.[5] It is not required that a speaker, when transmitting the reference of a term, focus on or could ever have focused on the referent of the term. Further, the speaker need neither know what descriptions were originally used nor be aware of which object was focused on in fixing the reference in order to succeed in referring with the term. Thus reference

---

4. See chapter 2 for further refinements concerning fixing the reference of a term by means of focusing.

5. See Saul Kripke, *Naming and Necessity,* 96.

determination for this sort of term requires only that the reference of the term is fixed by means of a focusing.

Any term whose reference for a given linguistic community is determined by *focusing* on a thing taken as having one or another property I call an *F-type term*. The process of determining reference in this manner I call *F-style rigid designation*.

This notion of F-type term does not require, however, that the reference of an F-type term must have been initially fixed by means of focusing. Later, we will see that certain terms initially fixed by description may later have their reference fixed for a linguistic community by means of focusing. These terms are thus F-type terms, even though initially they were not.

Every F-type term is linked to one or more background statements by a historical chain of intentions to corefer. These background statements play a central role in initially determining the term's reference. In the previous example, such statements are "There is (something taken to be) a very bright star out tonight" and "Let that star be called 'Hesperus'." Statements of this sort I call *anaphoric background statements,* and the anaphoric background statements of an F-type term I call the A-B-F statements of that term. So much for F-style rigid designation.

Naming an object by means of focusing on it usually involves certain presuppositions. For example, often we assume that we are focusing on a certain kind of entity, say a human being or *our* child. Consider the case of a doctor who confuses two babies and brings the wrong baby to each of the two pairs of parents. The parents, believing that they are looking at *their* babies, decide to name the baby in front of them, say, "Mary" and "Barbara," respectively. Suppose the error on the part of the doctor is soon discovered. Thereafter each pair of parents applies the name not to the baby they initially focused on, but to *their* baby. Thus if these presuppositions are violated, the act of naming by means of focusing may be annulled.

1.2   S-Style Rigid Designation

The second style, which I call *S-style rigid designation,* employs descriptions used *attributively*—Kripke's second way to fix the reference of a name.

When a description is used attributively to fix the reference, the referent of the description is whatever object actually satisfies that description. For example, the expression 'the actual murderer, whoever that person may be, of the shortest Soviet spy' refers to whoever actually murdered the shortest Soviet spy. Now in such a case, we may have no knowledge, not even a clue, as to who this murderer is. Still we may give a name to the murderer as follows: "let us call the (actual) murderer of the shortest Soviet spy 'John Doe'." If we assume that the context of this utterance is the actual world, 'John Doe' rigidly denotes whoever actually satisfies that description. For even if we say counterfactually "Had John Doe been bought off by the Soviet Union, he would not have murdered the shortest Soviet spy," still 'John Doe' refers to the actual murderer if there is one.

Kripke uses the case of 'Neptune' to illustrate how the reference of a name may be fixed by an attributive use of a definite description. Neptune was hypothesized as the planet that caused such-and-such discrepancies in the orbits of certain other planets. To quote Kripke, "If Leverrier indeed gave the name 'Neptune' to the planet before it was ever seen, then he fixed the reference of 'Neptune' by means of the description just mentioned."[6] For at that time, there was no heavenly body that could be seen (even with a telescope) or taken to satisfy the description. In other words, F-style rigid designation would not have been possible at that time.

Thus it is necessary to recognize that there are cases in which the fixing of a term's reference is based on what in fact satisfies the given description rather than on any ostension or focusing. In these cases, the reference of the term is not fixed by focusing on a particular object or on "ostending" that object. We are not focusing on some thing as the referent of a description and then naming it (while taking it to satisfy the description regardless of whether it does in fact satisfy the description).

What is important about fixing the reference of rigid designators by the attributive use of definite descriptions is that the terms so introduced rigidly denote *whatever objects actually turn out to satisfy the descriptions* (in a given context of use). Such terms may be thought of as designating or referring to the satisfier of the open sentence formed by removing the quantifier that binds the variable in the description in the sentence containing it.[7] For example, suppose a speaker says that some woman (or other) will be the forty-fifth president of the United States, and continues with "She will be a Democrat. Let that woman—whoever she may be—be

6. See Kripke, *Naming and Necessity,* 79n.33.

7. For details, see chapter 8, which presents a formal semantics for these terms.

called 'Alice'." The pronoun 'she' in this context does not refer to any particular person being focused on or taken under consideration. Yet the pronoun does act as a rigid designator referring to the *satisfier* of the matrix of the following bound variable sentence:

($\exists!x$)A(x is a woman & x = 45th president of the United States & (x is a Democrat)),

where 'A' stands for the actuality operator (to be read "it is actually the case that").[8]

In the case of terms of this sort, a speaker may never be aware of what actual description, attributively used, was initially employed to fix the reference. A speaker may not know, for example, what description was initially given in fixing the reference of 'Neptune'. Nonetheless, if the reference of the term is fixed by the original description, its reference is grounded in, or rests on, a description used attributively.

Any term whose reference is obtained by letting the referent be whatever actually satisfies a given description, I call an *S-type term*. This manner of determining the reference of a term I call *S-style rigid designation*. The anaphoric background statements that play a central role in initially determining the reference of an S-type term I call its A-B-S statements. In the previous example, "Some woman will be the forty-fifth president of the United States" and "Let that woman—whoever she may be—be called 'Alice'" are the A-B-S statements.

1.3   F-Type and S-Type General Terms

In developing the distinction between F-type and S-type terms, I have used as examples chiefly singular terms, such as 'Hesperus' and 'Cicero'. It is my contention, however, that the distinction also applies to general terms, such as 'mass'. Many general terms name kinds, and although we cannot *focus* on a kind, we can and do focus on things or samples that instantiate it. This, in fact, is what we do in the case of F-type general terms. Examples of F-type general terms include 'water', 'gold', 'cat', and 'tiger'. Examples of S-type general terms include 'H_2O', 'Au_{79}', and 'mass'.

8. For purposes of the present discussion, I formalize the rigidity of the variable with an actuality operator, but I do not consider this strictly correct. See chapters 3 and 8 for detail.

This distinction between F-type and S-type terms, however, does seem to run into certain problems when it comes to general terms. Here I wish to discuss two particular difficulties.

First, recall that in introducing F-type *singular* terms, we often use descriptions (or sortals). But as we saw earlier, these descriptions are used *ascriptively* or *referentially*. Now we also use descriptions in introducing rigid *general* terms. Here it might be supposed that not only do we always use descriptions when introducing a general term, but also these descriptions are used *attributively*. Now if this is the case, then general terms can only be S-type and not F-type. Various philosophers, such as John Searle and Alvin Plantinga, hold to this "descriptivist" view for general terms.[9] A descriptivist might claim that the term 'water', for example, refers to the kind that is instantiated by typical samples of the clear liquid that actually is in the lakes, rivers, and oceans that we bathe in and drink from. If the descriptivist is correct, then general terms that denote kinds are all S-type.

My claim is that there are general terms such that whatever descriptions may be used in introducing them, these descriptions are used *ascriptively* (or *referentially*), not attributively. Such general terms are F-type.

Consider some of the ways in which we may introduce certain general terms with the aid of a description. We may use a description in introducing certain general terms by describing a stereotypical member or sample of the *kind* that the general term is to denote. In this case, however, my contention is that one's description of the stereotype invariably derives from some past or present *perceptual acquaintance* with an object that instantiates the description. The introduction and transmission of the term must involve a *focusing* on a member or sample. For example, in introducing the general term 'dog', we are not simply specifying some satisfaction condition independently of past or present perceptual acquaintance that a stereotypical member of the species *dog* must meet, such as having a certain color, size, and shape, making certain sounds, and the like. (Further, any claim that the term is introduced and transmitted by means of a description of a stereotypic dog-like gestalt is very dubious. For a stereotype

9. See Alvin Plantinga's *The Nature of Necessity* (Oxford: The Clarendon Press, 1974), and "The Boethian Compromise," *American Philosophical Quarterly* 15 (April 1978): 129–138, and see John Searle's *Intentionality* (Cambridge: Cambridge University Press, 1983). They would also make this claim for singular terms as well. However, their arguments are less convincing for singular terms.

can vary from person to person as widely as the range of variation among the members of the species. An individual familiar only with Great Danes will have a very different stereotype of a dog than an individual familiar only with dachshunds.)[10]

Descriptions used in introducing general terms often include some phrase such as "a typical sample" or "under normal conditions." But such descriptions can never fully specify in purely qualitative terms (or in any terms, for that matter) a satisfaction condition that members or samples of the kind must meet—a condition that avoids dependence either on a focusing or on the making of a new scientific discovery that specifies what may count as a "typical sample" or a "normal condition." Thus such descriptions fail to fix the reference of the term attributively. For example, in introducing the term 'water', the only way we can specify what is to count as a typical sample is by focusing on such a sample or by awaiting the scientific discovery that a typical sample must be H_2O. In either case, the phrase "typical sample" when used with a description introducing a general term cannot be used attributively.

Finally, certain cases in which the claim is made that descriptions are being used attributively in the introduction of general terms turn out on examination to involve a circularity. For example, the claim may be made that in introducing the term 'water', the description 'typical sample of the clear liquid found in the lakes, rivers, oceans, and the like' is being used attributively. But in order to accept the description as attributive, we must first have introduced the general terms 'lake', 'river', and 'ocean'. But these general terms must either have been introduced as F-type terms or depend for their introduction on the very term 'water' that they are now being used to introduce. Thus *Webster's New Collegiate Dictionary* defines the term 'river' as "a natural stream of *water* of considerable volume" (my emphasis).

The second difficulty that I wish to discuss is the following: It can be argued that sometimes the initial samples that we focus on in naming a kind may not actually be instantiations of the kind *k* that is the referent of the general term whose reference we are fixing with the aid of these samples. But if the *initial* samples can turn out not to be instantiations of the kind *k*

10. See Hilary Putnam's *Representation and Reality* (Cambridge, MA: MIT Press, 1988) for an analogous point regarding whether stereotypes can serve as the mental content that fixes the reference of natural kind terms.

that we name in focusing on these samples (and assuming, of course, that there is no change in the reference of the term), then seemingly this would be possible only if these samples failed to *satisfy* certain descriptive criteria we have for an object's or sample's being an instantiation of k. That is, the description in introducing the general term would have been used attributively, in which case the general term would really be S-type and not F-type.

Concerning this objection, recall that in the case of a general term we cannot focus on the kind that we are naming. We can only focus on things or samples that instantiate the kind. Hence, in focusing on initial samples, we could be mistaken in *taking* them to be samples of the kind. This may occur, as in our example of the baby mixup case, when any of the suppositions that underlie the naming a kind fails to be met.[11] For example, the initial samples may not belong to one uniform kind, the kind may have been already named,[12] or the initial samples may fail to be "typical members" of the class typical members of which we would be prepared to accept as samples of that kind. To illustrate, we may think that in introducing the term 'water', we are focusing on typical samples of the clear liquid found in the lakes, rivers, oceans, and the like with which we have had perceptual encounters. But it may then turn out that these particular samples all happen to be a clear liquid other than water, not identical to H_2O.

When the underlying suppositions for naming[13] fail to be met, various social factors determine whether the term still succeeds in naming and whether these initial samples are to count as belonging to the kind we are naming. Such factors include how much time has elapsed from the initial naming of the kind, our interest in what we currently focus on when we use the name for the kind, and how strong the original intention still is to name the kind. I have more to say about these factors in chapter 2, where I present an account of reference change. The important point for now is that the initial samples used in fixing the reference of a general term may not be members of the kind named by that term, and yet we needn't claim

---

11. I owe to Sidney Morgenbesser this general view that there are suppositions that underlie naming.

12. See Kripke, *Naming and Necessity,* 136, for details of how this can come about.

13. We leave open whether there is a priori knowledge connecting the term being introduced with its underlying suppositions.

that the description or sortal used in introducing the term is used attributively, in which case the general term would really be S-type and not F-type.

The central difference between an F-type and an S-type natural kind term is that in the case of an F-type term, the kind that is being referred to by the term is in one way or another being determined by perceptual encounters with members of that kind. I make further refinements of the distinction between F-type and S-type terms throughout the book, especially in chapters 2 and 3.

2

A Theory of Reference Transmission and Reference Change

My aim in this chapter is to use the distinction between F-style and S-style rigid designation to develop what I call an *anaphoric* theory of reference transmission and reference change for directly referential rigid designator terms. I formulate a necessary condition for a rigid designator term to undergo a reference change, that is, for the term to acquire a different referent from the one it had initially or previously. I also suggest the sort of conditions that in conjunction with the necessary condition would, for a variety of situations, provide the desired necessary and sufficient conditions for reference change.

As observed in chapter 1, a standard (Kripkean) account of reference determination for names and certain other directly referential rigid designators holds that reference determination is essentially a two-step process: an initial or baptismal step and a subsequent transmission phase. Reference transmission is viewed as a causal or historical process such that the referent of the name can be traced back to the initial baptism or dubbing. The object baptized at that initial step remains the referent of the name.

This account, however, does not include a theory of reference change. The absence of such a theory seems to make the standard account vulnerable to certain "counterexamples," all of which involve instances of unintended reference change. It will be shown below that the theory developed here can accommodate these purported counterexamples.

A word of caution. When I talk of a name undergoing a reference change, I am not talking about the term merely as a *syntactic item*. Rather, what I have in mind is a name together with certain occasions of use. More precisely, I am interested in a name and a particular set of anaphoric background statements ("A-B statements," hereafter) that introduced that use of the name into the language community. Accordingly, I am concerned with the reference of a name only relative to a particular set of A-B statements associated with that use (or with a certain set of occurrences) of a name, although I note that several people may have the same name, and in that sense the name may be said to have multiple reference. (Reference change may involve a change in the A-B statement(s) associated with the term; where this is the case, I speak of "conceptual change," a topic discussed in section 2.6 of this chapter.)

In addition to the notion of A-B statements, I make use of the notion of an *anaphoric chain* and the notion of a chain's being *grounded* in an object. An anaphoric chain is a chain of communication where a name is passed on "from link to link" by means of a mode of transmission going back to the object, if any, to which the name refers or to the relevant A-B statements that introduced this use of the name otherwise. If the anaphoric chain ultimately goes back to an object, we say that the chain is *grounded* in that object. I also make use of the notion of an *anaphoric background condition* ("A-B condition," hereafter). This condition is the condition that a name must satisfy at the initial introduction of the name into the language in order for the name to designate. For example, if the name is F-type, its A-B condition that must be satisfied is that the speaker in introducing the name succeeds in focusing on the object that the name is intended to designate. (A more precise formal account of anaphoric chains, grounding, and A-B conditions is presented in chapters 5 and 8.)

2.1   Reference Transmission for F-Type Terms

First, let us examine how we transmit the reference of an F-type term. This takes place in two ways. To illustrate them, let us consider two cases, one in which we cannot currently focus on the referent of the term, the other in which we can.

Take, for example, the F-type term 'Aristotle'. Obviously since Aristotle has long been dead, there is no object that we can *now focus* on and call 'Aristotle'. There is no entity that any member of the community can point to and refer to by direct ostension or by a demonstrative (excluding, of course, deferred ostension or deferred use of a demonstrative). Moreover, no one around today was once acquainted with Aristotle or was once able to refer to him by direct ostension. So even though the term 'Aristotle' may have been introduced at the initial baptism stage by an ordinary focusing on the object, the current transmission of its reference can not take place in that manner. Instead, when we transmit the reference of the name 'Aristotle', we do so by giving a definite or indefinite description. We may say something like "Aristotle was a famous Greek philosopher who wrote the *Nicomachean Ethics.*" But for reasons now well known,[1] this description does not give the meaning of the term 'Aristotle'. In fact, it does not even fix the reference of the term 'Aristotle'. We do not say "Let the famous Greek philosopher, whoever that person is, who wrote the Nicomachean Ethics be called 'Aristotle'." For we agree that we may discover that Aristotle did not write the *Nicomachean Ethics,* that he was not a philosopher, or even that he was not Greek. Similar remarks apply, of course, to any definite description that one might think fixes the reference of 'Aristotle'.

How, then, is a description used to transmit the reference of 'Aristotle'? The description is used to indicate something the speaker or the linguistic community, by and large, *believes* is true of the referent of the term. By the use of a description, then, a speaker helps to indicate which historical chain (of intentions to corefer) he is on when he uses a given occurrence of the term 'Aristotle'. The historical chain determines the referent of the name 'Aristotle', but the use of a definite description helps indicate who the speaker or the linguistic community believes is the referent of the term. Thus in transmitting the reference of the F-type term, 'Aristotle', we may use a definite description as follows: 'Aristotle' denotes whomever the historical chain of intentions to corefer ultimately goes back to, whomever that may be, and we *take* it that that person is the famous Greek philosopher who wrote the *Nicomachean Ethics.* Descriptions are thus akin to Hilary Putnam's stereotypes with natural kind terms. Although the stereotypical tiger is striped, this may not be true of all tigers. Nevertheless, we may communicate which species we believe we are referring to by the use of stereotypes.

This account describes the way in which the reference of an F-type name is commonly transmitted. We use the term 'Aristotle' to refer to the individual who was initially focused on and baptized with this (or a phonetically or syntactically similar) name. Since we are often no longer in an epistemic situation in which we may focus on the object named, we can

1. See Kripke, *Naming and Necessity.*

usually help to indicate which object we believe we are referring to only by stating one or more conditions that we currently *take* that object to satisfy. By using these descriptions, the speaker who is passing on the name directs attention to the specific historical chain (of speakers' intentions to corefer) along which he or she believes the name is being passed. The specific chain (if it is the correct one), in turn, determines the referent of the given term.

This process, or mode of transmission, I call *mock-focusing*. It is a process in which what we ascribe to—say, Aristotle—may not be true of him, even though when we pass on the reference of the F-type term 'Aristotle' along a historical chain of speakers' intentions to corefer, the ascriptive use of descriptions (i.e., descriptions attributed to an object that may not apply to it) plays a central role in determining the particular historical chain along which we believe the term is being passed. This process, or mode of transmission, also links a particular occasion of use of the term 'Aristotle' to its referent. By means of this process, the community passes the term 'Aristotle' from link to link along an anaphoric chain that is grounded in the object initially focused on when the object was baptized with that (or a recognizably similar) name.

Consider next the case in which we can focus on the referent of an F-type term, say, 'Alan Berger'. How does the reference of this term get transmitted? Here the referent is still alive. People can, and do, focus on the referent of this F-type term by pointing to him and referring to him by direct ostension or by a demonstrative. In that sense we may say that various members of the community are acquainted with him. To be sure, not all focusings by community members will count as correct focusings on the referent of this (or any other) term. Indeed, many focusings will not be accepted as reliable. But, in the spirit of Hilary Putnam's thesis of the division of linguistic labor (see chapter 6 for detail and further development), various members of the community count as experts in focusing on the referent of a term. In the case of 'Alan Berger', they would include the referent's immediate family, close personal friends, and so on. When in doubt, it is usually focusings by these experts to which the community defers, even though experts may fail to focus on what, in fact, is the term's referent.

Furthermore, a description, definite or indefinite, may accompany a focusing on an object in transmitting the reference of a term. An example might be "Alan Berger is the guy in the room pounding away at the type-writer." A description used in transmitting reference by focusing serves merely to help to convey which object is being focused on. It does not matter whether or not the description is true of the object, as long as it helps to indicate which object is being focused on. The description is being used merely ascriptively.

This mode of transmitting reference I call *genuine focusing*. It is a process through which a linguistic community passes an F-type term along a historical chain (of speakers' intentions to corefer) by means of currently focusing on an object—an object that the community *takes* to be the referent of the term. Through this process, the community passes the F-type term from link to link along an anaphoric chain that is grounded in the object focused on at the baptismal step.

Transmitting the reference of the term by mock-focusing is therefore to be distinguished from transmitting the reference by genuine focusing. The difference is this: when we transmit the reference of an F-type term by mock-focusing, there is not even an object available that we are currently taking rightly or wrongly to satisfy certain conditions (or, at least, there are no experts in focusing on what they take to be the referent that we are relying on); but when we transmit the reference of an F-type term by genuine focusing, there must be an object on which we are focusing, and any description (correct or incorrect) of the object only serves to help to convey what object we are focusing on.

Of course, we usually do not focus on the referent of an F-type term when we transmit its reference even when the referent and experts in focusing on the term's referent are currently available. Usually we rely only on descriptions (such as "the author of this manuscript") in order to transmit the reference of a term, if anything at all. This does not mean, however, that the transmission of the reference of the term 'Alan Berger' occurs by means of mock-focusing, as it does in the case of the term 'Aristotle'.

One important difference is that whereas no one around today is or has been acquainted with Aristotle, people living today are and have been acquainted with Alan Berger. Hence, for the term 'Aristotle', the community can rely only on descriptions used ascriptively to indicate to whom they are referring. On the other hand, a linguistic community is not forced to rely only on the mock-focusing mode when transmitting the reference of the term 'Alan Berger', for both the referent and the experts on focusing on the referent are available to the community. Hence it may transmit the term's reference by focusing on the referent.

Further, when both modes of transmission are available to a linguistic community, the referent of the description in the mock-focusing statement may differ from the referent of the object currently focused on. For example, suppose someone uses the description "the author of this manuscript" in transmitting the reference of the F-type term 'Alan Berger' by means of a mock-focusing, and suppose further that he is not the author of this manuscript. Then the object that satisfies this description may not be the person focused on by focusing experts of the referent when they transmit the reference by means of a genuine focusing. In that case, the mode of transmission used by the linguistic community is either a genuine focusing or a mock-focusing, depending upon which of these two modes the community relies on in transmitting the term's reference during a given period of time.

When both modes of transmission are available, if the referent of the description in the mock-focusing statement differs from the object currently focused on, the community as a rule does not rely on mock-focusing. Usually the community defers to the focusings carried out by those who are focusing experts with respect to the referent of that term. Recall that the use of descriptions with F-type terms is always merely ascriptive, that is, they may not be true of the object. They are used to indicate which object we currently take to be the referent of the term and which anaphoric chain we take to be the one the F-type term is passed along. In general, then, a genuine focusing transmission mode takes precedence over a mock-focusing transmission mode for a given community. When an F-type term can be transmitted by both modes, and thus the possibility arises of disagreement concerning what is taken to be the referent, we assume that the community will defer to the genuine focusings of the community's experts and thus that the mode of transmission for the community is a genuine focusing.

2.2   Reference Change for F-Type Terms

I now formulate and explain a necessary condition for reference change of F-type rigid designator terms: An F-type term can undergo an unintended reference change at a particular stage in its reference transmission only if at that stage the term's reference is transmitted by a *genuine focusing* on a new referent. Here, current or later focusings can supplant previous or even initial focusings. This condition holds regardless of whether the F-type term is a singular or a general term. Later, I suggest the sort of conditions that, taken with this necessary condition, provide necessary and sufficient conditions for reference change of F-type terms.

Before I do so, however, let us note and discard two kinds of situations in which we loosely speak of reference change. First, there is the situation in which we incorrectly introduce a term from one language into another. In such a case, there are no rules governing the kind of mistakes that we can make. F-type terms can become S-type terms and vice versa, singular terms can become general and vice versa, and so on. The anaphoric chain of the term is broken when the term is introduced into a given language by mistranslation. In such a case, a new A-B condition is introduced for the term.

Second, an F-type term may at some point come to acquire a mythical or fictional character as its referent, as for example in the case of Santa Claus. These are cases of fictional characters created by grossly exaggerating features attributable to the actual person with the same phonetic name.

I first examine three purported counterexamples to the standard account (see earlier) of reference determination. In each case, there is a term that undergoes an unintended reference change. First, I show that in each case our necessary condition is fulfilled. Second, I suggest the kinds of conditions that would supply sufficient conditions as well. Finally, I conclude that the historical chain view of reference determination, when supplemented with my theory of reference change, is immune to these three counterexamples.

First, there is the well-known "Madagascar case" due to Gareth Evans. According to him, 'Madagascar' was a native name for a part of the continent of Africa. Marco Polo erroneously took the natives to be using that name to refer to an island off the coast of Africa. Today the term is so widely used as a name for the island that this usage has overriden the earlier historical connection to the referent assigned to 'Madagascar' at the initial baptism.

In this case, we have an F-type singular term. At a certain stage in the transmission of its reference, there is a genuine focusing not on its original (or previous) referent, but to an island off the coast of Africa. Since then, the mode of transmission of the reference of 'Madagascar' has continued to be a genuine focusing—but we focus on the region now taken to be the referent of the term 'Madagascar'. Thus the necessary condition for reference change formulated above is fulfilled.

It is true that most of us have never seen Madagascar and perhaps are not able even to transmit the term with a description. Or perhaps, at best, we can find the place on the map and then describe its location as such-and-such longitude and latitude. But still, the community at large does not rely on these descriptions to determine the referent of this term. Thus the current mode of transmission of the term is not a mock-focusing as in the Aristotle case. There, the term referred to the thing focused on initially. Here, when an *individual* who has never seen Madagascar transmits this reference in a mock-focusing manner, reference is merely derivative from what the community's experts—the geographers and the travelers—focus on. The community relies on these people for the correct transmission of the term's reference, and these people, in turn, rely ultimately on their focusings when they transmit the reference of the term. In transmitting the reference of the term 'Madagascar', they focus on a place that they take to have certain properties, say latitude and longitude. The experts may, of course, be mistaken in what they ascribe to Madagascar. For example, there may be geological shifts in position of a whole continent that change the latitude and longitude of Madagascar. Nevertheless, for the linguistic community, the current stage in the transmission of the term's reference, as determined by experts, rests on a genuine focusing.

So much for the necessary condition in the Madagascar case. I suggest that to find conditions that together with the necessary condition would give us necessary and sufficient conditions, we must, first, look to social, legal, and institutional conventions (for example, those governing naming rights and the selection and status of names) and to special interests associated with certain kinds of referents. (These matters are discussed in chapter 6 in my development of Putnam's "socio-linguistic hypothesis.") Second, we must look to the time period during which a community focuses (genuinely) on the new referent.

As a second case, let us imagine that at the initial baptism of the word 'water', all the lakes, rivers, oceans, and so on were filled with the substance xyz, the clear liquid that people drank and bathed in was xyz, and so on. Here 'xyz' is the name for a substance the molecular structure of which is not identical with H_2O, but which has all the phenomenal qualities of H_2O (as described in Putnam's famous Twin Earth example.)[2] In the course of natural change, xyz was replaced everywhere on earth by H_2O. But the community continued to use the term 'water' to refer to the liquid in the lakes and the present clear liquid that we drink and so on. Thus what we currently take to be the referent of the term 'water' came to override the referent of the term at the initial baptism.

This example is better than the Madagascar case since it does not depend upon translating a term into our language, where the introduction by mistranslation of the term into our language could be considered a second baptism.

Note that not only is the term 'water' an F-type term, but the current mode of transmission of 'water' is a genuine focusing. We focus on samplings of water when we drink a certain clear, odorless liquid, point to the lakes, rivers, oceans, and so on, even now when we currently transmit the term. In this example, the thing initially taken to have these properties (i.e., the thing initially taken to have the properties of being a clear, odorless liquid filling the lakes, rivers, and so on) is not the thing that we currently take to have these properties. The thing that we now take to have these properties is phenomenally identical with the thing we initially took to have these properties and is located in the same natural places where the thing we initially took to have these properties was located. Thus it confounded even our focusing experts! The thing that they currently focus on is not the same thing that we initially focused on.

It is true that, as in the case of the F-type singular term 'Alan Berger', we do not always focus on samplings of the referent when we currently transmit the reference of the term 'water'. Sometimes we rely on descriptions, such as those above, to transmit the reference of this term. Moreover, as in the case with the term 'Aristotle', no one around today is or has been acquainted with the initial referent of the term 'water' at the baptismal step. Nonetheless, this does not make the current mode of transmission of the term 'water' a mock-focusing. One fundamental difference is that whereas

2. See Hilary Putnam, "The Meaning of 'Meaning'," in *Minnesota Studies in the Philosophy of Science VII: Language, Mind, and Knowledge,* ed. K. Gunderson (Minneapolis: University of Minnesota Press, 1975), 131–193. See also Hilary Putnam, "Meaning and Reference," *The Journal of Philosophy* 70 (November 8): 699–711; also in *Naming, Necessity, and Natural Kinds,* ed. S. P. Schwartz (Ithaca: Cornell University Press, 1977), 119–132; all page references given in this work are to the latter.

no present community expert purports to focus on Aristotle, the same is not true of water. And again, as in the case of the name 'Alan Berger', should the referent of the description in the mock-focusing statement differ from the object currently focused on by community experts, it is the focusing by experts to which the community defers.

A second fundamental difference is based on the institutional convention that grants certain members of the community certain *rights of entitlement* to introduce a name for certain entities that have a special relation to them. Names introduced into the community this way often carry a special legal status. For example, in the United States, the parents of a baby have an entitlement right to name their baby, and that name is the legal name of their baby. (For further discussion of these semantic institutional competencies, see chapter 6.) Thus, while Aristotle's parents have entitlement rights to so name him, current focusing experts do not. The same is not true of the natural kind F-type term 'water'. In fact (as we see in chapter 6), focusing experts on natural kinds have a certain institutional competence that allows them to name such kinds. Thus the current mode of transmission of the F-type term 'water' is, indeed, a genuine focusing.

Note that our necessary condition stated above for a term changing its referent has been met: The term is F-type, and its current mode of transmission is a genuine focusing. Our community interest in focusing on the thing that we currently take to have these properties seems to override the term's designating what it did at the initial baptism stage. Our social interests, such as our interests in the thing we currently take to be a clear liquid and so on, together with the long lapse of time since the initial baptism stage, seem to give us a sufficient condition for the term's having a change in reference from the initial baptismal stage.

Finally, let us imagine, as in Putnam's Twin Earth example, that while on Earth originally all the lakes and so on were filled with H_2O and the clear liquid that we drank and bathed in was H_2O, on Twin Earth originally all the lakes and so on were filled with xyz and our Twin Earthian counterparts bathed in and drank the clear liquid xyz. Suppose further that although our science of space travel has advanced immensely, and we have had interplanetary contact with Twin Earthians, no one has yet discovered the molecular structure of either the stuff that was originally in the lakes on earth or those on Twin Earth. Now also imagine that it has become a common practice for Earthians and Twin Earthians to trade back and forth in "water." (There is a snooty part of Twin Earth, for example, that bottles its water for a mere $1.50 a bottle. They call it 'Perrier'.) Finally, imagine that, after a widespread mixing of the two liquids had occurred, it was discovered that what is called "water" has two molecular structures, H_2O and xyz. In such a situation, since both molecular structures are present in abundance and since we referred to both as "water" prior to the discovery that there are two structures, it is natural to think that our term 'water' would still continue to refer to both H_2O and xyz despite the initial baptism of the term 'water' on Earth.

Perhaps we might distinguish the two molecular structures for water as we presently distinguish between "heavy" water, or deuterium oxide, which has an extra neutron in its hydrogen atoms, and regular water. But nevertheless, we still refer to both structures by the generic name 'water', and I surmise that we would do the same in the situation described above.

Once again, we have an F-type term, 'water', the reference of which is transmitted by a community through a genuine focusing. Here again our necessary condition is met for a change in reference from that of the initial baptismal step. The word 'water', which initially referred by genuine focusing to H_2O, now refers by genuine focusing to either or both of H_2O and xyz. And once the necessary condition has been met, social factors would seem to provide sufficient conditions for the change in reference from the initial baptism stage. We are unable to distinguish which microstructure was initially dubbed with the term 'water'. There is an abundance of stuff around us that we currently focus on, and our interest is in this stuff, whether it has one microstructure or two. Finally, there is a long-term history in our linguistic community of referring to both H_2O and xyz as "water."

We proposed above that the necessary condition for a term to undergo a reference change is that the mode of transmission at which the change occurs be a genuine focusing on a different referent. Now it might be objected that natural kind terms, such as 'water', 'tiger', 'gold', and the like, are really F-type general terms for which reference change nonetheless occurs through a purely *descriptive* mode of transmission. Once we discover that water = H_2O and that gold = Au_{79}, the referents of the terms 'water' and 'gold' may be thought of as being whatever objects satisfy the descriptions 'the property of being H_2O' or 'the property of being Au_{79}', respectively. But when we use these descriptions to determine the extensions of these terms, many of the objects originally focused on with these terms no longer count as part of these extensions. We may have been mistakenly taking certain samples to be samples of water or gold when in fact they were samples of something else. From this it might be concluded that natural kind terms, such as 'water' and 'gold', are F-type terms, and that the discoveries that water = H_2O and gold = Au_{79} has produced a change in referents when the references of these terms are transmitted by a purely descriptive mode.

All this objection shows is that sometimes we discover that many of our focusings are misfocusings, mistakes where we fail to focus on what we intend to focus on. When we name a natural kind or substance with a general term, we are also naming anything which is the same stuff or kind. Unlike in the case of a singular term, we can focus on only samplings, or parts, of a general term's referent. Since focusings on each of these samplings are attempts to focus on the *same stuff* or *kind,* many of these attempts may fail, especially in the absence of a theory of what constitutes the same stuff or kind. Thus it should come as no surprise if experts later discover, on theoretical grounds, that many of our focusings on samplings, even original focusings, are mistaken, that is, they are not focusings on what we intended to focus on.

A comparison with mistaken focusings having to do with singular terms may help to convince us that this is the correct way to view the matter. Suppose in some early civilization, a woman gives birth to identical twins whom she names 'Johnny' and 'Steve'. Now suppose that from their birth on, everyone, including the mother, is constantly mistaking one child for the other. Further, suppose that since this takes place in an early civilization, there is no known epistemic criterion to distinguish one twin from the other, let alone any metaphysical criterion based upon a person's essence. Finally, imagine that at some later date, some criterion is established to distinguish one twin from the other. When applying that criterion, we find that some, perhaps most, of our early focusings in connection with the use of these names do not in fact focus on the same person focused on at the very first use of the names. In such a case, we would not say that, thanks to some theoretical advances, we have changed the referent of the name back to the very first focusing. Rather, we would say that, thanks to these theoretical advances, we have discovered that most of our focusings were mistaken.

Now the situation with respect to general terms is admittedly not perfectly analogous to the case of the twins. It is harder to claim that due to theoretical advances we can show that our very first focusing was a mistaken focusing on the referent of a singular term. The reason for this is that a focusing on the referent of a singular term, in contrast to a general term, is a focusing on the entire referent. Nevertheless, I think that the use of theoretical identifications of natural kinds and substances to correct earlier focusings on samples should be viewed in the same way as the use of theoretical advances to provide criteria for the correctness of focusings on individuals. The theoretical identification of gold with Au_{79} distinguishes real gold from fool's gold, even if the very first focusing was on fool's gold; the identification of water with H_2O distinguishes water from anything else that is a clear and odorless liquid with which water may initially have been confused. But this should certainly not be viewed as a change in the reference of these terms, but rather as a means of distinguishing correct from incorrect focusings.

Thus far, we have been examining only F-type terms with a genuine focusing mode of transmission. Can we now generalize our necessary condition for reference change to all rigid designator terms, F-type or S-type?

2.3   Reference Transmission for S-Type Terms

Before we consider reference change for S-type rigid designator terms, let us first discuss briefly the transmission of reference for such terms. An S-type term, recall, is a rigid designator term that refers to the satisfier of its A-B sentence. An A-B sentence has the form of an existential statement. Hence, the referent of an S-type term is the satisfier of its A-B condition formed by removing the existential quantifier from the term's A-B sentence. As an example of A-B sentences, consider the following pair:

(3)   Some woman or other will be the first woman to land on Mars in the year 2051. Let that woman—whoever she may be—be called 'Sonia'.

Here 'Sonia' is an S-type singular term whose referent is the object in virtue of which the above existential prediction is true.

Now one obvious, indeed, usual way in which the reference of an S-type term is transmitted is by the attributive use of a description. Generally we take the existential A-B sentence itself as the description used in transmitting the reference of the S-type term. In answering the question "Who is Sonia?," we may say "She is whoever will be the first woman to land on Mars in the year 2051." That is to say,

(4) $(\exists x)(x$ = the first woman to land on Mars in the year 2051 & x = Sonia)).

Note that here, unlike in reference transmission by genuine focusing or mock-focusing, the description itself is used attributively and is in an extensional context. The referent of the S-type term must satisfy this description used in its A-B statement regardless of whether the speaker attributes to the referent the property of satisfying this description. What the speaker takes the referent of the term to satisfy, that is, what the speaker ascribes to the referent, is irrelevant to transmitting the reference at this stage of transmission. We cannot discover that we were wrong about the referent of the term satisfying the description. We cannot discover, for example, that Sonia really isn't the first woman to land on Mars in the year 2051, if such a person exists.[3]

This mode of transmission, which I call *purely descriptive,* is in sharp contrast with the two modes of transmission—genuine focusing and mock-focusing—discussed above. For example, when we transmit the reference of the F-type term 'Aristotle' in a mock-focusing manner, say, by the description 'the famous Greek philosopher who wrote the *Nicomachean Ethics',* we may discover that we are wrong in ascribing one or all of the properties we thus ascribe to Aristotle. We saw that there the description is embedded in a nonextensional context. Letting Jones be the speaker, we have in contrast with (4):

(5)   Jones takes it that: $(\exists x)(x$ = Aristotle & x = the famous Greek philosopher who wrote the *Nicomachean Ethics).*

We may discover that the speaker is wrong in ascribing one or all of the properties he ascribes to Aristotle.

Is it possible to transmit the reference of S-type terms by either a genuine focusing or a mock-focusing mode? Consider again the S-type term 'Sonia'. At some later date, in the year 2051, say, someone may believe he knows who Sonia is and focus on her. That is, someone may believe he knows who the first woman to land on Mars in the year 2051 is, and be in an epistemic position to focus on her. In such an event, at that future time, that person can transmit the reference of the S-type term 'Sonia' by a genuine focusing. Moreover, if the person has certain beliefs about Sonia, say

---

3. The implications of this in connection with contingent a priori statements have been discussed by Saul Kripke and Keith Donnellan.

that she is married to Mr. Jones, that person can refer to Sonia through a mock-focusing mode. When asked "Who is Sonia?," that person can say, "(I take it that) she is the wife of Mr. Jones."

That an *individual* of a given community may transmit the reference of an S-type term by a genuine or a mock-focusing mode does not mean that the term is transmitted by one of these modes *for that linguistic community.* Many people or even perceived experts of the community may not be in an epistemic position to transmit the reference of an S-type term by one of these modes.

When more than one mode of transmission is available to various members of a linguistic community, the objects referred to by these different modes may differ. The wife of Mr. Jones, the person who is taken to be the first woman to land on Mars in the year 2051 and the first woman to in fact land on Mars in the year 2051 may turn out to be different individuals. As in the case of F-type terms, we define the mode of transmission for a linguistic community to be the mode the community relies on (i.e., the mode the community will rely on even though it may not determine the correct referent of the term) when different modes determine a different referent for the term in question. Again as in the case of F-type terms, the community usually defers to those whom they perceive to be experts. And again, genuine focusing in general takes precedence over any other mode when there is no violation of any institutional or social convention, such as entitlement rights to name a certain person (such as your child) and so on. This precedence of genuine focusing over other modes of transmission is especially clear when either the community experts or a significant number of community members are in an epistemic position to transmit the reference of the term by means of a genuine focusing.

When a term initially introduced as an S-type term becomes transmitted by the linguistic community through a genuine focusing, the referent is no longer determined by the initial satisfaction condition. The community will now determine the referent of the term by the epistemic condition of focusing on the object. Since we wish to preserve the distinction between an F-type term and an S-type term as a distinction between whether the referent of the term is determined by an epistemic condition or a satisfaction condition, we adopt the following convention: If for a given stage in the transmission of the reference of a term, the reference is transmitted by means of a genuine focusing, then, regardless of how the term was initially introduced, we say that at that stage in the transmission of the term, the term is F-type. Thus what is initially an S-type term may cease to be an S-type term and change its status to an F-type term.

Can we transmit the reference of an S-type term by means of a mock-focusing mode without ever having been in an epistemic position to focus on the referent? Suppose, for example, we believe that whoever will be the first woman to land on Mars in the year 2051 will also be the first woman to be president of the United States. Thus, when asked, "Who is Sonia?," we might on occasion say "She will be the first woman president of the United States." When we transmit the reference of the term 'Sonia' with this description, by which mode have we transmitted the reference of this term and which mode dominates if the descriptions in the two modes refer to different objects?

The answers to these questions are not always so clear-cut. Additional descriptions sometimes place further constraints on what can count as the referent of an S-type term. For example, if after someone utters, "Some woman will land on Mars in the year 2051," someone else then interjects, "Yes, *she* will be the first woman president of the United States," the S-type term 'she' in subsequent uses of the term 'she' seems to refer to whomever satisfies both descriptions. If, on the other hand, someone says after the two A-B sentences in (3) above, "I'll bet she will be the first woman president of the United States," it is less clear whether the S-type term 'she' must refer to an object that satisfies this description as well. If the person feels confident that, in fact, the term 'she' satisfies the above description as well, the person may answer the question, "Who is she?," by saying, "She will be the first woman president of the United States." But this use of a description is ascriptive and tantamount to transmitting the reference of the term in a mock-focusing manner. Since the description is inside an intentional context, we may discover that we were wrong in attributing this property to Sonia. Moreover, the description used in this manner is derivative from the description formed with the A-B sentence in this example, and thus the community would rely upon the later description at this stage of transmission.

When an S-type term is transmitted by a description used ascriptively, the referent of the term is still determined by the satisfaction condition derived from the term's A-B sentence by removing the existential quantifier of this sentence. For this reason we call such a mode of transmission *mock-*

satisfying. This mode links a particular occasion of use of an S-type term to its referent. By means of this process, a community passes an S-type term from link to link along an anaphoric chain, which is grounded in the satisfier of the term's A-B condition that is derived from its set of A-B sentences.

A general remark about reference determination is in order. We remarked earlier that terms, such as proper names, may have multiple reference in the sense that more than one person or object may have the same phonetic or orthographic name. A natural question arises: How can we determine on a given occasion of use who is the referent of the term, that is, which set of A-B statements associated with the term is the relevant set, given a particular occasion of use of the term? Our answer is given by determining which description in a given mode of transmission is used with a given occurrence of the term when the speaker is asked "to whom are you referring?" For example, if the question is "To whom are you referring by 'Aristotle'?" and the response is "the famous Greek philosopher," that indicates that the occasion of use of the term 'Aristotle' was not in the anaphoric chain grounded in the shipping magnate.

2.4   Reference Change for S-Type Terms: Singular Terms

We turn now to the question of reference change for S-type terms. Our thesis is that S-type terms may undergo a reference change in two ways. First, the term may change its status and become an F-type term. As such, it may undergo a change in reference when transmitted by means of a genuine focusing as described above for F-type terms. Second, unlike F-type terms, which cannot undergo a reference change when transmitted in the mock-focusing mode, S-type terms can undergo a change in reference when they are transmitted in the mock-satisfying mode. Such changes of reference I consider to be a conceptual change and discuss in fuller detail in section 2.6 of this chapter. Thus, the only way a term can undergo a simple change in reference (without thus also undergoing a conceptual change) is when it is transmitted by means of a genuine focusing.

We wish to illustrate how an S-type singular term changes its status to an F-type term and also undergoes a simple reference change. Let us consider the introduction of the name 'Neptune'. Recall that Neptune was hypothesized as the planet that caused such-and-such discrepancies in the orbits of certain other planets. At that time, there was no object that both satisfied the description and could be focused on with the aid of existing telescopes. Thus the term 'Neptune' was introduced at the baptismal stage as an S-type term. Although there is no focusing on an object at this initial stage, the term is a rigid designator denoting whatever actually satisfies the description.

Later on, however, after the development of more sophisticated telescopes, it became possible to focus on a heavenly body that our focusing experts on such heavenly bodies, that is, our astronomers, took to satisfy the above description. These experts then began to transmit the reference of the term 'Neptune' by focusing on the object that they took to satisfy the above description. After a while, these experts and the community, when transmitting the reference of the term 'Neptune', began to rely more on the *focusings* on the object rather than on the original description used when the term 'Neptune' was introduced. At this stage, the transmission for the community of the reference of the term 'Neptune' occurs through a genuine focusing. Thus far, what changed was the term's status from S-type to F-type and the mode of transmission, not necessarily the reference. (In fact, that is pretty much our current situation.)

Now suppose that we were to discover that, in fact, we are wrong in thinking that the heavenly body focused on is the planet that caused such-and-such discrepancies in the orbits of certain other planets, and that, in fact, some other planet satisfies this description. It does not seem likely to me that our newspapers and television would then report this new discovery as the "true" discovery of the planet Neptune. That is, they would not say that Neptune is the planet that caused such-and-such discrepancies in the orbits of certain other planets and that we have now discovered Neptune to be a different planet than the one we focus on and have been taking to satisfy the above description. Rather, it seems to me that we would still call the original planet focused on 'Neptune' despite the fact that it fails to satisfy the above definite description and that the planet that does satisfy the above description we would call something else. Newspapers and television would more likely report this new discovery as the real discovery of the planet that causes such-and-such discrepancies in the orbits of certain other planets and would report the discovery that our long-held belief about Neptune's being the cause of these discrepancies is erroneous.

The reason why we would have a change in the reference of the term 'Neptune' from its original reference (i.e., the satisfier of its A-B sentence) is twofold: first, in the current stage of transmission, the reference of the term is transmitted through a genuine focusing; thus the necessary condition for reference change of an F-type term is fulfilled. Second, the long period of time in which reference transmission for 'Neptune' is through a genuine focusing and various other social factors, such as the role of naming heavenly bodies by experts in astronomy, provide the sufficient conditions as well.

2.5   Reference Change of S-Type General Terms

We turn next to a discussion of reference change in the case of S-type general terms. Take, for example, the term 'mass'. We first describe how the term is used in Newtonian mechanics. We then consider a hypothetical situation in which certain discoveries could have led to a change in the reference of this term. (Later, in section 2.6, I compare the term's referent in Newtonian mechanics and in relativity theory and argue that in both theories the referent is the same.)

In his *Lectures on Physics,* the distinguished Nobel Laureate physicist, Richard Feynman, describes mass as "the quantity (measure) of how hard it is to get something (some physical thing) going."[4] Just how hard it is to get something going, that is, the property of resisting acceleration (or change in dynamic state), is what we call "inertia." Thus mass is a quantitative measure of the inertia of an object. I take these statements to be or to approximate the A-B statements for the terms 'mass' and 'inertia' and to describe their interrelationship as these terms are used in Newtonian mechanics. I view these terms as S-type general terms: mass is whatever quantity satisfies the condition 'x is the measure of how hard it is to get something going'; inertia is whatever property satisfies the condition 'x is the property of a physical thing being more or less hard to get going', that is, 'x is the property of resisting acceleration'. The picture presented in Newtonian mechanics is clear: Physical objects have a certain intrinsic resistance to movement or change of movement, that is, a resistance that is independent both of any forces acting on the object and of its acceleration. Since the force acting on an object can be used to measure how hard it is to get something going, when no other forces are acting on the object and

4. Richard Feynman, *The Feynman Lectures on Physics* (Reading, MA: Addison Wesley, 1963–65), 9-1.

the object is moving at a constant velocity, we can say that the mass of an object is the amount of force needed to overcome its inertia.

Now let us consider a hypothetical situation in order to see how the reference of the S-type general term 'mass' can change. Imagine Twin Earthians who live in a world governed by the same laws of Newtonian mechanics that (approximately) govern our world and who accept Newton's laws of motion. They introduce their term 'mass' by the A-B statement "Mass is the amount of force needed to get an object going," and they are aware that the A-B sentence holds only when there are no other forces acting on the object and the object is moving at constant velocity. Note that their term 'mass' is an S-type general term. Now suppose either that there is no place other than Twin Earth in the universe, that is, there are no other heavenly bodies and so on, or that Twin Earthians do not postulate universal forces that apply to other regions of the universe. We make this last pair of assumptions in order to block the Twin Earthians from deriving Newton's law of gravitational forces ($F = G\frac{m^1 m^2}{r^2}$) from Newton's second law of motion ($F = ma$). In order to derive Newton's law of gravitational forces from his second law of motion, we need to make two additional assumptions: first, we need to assume Kepler's laws in order to calculate what acceleration and force there must be to hold the planets in their elliptical orbits; second, we need the assumption that there are universal forces. Finally, we also assume that Twin Earth is a perfect sphere so that the same body always receives the same acceleration due to gravity on different parts of Twin Earth's surface.

Given the hypothetical situation, the above two assumptions would not be available to Twin Earthians. Thus they would not be able to distinguish between what we call "mass" and what we call "weight." Hence, they would not be able to determine which of the two, if any, is the satisfier of the Twin Earthian's A-B condition when they introduced their term 'mass'.

As a matter of historical fact, Galileo, Descartes, Leibniz and even Huygens had no clear conception of mass. "[W]*eight* and *mass* were taken interchangeably; these terms were one and the same thing. The real distinction between the two became evident when it was discovered that the same body may receive different accelerations by gravity on different parts of the earth's surface."[5] Newton, in his extension of the laws of

5. Florian Cajori, *A History of Physics* (New York: Dover, 1962), 60.

dynamics to heavenly bodies, clearly perceived the distinction between mass and weight.[6] Newton's extension of these laws thus delimited the class of satisfiers of the A-B condition for the S-type term 'mass'. Future Twin Earthian theories or extensions of their theories (say, accepting the existence of universal forces) might enable Twin Earthians to make this distinction and to discover that it is mass and not weight that satisfies their term 'mass'.

Now imagine that at some later stage, the Twin Earthians develop operational procedures, such as the use of scales, that enable them to measure easily the quantity they *take* to be the amount of force needed "to get an object going." Although the determinable quantity, weight, may not be something with which we are directly acquainted, the determinate feature that is the particular weight of a given object is epistemically accessible to us. We may take that determinate feature, say, the weight of a given object, to be that amount of force needed "to get *that* object going." The Twin Earthians, of course, believe they are measuring the "mass" of the object. Since the new procedure is so easy, it can be quickly and widely adopted: it requires merely focusing on meter readings, and so on. Thus the new stage in the transmission of the reference of the term 'mass' for Twin Earthians takes place through a genuine focusing. Since the new procedure can be carried out so easily, in the course of time, the term 'mass' for Twin Earthians comes to refer to what we would call an object's weight on Twin Earth. Thus our hypothetical example illustrates how an S-type general term can undergo a change in reference, and that when such a change takes place, it does so through a genuine focusing.[7]

We are now in a position to draw several conclusions from the hypothetical Twin Earth case. First, observe that initially the Twin Earthians' laws are the same (orthographically) as ours, and yet the referent of their term 'mass' is not the same as ours. Their term 'mass' at this stage refers to what we would call 'weight on Twin Earth'. Indeed, Newton's laws of

---

6. Ernst Mach, "On the Part Played by Accident in Invention and Discovery," *The Monist*, vol. 6, 166.

7. The determinate weight of a given object may arguably be considered an S-type term since it is debatable whether we can focus on a determinate weight. If so, I would then maintain that we achieved a reference change by mock-satisfying. This would then lead to a change in the concept expressed by their term 'mass' to denote the quantity measured by such-and-such meter readings and scales.

dynamics would be the same as they currently are even if he had not postulated the existence of universal forces and even if he had not been aware of a distinction between 'mass' and 'weight'. Newton and many of his predecessors would have had to rely on future theory to learn the referent of their term 'mass'. Here the moral is: contrary to a current view, we cannot simply look at *just* the laws of a given theory to determine the referents, let alone the meanings, of the terms in that theory. For in the case described above, the laws are the same (orthographically) as ours, and yet the referent of their term 'mass' differs from the referent of our term 'mass'.

Second, observe that even in cases where the laws express identities, and where these identity statements, such as '$p = mv$' (where 'p' denotes momentum), contain terms that seem to have a unique reference, there can still be more than one satisfier for a given term in the identity statement. In the hypothetical case of Newton and in the actual case of many of his predecessors listed above, as well as in the Twin Earth case prior to the use of procedures to measure how hard it is to get an object going, both quantities, weight and mass, satisfy the above identity statement for the term 'm'. Future theories or hypotheses can reduce the class of satisfiers of the term to a unique satisfier. For example, Twin Earthians may later come to believe that there are heavenly bodies and that their laws apply to the entire universe. Such a development would prevent the quantity weight from satisfying, say, the above equation '$p = mv$'.

Thus the example of mass illustrates how an S-type general term may undergo a reference change if (i) its status is changed to that of an F-type term, and (ii) its reference is then transmitted by means of a genuine focusing.

2.6 Conceptual Change

In this section we are concerned with concepts, conceptual change, and the relationship between conceptual change and reference change. The notion of conceptual change, and the necessary and sufficient conditions for it, is notoriously elusive. Moreover, there does not appear to be any received view as to what constitutes such a change. For example, one notion of conceptual change is that of a term's having associated with it first one concept, then another. This notion of concept too is very elusive. One common and legitimate use of this notion is to identify a concept with the meaning of a term. Our notion does not necessarily have these consequences. For our purposes we say that an S-type has underwent an unintended *genuine conceptual change* when the term has a different A-B condition than it initially had, yet remains an S-type term.

There is also a situation in which we loosely speak of a conceptual change: where there is a mistake or where we *intend* to change the current use of a given term, usually to correct a mistake. The new use may be only very remotely, if at all, connected with a previous use. We call such a change in usage *trivial conceptual change*, since we can always form the intention to use a given term in a new or a different way. As in situations in which we introduce a term from one language incorrectly into another, there are no rules governing the connection between the earlier and later use of the term. F-type terms can become S-type and vice versa, singular terms can become general and vice versa, and so on. We illustrate this trivial notion of conceptual change only because of its commonality, especially in certain theoretical contexts in which it is often confused with a more interesting notion of conceptual change.

To illustrate both kinds of conceptual change, we consider two examples: the first is the concept of mass in Twin Earthian classical mechanics and Twin Earthian relativity theory; the second is the concept of mass in Newtonian mechanics and in relativity theory.

2.7   Trivial Conceptual Change and Conceptual Confusion: Relativity and Twin Earth Relativity

To illustrate how a trivial conceptual change may take place, let us expand on the previous hypothetical example in section 2.5 by imagining that Twin Earthians have in the course of time developed their own theory of relativity. Like us, for centuries they accepted the law of inertia as a fundamental law of classical mechanics: A body removed sufficiently far from other bodies continues in a state of rest or of uniform motion in a straight line (with constant velocity). Let us also imagine that they too have determined that all systems of coordinates for which this law of inertia holds are to be regarded as equivalent for the purpose of formulating the laws of mechanical motion. They too call such systems Galilean; the transformation equations that enable descriptions of motion relative to one Galilean system to be transformed into descriptions relative to another they too call Galilean transformations. For them, as for us, such systems are equivalent in the sense that the laws of mechanical motion are invariant with respect to Galilean transformations.

One day, while thinking about the simultaneity of events and other physical phenomena, a Twin Earthian Einstein makes two ingenious discoveries. First, he discovers that there are two notions, both of which satisfy the equations for the term 'mass'. One is the notion of how hard it is to get something going independently of any other variable, such as acceleration due to gravity on Twin Earth, that is, the original A-B condition for their term 'mass'. The other is the notion of how hard it is to get something going, given its acceleration due to gravity on Twin Earth (or any other gravitational forces), that is, what Twin Earthians now focus on and call 'mass' and what we on earth call 'weight'. Second, he discovers that certain assumptions made in their classical mechanics regarding the time-interval between two events and the space-interval between two points of a rigid body are unjustified. In order to correct these assumptions, he has to modify the Twin Earthians' laws of classical mechanics in such a way that the new laws will be invariant with respect to an appropiate set of transformation equations (the Lorentz transformations). The resulting new principle he calls the "special principle of relativity," which requires that all the basic laws of physics be invariant with respect to inertial frames.

Now suppose this Twin Earthian Einstein finds that the way to make Twin Earthian classical mechanics Lorentz-invariant is to substitute for 'm' in all Twin Earthian physical laws $(m_0/g)\sqrt{1 - v^2/c^2}$, where g is the constant acceleration due to gravity on Twin Earth and m_0 is rest mass, that is, the mass of a body that is not moving. We still assume that the laws of physics are supposed to apply only to Twin Earth, that is, that the Twin Earthians do not assume the existence of other heavenly bodies or of universal forces. We may now raise the question: does relativistic Twin Earth mass ('mass$_{RTE}$') refer to the same quantity as prerelativistic Twin Earth mass ('Mass$_{CTE}$')? Clearly the answer is no: 'Mass$_{CTE}$' refers to the weight of an object on Twin Earth, whereas 'mass$_{RTE}$' refers to the object's mass. The Twin Earthians' term 'mass' when used in their classical mechanics does not have the same reference as their term 'mass' when used in their relativity theory.

The question now arises: Is the Twin Earthians' term 'mass' a counterexample to our claim about a necessary condition for a change in reference? We have argued that the mode of transmission of an F-type term's undergoing a change in reference must be a genuine focusing. The Twin Earthians' term 'mass' when used in their classical mechanics was transmitted by means of a genuine focusing, and consequently its status had changed to F-type. But later, in their relativity theory, when their term 'mass' underwent a change in its referent, the term was transmitted through a purely descriptive mode, and thus became an S-type term.

I maintain that this is not a counterexample to our claim because the use of the term 'mass' in their classical mechanics is *intended* to be used differently than their use of this term in their relativity theory. Their new theory acts as a new introduction of their term 'mass' and this theory contains its A-B statements. This use of the term 'mass' has no more in common with the use of 'mass' in Twin Earthian classical mechanics than does the use of the term 'mass' (or its equivalent) in Greek antiquity with its use in Newtonian mechanics.

That the term 'mass' in Twin Earthian relativity theory is *intended* to be used differently than in Twin Earthian classical mechanics is evidenced by their introduction of the notion 'acceleration due to gravity on Twin Earth' in their relativity theory. This notion is precisely what was not properly understood in their classical mechanics. But now, as evidenced by their introduction of the notion, they are aware of the distinction between the mass of an object and its weight (mass multiplied by acceleration due to gravity) on Twin Earth. And by introducing the constant g along with the term 'mass', they are carefully and intentionally distinguishing the two. The term 'mass' in their relativity theory is used the way it was *originally* used. After the term was originally introduced, it became confused with weight on Twin Earth. A return to a prior usage in order to correct a mistake is probably a common reason why linguistic communities may use a given term in a way different from the way they have been using it just before.

2.8   Genuine Conceptual Change, Newtonian Mass, and Relativistic Mass

We present two sufficient conditions for a conceptual change. We will then be in a position to apply our theory of reference change to the current debate concerning whether the term 'mass' in Newtonian mechanics refers to the same object as the term 'rest mass' in relativity theory.

We argue that not only do the two terms refer to the same physical quantity, but that no genuine conceptual change has taken place.

We said earlier that systems of coordinates whose relative motions are in accord with the law of inertia, are called "Galilean systems." We are concerned with such systems because the laws of classical mechanics hold only for such systems. That is, the laws of Newtonian mechanics are invariant with respect to these systems.

Analogously, a system of coordinates relative to which the state of motion accords with the laws of electrodynamics, the law of the propagation of light, and the simultaneity of events is called a "Minkowski space-time." All the laws of physical motion hold only for such a system of coordinates, and thus these laws are invariant with respect to such a system of coordinates. The system of equations from which we can transform a physical system from one Minkowski space-time to another is called a "Lorentz transformation." These laws and facts of physics are obviously invariant with respect to such a transformation.

Physicists seek to establish systems of coordinates and their transformations that leave the laws of physics invariant, since that gives them a formulation of their laws independent of any such reference frame. These coordinate systems and their transformations give, in this sense, an intrinsic characterization of the laws of physics. The Galilean transformation gives an intrinsic characterization of the laws of classical mechanics, and the Lorentz transformation gives an intrinsic characterization of the laws and facts of physical motion referred to above. We thus speak of coordinate systems and their transformations that leave a given set of laws invariant as "law-preserving coordinate systems" and "law-preserving transformations," respectively.

It seems natural to speak of a property or relation of objects or events that remains invariant with respect to a law-preserving transformation as an "intrinsic property" of the object or event. That is, we define a property as *objective* or *intrinsic* if and only if the property or quantity of the concept does not change (is invariant) when we consider the value of the property before and after undergoing a law-preserving transformation. For if a given property does not remain invariant with respect to various equivalent formulations of the same laws, it is not objective or intrinsic. On the other hand, if a given property does remain invariant with respect to a law-preserving transformation, this means that the property can be attributed to the object or event, to the same degree, regardless of how these laws are formulated. We obtain the same results in measuring this property for a given object or event from any law-preserving system of coordinates.

We now give some examples of properties that are and properties that are not intrinsic with respect to law-preserving transformations. The simultaneity of two events is a property that is intrinsic with respect to a Galilean transformation, since if two events are perceived as simultaneous in one inertial frame they will be perceived as simultaneous from every inertial frame. The elapsed time between two events is also intrinsic with respect to a Galilean transformation since the elapsed time between two events is invariant. On the other hand, the spatial distance between two events is not an intrinsic property with respect to a Galilean transformation, nor is the relation of moving faster than. In both these cases, we in general get different results when we evaluate these notions in different inertial frames. Rest mass is intrinsic with respect to a Lorentz transformation, since its value remains invariant with respect to this transformation, whereas simultaneity of two events is not.

The previous considerations seem to suggest the following sufficient condition for a conceptual change. If a term signifies a property that is intrinsic in one theory, but not in another theory, we say that the term expresses different concepts when used in the different theories. Two examples of terms satisfying this sufficient condition are 'length' and 'time'. Both terms denote intrinsic properties in Newtonian mechanics, but do not in relativity theory. Perhaps this fact can help shed light on some of the famous paradoxes of relativity, such as length and time dilation.

Another sufficient condition applies to individuals in a theory. Suppose a term in a given theory denotes an individual to which a class of predicables apply, and the term in another theory denotes an individual to which that class of predicables does not apply. Then the term expresses different concepts when used in the different theories. An example of the latter may be the notion of a physical entity as used in quantum mechanics when compared with how this term is used in other physical theories. The predicables of position and momentum no longer apply conjointly to a physical entity in quantum mechanics. For our purposes here, we need not discuss this latter sufficient condition for a conceptual change.

A current debate in philosophy of science is whether the term 'mass' as used in Newtonian mechanics and as used in relativity theory expresses different concepts. Our discussion of sufficient conditions for a change in concept sheds light on the matter to this extent: The term 'mass' as used in both theories does not satisfy either of the two above sufficient conditions for a conceptual change. This, of course, does not mean that a conceptual change has not taken place, but it may suggest that such a change has not occurred.

Further arguments that such a change has not taken place are provided, first, by the role that both terms 'mass' and 'rest mass' play in Newtonian mechanics and relativity theory, respectively. In a four-dimensional coordinate-free form, John Earman explains:

three principles of Newtonian Mechanics appear as

(N1) m_N is a scalar invariant
(N2) $P_N = m_N V_N$
(N3) $F_N = m_N A_N$

where M_n, P_n, V_n, F_n, A_n are, respectively, the Newtonian mass, the Newtonian four-momentum, four-velocity, four-force, and four-acceleration. In the SRT [special theory of relativity] there are *exact* analogues (R1), (R2), (R3) of (N1), (N2), (N3) with proper mass m_O in place of m_N, the relativistic four-momentum P_R in place of P_N, etc. . . . The exact parallelism between these two sets of principles supports the hypothesis that m_N and m_O have the same denotation.[8]

Second, it does not seem plausible that 'rest mass' and 'relativistic mass' denote physical quantities that are on the same footing. As Earman points out, the "so-called 'relativistic mass' comes from a three-dimensional coordinate-dependent effect associated with inertial coordinate systems. If, therefore, 'relativistic mass' denotes a new kind of mass, then for every distinct kind of non-inertial coordinate system there will be yet another new kind of mass."[9] Note the appeal in this second argument to an intrinsic, coordinate-free, form of the laws of physics. Apparently we have a strong intuition that a sufficient condition for a term having the same denotation in two theories is its having an intrinsic property associated with it *and* its playing the same role in both theories.

Finally, we note that both 'proper mass' and 'Newtonian mass' appear to have the same A-B statement, namely, "let 'mass' denote the measure of how hard it is to get something going."

8. John Earman, "Against Indeterminacy," *The Journal of Philosophy* 74, 9 (September 1977): 535–538.

9. Earman, "Against Indeterminacy," 537.

3

S-Type Terms and Their Anaphoric Chains

S-type terms and their anaphoric chains constitute a deep, pervasive feature of the process whereby linguistic information is conveyed. Pronouns are often paradigm cases of such a feature. For example, imagine the following conversation. "A man was in my room smoking a cigar earlier today." "How do you know?" "He left a trail of ashes, and the room has the odor of his cigar smoke." In this conversation, the pronoun 'he' is used as an S-type term the referent of which cannot be determined independently of the anaphoric chain of sentences making up the conversation: The pronoun 'he' refers to the man who was in the initial speaker's room smoking a cigar earlier on the day of the conversation.

In this chapter, I hope to do three things. First, I wish to provide a brief informal account of the semantics of S-type terms and their anaphoric chains. (Later, in chapter 8, I present a formal semantics for these terms.) Second, I argue that the notion of anaphoric chain is *required* to give a satisfactory account of how reference is determined for S-type terms in general and S-type pronouns in particular. As far as I know, there is no analysis in the literature of anaphoric chains[1] that includes an account of the rigidity of such terms and consequently no adequate account of the semantics of S-type terms. Since the predominant occurrence of indexicals is in this S-type anaphoric use, the lack of such a semantics constitutes a serious limitation on current accounts of indexicals. I illustrate this point in a brief

---

1. See chapters 7 and 8 for a discussion of Discourse Representation Theory (due to Hans Kamp and Irene Heim) and Dynamic Predicate Logic (Jeroen Stockhoff and Martin Groendijk) for attempts to develop something close to anaphoric chains and for criticisms of these attempts. Those attempts do not deal with the question of rigidity, which is essential for a full account of S-type terms and pronouns.

discussion of some aspects of David Kaplan's work on indexicals. Last, as a further illustration of how the F-type/S-type distinction and the semantics of S-type terms can be applied, I present a new puzzle about certain kinds of identity sentences and suggest how the introduction of such a distinction can lead to a solution to the puzzle.

3.1   F-type and S-Type Terms and Their Semantic Contributions to Sentences

I begin this informal account of the semantics of S-type terms by showing that F-type terms and S-type terms determine their referents in significantly different ways. As a result of this difference, they make different contributions to the semantic information conveyed by the sentences in which they appear, even though these sentences may express the same proposition (i.e., have the same content). To make this clear, let us examine how the same sentence conveys different information depending upon whether the designator term in the sentence is F-type or S-type.

Consider the imaginary conversation at the beginning of the chapter:

Ms. A: A man was in my room smoking a cigar earlier today.
Mr. B: How do you know?
Ms. A: He left a trail of ashes and the odor of cigar smoke.

In this dialogue between Ms. A and Mr. B, we have the S-type pronoun 'he' and its A-B sentence, which is the first sentence of the dialogue. The three sentences we call the *anaphoric chain* of the S-type term 'he'.

To ascertain to whom the term 'he' refers, we would go back to the A-B sentence on the basis of which Ms. A introduces the pronoun 'he'. In quantification theory, we may loosely formalize the A-B sentence as follows:

(1) $(\exists x) (Mx \ \& \ Rx \ \& \ Cx)$,

where the predicates 'Mx', 'Rx', and 'Cx' stand for 'x is a man', 'x is in my room' and 'x is smoking a cigar earlier today', respectively. Recall that in chapter 1, in order to determine the referent of an S-type term, we made use of the truth conditions of its A-B sentence. There we said that the S-type term rigidly refers to a satisfier of the open sentence formed from the A-B sentence after removing the appropriate quantifier. Thus in the previous example, the relevant satisfier class from which we may arbitrarily select a member that the S-type term rigidly refers to is

(2)   (Mx & Rx & Cx).

We called this open sentence the A-B condition for the S-type term.

It may be helpful here to suggest an analogy between how an S-type use of a term refers to its referent and how a term obtained through existential instantiation (in a natural deduction system) refers to its referent.[2] A term introduced by an existential instantiation denotes an arbitrarily chosen satisfier (i.e., some satisfier or other of the open sentence formed by removing the existential quantifier) taken from the range of values of the variable previously bound in the existential sentence prior to removing the existential quantifier. Similarly, the S-type term denotes an arbitrary satisfier of the open sentence formed from its A-B sentence after removing the relevant quantifier (i.e., its A-B condition) taken from the range of values of the variable previously bound in the A-B sentence prior to removing the relevant quantifier. A term introduced in an existential instantiation refers back to an arbitrarily chosen satisfier of the existential sentence after removing the existential quantifier on which the existential instantiation is based. Simlarly, an S-type term refers back to an arbitrary satisfier of its A-B condition.

When we say "Something has property P" ("∃x(Px)"), this sentence is true just in case there is an assignment for x that satisfies the open sentence Px. There may, of course, be more than one assignment for x that satisfies Px. A term used in an existential instantiation of a sentence is an arbitrary constant. It "names" an "arbitrarily selected object" from the range of x that satisfies the existential sentence.

Note that it clearly does not make sense to ask, with respect to an arbitrary constant introduced through an existential instantiation, which object satisfying the existential sentence after removing the quantifier in question is referred to by that constant. So too it does not make sense to ask which member of the class of satisfiers of its A-B condition is referred

---

2. This analogy is used only as a heuristic device. In chapter 8, where we present the formal semantics of S-type terms, it is shown that this analogy does not literally hold. For important views that base their semantics of anaphoric pronouns on their semantics for existential instantiation in a natural deduction system, see George Wilson, "Pronouns and Pronominal Descriptions: A New Semantical Category," *Philosophical Studies* 45 (1984): 1–30; Jeffrey King, "Anaphora, Instantial Terms, and Pronouns," *Philosophical Studies* 61 (1991): 239–265, and Kit Fine, *Reasoning With Arbitrary Objects* (New York: Blackwell, 1985). It would be a worthy project to compare these interesting approaches with my own.

to by an S-type term. (Of course, when a uniqueness condition, as in Russell's theory of descriptions, is placed on the existential sentence, the problem of which object the S-type term refers to does not arise. The S-type term, in such a case, refers to the unique satisfier of its A-B condition, whatever that object may be.)

We discover another aspect of the analogy if we examine the truth conditions of sentences containing arbitrary constants on the one hand, and the truth conditions of sentences containing S-type terms on the other. The truth condition for a sentence containing an arbitrary constant introduced by existential instantiation, is obtained as follows.

Consider the arbitrary constant, μ, introduced by an existential instantiation, $F\mu$, of an existential sentence $\exists x(Fx)$. If we use the term μ in another sentence, $G\mu$, then the truth condition for $G\mu$ is

$G\mu$ is true iff $\exists x(Fx \, \& \, Gx)$.

For since μ denotes an arbitrarily chosen satisfier of Fx, what $G\mu$ says is not

$\exists x(Fx) \, \& \, \exists x(Gx)$.

Rather, what it says is that some arbitrarily chosen object that has the property F also has the property G:

$\exists x(Fx \, \& \, Gx)$.

Similarly, the truth condition for a sentence Hs containing the S-type term s, the A-B condition of which is, say, Px, may be expressed as follows:

Hs is true iff $\exists x(Px \, \& \, Hx)$.[3]

The following dialogue between Smith and Jones can help to illustrate how truth conditions are determined for sentences containing S-type terms. Smith starts the dialogue by making the following prediction:

Smith: A woman (some woman or other) will land on Mars in the year 2051.
Jones: She will be an American.

Here Smith's first sentence is the A-B statement for the term 'she', and this term as used in the sentence uttered by Jones is an S-type term. It refers to a member of the class of women-who-will-land-on-Mars-in-the-year-2051, that is, to a member of the class of satisfiers of the A-B condition.

---

3. We are ignoring for the moment that an S-type term is rigid.

After Smith's A-B statement, Jones says, "She will be an American." We may then state the truth condition for his utterance as follows:

"She will be an American" is true iff $\exists x$(x is a woman who lands on Mars in the year 2051 & x is an American).[4]

It should now be clear from the truth condition for this sentence that the S-type term 'she' must refer to an object that satisfies *both* conjuncts contained in its truth condition (after removing the existential quantifier).

But the analogy between S-type terms and arbitrary constants introduced by existential instantiation should not be pressed too far. S-type terms are rigid designators: they pick out the same object in all possible worlds. On the other hand, terms introduced merely to refer to the satisfier of an open sentence formed from an existential sentence by removing the existential quantifier do not in general refer to the same object in all possible worlds.[5]

To see that the S-type term 'she' in our example above rigidly refers to some woman under consideration, we can imagine Smith going on to say the following:

Smith: Were she to have earned more money as a musical conductor than as an astronaut, she would have been conducting on Earth rather than preparing for her voyage to Mars.

The S-type term 'she' still rigidly refers to the same woman who actually became an astronaut, even when we consider the possible circumstance in which she chose not to become one.

What limits the analogy between the two kinds of terms is that an S-type term's A-B statement plays a significant role in determining the class from which we select the term's referent. But there is no proposed semantics for an existential statement to play the same role in determining the referent of an individual constant introduced by existential instantiation of this statement.

In determining the class from which we select S-type term's referent, we first turn to where, when, and by whom (as well as other relevant param-

4. Further refinements are required to state correctly the truth conditions for S-type terms. See this chapter and chapter 8 for details.

5. Some people may hold that arbitrary constants introduced by existential instantiation are rigid designators, in which case, the analogy does not break down at this point.

eters) its A-B sentence is introduced. We call the context specified by these various parameters in which the A-B sentence is introduced the *context of introduction* of the A-B sentence. The A-B statement makes a claim that the proposition expressed by the A-B sentence is true with respect to (wrt, hereafter) the context of introduction. But in order for this proposition to be true wrt the context of introduction, often some other proposition must be true wrt to some (other) possible world, time, agent, or other parameters. For example, if the A-B statement makes a claim that P could have been the case, then in order for the A-B statement to be true wrt its given context of introduction, presumably the actual world, P' must be true wrt some possible world accessible to the actual world, where 'P'' is the indicative form of 'P'. Suppose that the A-B statement is a claim that P will be true in the future. For this A-B statement to be true wrt its context of introduction, that is, the actual world at the time of utterance of the A-B sentence, P' must be true with respect to the actual world at a time later than that of the A-B statement's context of introduction. We call these possible worlds, times, or other relevant parameters in which P' must hold the *relevant indexes* or the *relevant context*. We also say that *an A-B statement makes a claim about the domain(s) of the relevant index(es)*.

Now consider an S-type term with a given A-B statement. The domain from which that A-B statement makes a claim (that is, the domain of its relevant index), is the domain from which the S-type term rigidly designates a member.[6] This domain we call the *pronominal satisfier class* for a given S-type term ('PSC', hereafter). It is the class from which we may choose a referent for the S-type term the A-B condition of which helped to determine this PSC. Also, later sentences of the discourse may or may not further restrict the PSC. Thus the PSC is not always identical with the domain about which the A-B statement makes a claim. When they differ, it is the PSC from which the S-type term rigidly designates a member.[7]

No analogous claim must hold for individual constants introduced by an existential instantiation of an existential sentence in a formal deductive system, or at least no such development of its semantics has been proposed.

---

6. For further discussion of contexts, see section 3.2 on David Kaplan. For further discussion and application of the relevant index, see chapters 5 and 7.

7. Also, later sentences of the discourse may or may not further restrict the PSC. Another main difference between the semantics for S-type terms and such constants is that my semantics for S-type terms permits intersentential binding. See chapter 8 for details.

In fact, generally there is no claim that there is a specific domain from which we may choose a referent for an individual constant introduced by existential or universal instantiation.

To see how the referent of an S-type term is determined from the domain of the relevant index, consider our dialogue above where Smith predicts that a woman will land on Mars in the year 2051. This prediction is the A-B statement, and its context of introduction is the actual world at a time prior to the year 2051. The prediction is true just in case in the actual world, in the year 2051, there is a satisfier of the open sentence that results from removing the existential quantifier (i.e., the A-B condition of being a woman landing on Mars in that year). Thus the relevant index is the actual world in the year 2051, and hence the domain about which the A-B statement makes a claim is, in this case, the domain of the actual world in the year 2051. Restricting this domain to the class of women who land on Mars in the year 2051 yields the PSC for the pronoun 'she', and this pronoun must rigidly refer back to a specific satisfier from this class.

We now show the semantic role of the A-B condition for an S-type term by comparing it with that of the A-B condition for an F-type term.

Consider the sentences

(3)   Some professional football player is very rich.

(4)   He (pointing) travels to Europe several times a year.

Suppose that in asserting (3) and (4), the speaker focuses epistemically on a certain individual taken to be a very rich professional football player. Then the pronoun 'he' serves as an F-type term. It rigidly refers to that individual, whether or not the speaker is correct in ascribing to him the property of being a rich professional football player. It seems then that the "propositional content" of (4), when the term 'he' is F-type, is something like the following:

(4a)   That guy (pointing) travels to Europe several times a year.

Here the role of the A-B statement, (3), is only ascriptive: the speaker need not be correct in ascribing to that person the property of being a professional football player. The use of the ascription seems to serve only to draw attention to the thing the speaker wishes to focus on and refer to with the F-type term 'he'. But the ascription in (3) does not provide an A-B condition (by removing the existential quantifier) that has to be satisfied in order for the sentence (4) to be true. Thus the referent of the F-type term 'he' does not have to satisfy this condition.

On the other hand, if the speaker does not have any particular individual in mind, the A-B statement and the A-B condition formed from this statement play a much more significant semantic role. The speaker simply means to assert that some professional football player—or other—is very rich, and he travels to Europe several times a year. Here the pronoun 'he' serves as an S-type term, and the statement then made by (4) (without indicating) has the following truth conditions:

(4b) $\exists x(A(x$ is a professional football player & x is very rich & x travels to Europe several times a year)),

where 'A' is the sentential actuality operator, to be read "it is the actually the case that" (since the actual world is the relevant index). This sentence, unlike (4a), is an existential sentence, and the pronoun 'he' refers to a member of the domain from the relevant context in which the A-B condition must be satisfied, and this member satisfies the truth condition sentence above after removing both the existential quantifier and the operator 'A'.[8]

Although the A-B condition is part of the truth condition for the pronoun 'he' when used as an S-type term, it is neither part of the meaning of the S-type term nor part of the propositional content of sentence (4) containing the S-type pronoun 'he' (and there is no indicating). To see this, consider the following variant of an earlier dialogue:

Smith: A woman (some woman or other) will be the first person to land on Mars in the year 2051.
Jones: Necessarily she will be an American.

Jones's statement can have two plausible readings. First, it could be interpreted less literally, but more plausibly, as not expressing a claim about any particular woman's necessarily being an American, but rather as expressing that necessarily, whoever will be the first person to land on Mars in the year 2051 will be an American. Based on this paraphrase, we would formalize the conjunction of Smith's and Jones's statements, that is, the entire anaphoric chain, as

(5) $\exists x[(Wx \ \& \ Lx) \ \& \ (\forall x((Wx \ \& \ Lx) \rightarrow Ax))],$

---

8. For further details on what constitutes the relevant context, see chapter 5. For further details on determining the domain of this context and a member of this domain, see chapter 8.

and we would formalize Jones's statement, that is, the second sentence of the anaphoric chain as

(5′)   [∀x((Wx & Lx) → Ax)].[9]

Second, it could be interpreted more literally, but less plausibly, as expressing a claim about the particular woman who lands on Mars in the year 2051: that she, whoever she may be, will necessarily be an American. Based on this reading, we would formalize the conjunction of Smith's and Jones's statements, that is, the entire anaphoric chain, as

(6)   ∃x[(Wx & Lx) & (Ax)].[10]

Now in both of these cases, we cannot interpret the A-B condition either as part of the content of the pronoun 'she' or as part of the content of what is expressed by the second sentence of the dialogue. For to do so would require formalizing the second sentence of the dialogue as

(7)   (∃x(Wx & Lx & Ax)).

But neither the first nor the second reading of the dialogue permits such a formalization of the second sentence of the dialogue. On neither interpretation are we claiming that it is a necessary truth that there exists a woman who will land on Mars in the year 2051 and that she will be an American. Rather, on the second reading, the S-type pronoun 'she' is assigned a referent from its PSC as determined by its A-B condition. We then attribute the property of being an American of necessity to this referent.[11] Thus on this literal reading of Jones's statement, it is only the referent, and not the A-B condition that determines it, that is part of the content of the S-type

9. For further discussion of these kind of sentences, see chapter 7.

10. In chapter 8, I show how to formalize the second conjunct alone, that is, the second sentence of the anaphoric chain. Of course, this will require assigning to the variable x a woman who lands on Mars in the year 2051. This example, slightly embellished, also illustrates that Frege cannot solve his puzzle regarding the cognitive significance of certain identity statements. Simply imagine that in the above dialogue, Jones points to a woman and says "Necessarily she is an American," and that in fact the woman demonstrated is the woman who lands on Mars in the year 2051. Then the current argument in the text shows that the content of Smith's occurrence of the pronoun 'she' in the dialogue in the text is the same as the content of the term 'she' made above together with Smith's demonstration (pointing). Yet clearly the cognitive significance of the two occurrences of the pronoun 'she' differ.

11. For details on how to formalize this sentence, see my formal semantics for anaphora in chapter 8.

term 'she' and, likewise, of what is expressed by the second sentence in the dialogue.

3.2   Kaplan on Directly Referential Terms, Character, Content, and Cognitive Significance

Recall that the term 'rigid designator' stands for an expression that designates the same object in every possible world in which the object exists and that otherwise fails to designate. According to this definition of a rigid designator, there are many rigid designator terms that require the mediation of a sense to determine their referents. The most obvious examples are complex mathematical terms, such as 'the square root of nine, plus two'. This complex term designates 5 in every possible world and thus is a rigid designator. Kripke calls such rigid definite descriptions "rigid *de facto*." Those rigid designators the referents of which are determined without the mediation of a sense, or "where the reference of a designator is *stipulated* to be a single object, whether we are speaking of the actual world or a counterfactual situation"[12] he calls rigid *de jure*.

Now consider a sentence that expresses an identity between the referents of a term, 'a', that is rigid de facto and a term, 'b', that is rigid de jure. Since 'a' is rigid de facto, it is associated with a Fregean sense, and thus it is easy to see how an identity sentence of the form 'a = b' expresses a different proposition from that expressed by a sentence of the form 'a = a'. Accordingly, Kaplan and others argue that a sentence of the form 'a = b' expresses the same proposition as a sentence of the form 'a = a', only when terms 'a' and 'b' are both rigid de jure, or what he calls "directly referential." For present purposes, an expression is directly referential if it is a rigid designator term and does not require the *mediation* of a sense to determine its referent (in any possible world). (We modify this definition in what follows.)

This is not to say, however, that directly referential terms do not have any sense or that they do not have any meaning. For example, Kaplan takes indexical expressions, such as 'I', 'here', and 'now', to be directly referential. At the same time, he is aware, of course, that indexical expressions do have meanings, or in his terminology, 'characters'—meanings that, in fact, play

12. Saul Kripke, *Naming and Necessity*, 21n.21.

a role in determining the referents of such expressions. 'I', for example, means the speaker in a given occasion of use, or "context of use" as Kaplan calls it. Other expressions, such as his dthat operator, may be *associated* with a full-blown Fregean sense used to fix the referent and yet be directly referential.

In order to distinguish directly referential expressions from other referring expressions, we need to distinguish Kaplan's notion of a *context of use* from his notion of a *possible circumstance of evaluation.* The context of use of an expression, or more simply a context, is the use of an expression by an agent at a particular time and place in a particular world. (The context may also include other parameters as well.) Indexicals, which are directly referential terms, will, perhaps by definition, in general designate different objects when used in different contexts.[13] On the other hand, a *possible* circumstance of evaluation, or for short a circumstance, is just a *counterfactual situation* (i.e., a possible world). Since an indexical is a directly referential expression, although in general its referent changes in different contexts of use, once its referent is determined in a given context of use, the indexical rigidly refers to its referent in all possible circumstances of evaluation in which its referent exists.

We must also distinguish Kaplan's notion of character from his notion of content. What is said in using a given indexical varies in different contexts. Borrowing Kaplan's example, if I say today,

I was insulted yesterday,

and you utter the same words tomorrow, what is said is different. Kaplan calls this first kind of meaning—what is said—content. The content of a sentence is what has traditionally been called a proposition. It is the *content* of an expression that is evaluated in circumstances of evaluation.

13. Often ambiguity and indexicality are treated as the same semantic phenomenon. I don't agree. Using Kaplan's basic machinery, an indexical term's content may be represented by one function that in general maps different contexts of use into different contents. A term is ambiguous if the term's content may be represented by more than one function that maps a given context of use into a content, that is, more than one content is designated for a given context of use of the term. But, unlike an indexical term, those same contents will be the only contents designated in different contexts of use. That is, the same function for the ambiguous term will map different contexts of use into the same content. (For the notion of content, see what follows.)

A second kind of meaning is that which determines the content in varying contexts. The rule

'I' refers to the speaker or writer

is what Kaplan considers a meaning rule of this second kind. Such meaning rules Kaplan calls "character." The character of an expression is set by linguistic conventions and determines the content of an expression in every context. In Kaplan's terms, we may represent contents by functions from possible circumstances to extensions (Carnap's intensions), and we may represent characters by functions from possible contexts to contents.[14] We thus get, schematically:

Character: Contexts → Contents

Content: Circumstances → Extensions

We call these functional representations of character and content principle (I).

In the case of referring expressions that are not directly referential, the referent is determined by the meaning in the first sense, that is, the content, of the expression, together with the "possible circumstance of evaluation of what is said on a given occasion of use." The most obvious examples are definite descriptions. On the other hand, in the case of directly referential expressions, if they have meaning at all, then they have it in the second sense, that is, the character, which in turn determines the referent in each context of use once and for all, independently of any possible circumstance. Thus an expression is *directly referential* if, once its referent is determined (say, by the expression's character in a given context of use), the referent remains fixed for all possible circumstances.

Consider the sentence "I exist." For any particular context of use, the sentence is true, since the referent of the term 'I' is the agent in that context, though of course the referent of 'I' will, in general, vary from context to context. On the other hand, given a particular context, the sentence will not be true in certain circumstances of evaluation, namely, those in which the speaker of the given context does not exist. Thus once we are given a context, the referent of the term 'I' remains fixed and is independent of the possible circumstances.

14. Kaplan notes that this functional representation of characters and contents has the drawback of identifying equivalent characters and of identifying equivalent contents.

For Kaplan, all demonstratives are directly referential. Once an associated demonstration is given with the demonstrative, its referent is determined and taken as fixed in all possible circumstances. In fact, Kaplan has introduced a singular term, 'dthat', intended to be a surrogate for a true demonstrative, and the description associated with the singular term that completes 'dthat' is intended to be a surrogate for the completing demonstration. The description, as Kaplan points out, "completes the *character* of the associated occurrence of 'dthat' but makes no contribution to content . . . It [merely] determines and directs attention to what is being said, but the manner in which it does so is not strictly *part* of what is asserted."[15]

According to Kaplan, we are to think of the vehicles of evaluation—the what-is-said in a given context—as propositions. Propositions are structured entities, and their constituents are generally taken to be complexes constructed from various attributes by logical composition. Such a complex, given a possible circumstance, determines an object. Singular propositions, on the other hand, are propositions that have as constituents individuals rather than individual concepts or manners of presentation. In the case of a singular proposition, then, the constituent is just the object itself. That is why Kaplan says of singular propositions, "it does not just turn out that the constituent determines the same object in every circumstance, the constituent (corresponding to a rigid designator) just is the object. There is no determining to do at all."[16] Thus Kaplan speaks alternatively of a term as directly referential if and only if in any context of use, the content of the term is the referent itself.

For Kaplan, all indexicals are directly referential terms. Their contents are their referents themselves. We call this claim about indexicals principle (II). Kaplan also maintains that character applies only to words and phrases as types, whereas content applies to occurrences of words and phrases in contexts. We call this principle (III).

According to Kaplan, it is a problem for the Fregean to account for the cognitive significance of a true identity statement of the form 'a = b' by

15. David Kaplan, "Afterthoughts," in *Themes from Kaplan,* ed. Joseph Almog, John Perry, and Howard Wettstein (New York: Oxford University Press, 1989), 581.

16. David Kaplan, "Demonstratives An Essay on the Semantics, Logic, Metaphysics, and Epistemology of Demonstratives and Other Indexicals," in *Themes from Kaplan,* ed. Joseph Almog, John Perry, and Howard Wettstein (New York: Oxford University Press, 1989), 494.

appealing to the different content of terms 'a' and 'b'. For, given his singular term 'dthat', the statement "a = dthat(a)" is a necessary truth. Thus if "a = b" is a true identity statement, so is "dthat(a) = dthat(b)." But the Fregean cannot account for the cognitive significance of the latter identity statement by appeal to the different content of these terms. For, since these terms are directly referential, they both have the same content, namely, the terms' (same) referent.[17]

If 'a' and 'b' differ in content, then 'dthat(a)' and 'dthat(b)' differ in character, the manner of presentation of the term. This suggests to Kaplan that it is the character of an expression that is to be identified with its cognitive significance of a thought. To make this claim more plausible, Kaplan presents the following Putnamesque thought experiment. Consider two identical twins raised under qualitatively identical conditions, stimuli, and so on, and further assume that they respond to all cognitive stimuli in identical fashion. Kaplan declares that in these circumstances the identical twins are in the same total cognitive (i.e., psychological) state. But they believe different things. Each sincerely says,

My brother was born before I was.

Kaplan thus concludes that it is an almost inevitable consequence of the fact that two people are in the same total cognitive state that they will disagree in their attitudes toward some object of thought. Now the fact that people could be in the same total cognitive state and still believe different things not only shows that cognitive significance cannot be identified with the thought, content, or proposition expressed by the sentence, contrary to Frege. It also strongly suggests to Kaplan that since people, such as the twins above, can have these different thoughts presented to them in the same manner, that is, by means of the same character, the cognitive significance of a single sentence or even a term should be identified with its character. Accordingly, we call Kaplan's view that the cognitive significance of an expression is identical with its character (schematically, cognitive significance = character) principle (IV).

---

17. For an argument that does not make use of any specially defined term, such as 'dthat', to show that the Fregean cannot account for the cognitive significance of certain identity statements, see section 3.1. See especially where I argue that F-type terms and S-type terms may have the same content, even though they clearly have different cognitive significance, and footnote 10.

3.3   Objections to Kaplan, and the Role of Anaphoric Chains and A-B Conditions

We now argue that Kaplan can neither provide a semantics for S-type (indexical) pronouns nor account for their cognitive significance. As for cognitive significance, I do not believe that Kaplan can account for this notion by the use of his notion of character any more than Frege can by the use of his notion of sense (or content). If two names (rigidly) designate the same thing, their character is represented by the same function. They have the same content, namely, their referent, given any context of use. But then, character cannot account for the difference in cognitive significance of, say, "Cicero = Cicero" and "Cicero = Tully." The problem of cognitive significance, as Kripke has shown in his "A Puzzle about Belief," is a genuine puzzle about cognition independent of any account of the semantics of proper names or other terms. (In chapter 5 I also argue that Kaplan cannot provide the correct formal semantics for proper names, even assuming that in general they are directly referential terms.)

Consider the sentences (3), (4), and (4′).

(3)   Some professional football player is very rich.

(4)   He travels to Europe several times a year.

(4′)   Well, he would be less rich if he were in philosophy.

Here (3) and (4) serve as anaphoric background for (4′). Now suppose that the occurrences of the term 'he' in the anaphoric chain have the same referent when used as an F-type term as when used as an S-type term. Still, the cognitive significance of (4′) will differ even though the content of (4′) (i.e., the proposition it expresses), as we argued in section 3.1, remains the same. This, as we noted above, is a problem for Fregeans, since they want to account for the difference in cognitive significance of expressions (or different occurrences of the same expression) by the difference in their content. But, as we will see, it is also a problem for Kaplan's account of cognitive significance.

Taking 'he' as an F-type term, the truth condition and cognitive significance for (4′) is something like

(4′a)   That guy (pointing) would be less rich if he (that guy) were in philosophy.

But, taking 'he' as an S-type term, (since the relevant index is the actual world) (4′)'s truth condition and cognitive significance seem to be something like the following:

(4′b)   ($\exists$x)A(x is a professional football player & x is very rich & x travels to Europe several times a year & if x were in philosophy, then x would be less rich),

where 'A' is a sentential actuality operator, read as "it is actually the case that." Since (4′b) is an existential sentence formalized with the actuality operator, whereas (4′a) is not, these sentences will in general have very different cognitive significance. When the occurrences of the pronoun 'he' in (4′) are S-type, the relevant context contains the actual world as its domain. Accordingly, the cognitive significance of (4′) is 'the person who actually is a very rich professional football player who travels to Europe several times a year would be less rich if he were in philosophy'. The same is obviously not true when the occurrences of the pronoun 'he' in (4′) are F-type.

But according to Kaplan's principle (IV), the cognitive significance of the expression is identical with its character. Moreover, the character of (4′) cannot differ depending upon whether the term 'he' is F-type or S-type. For that would violate his principle (III), that is, that "character applies only to words and phrases as *types*."[18] The pronoun 'he' is clearly the same type regardless of whether it is used as an F-type or S-type term. The property of being F-type or S-type applies to occurrences of terms, not types.

Nor can Kaplan assert that occurrences of the indexical pronoun 'he' have different contents even when they refer to the same entity depending upon whether the occurrence of the pronoun is F-type or S-type. We have seen in section 3.1 that in such a case, the content of the pronoun is the same whether it is F-type or S-type. Moreover, this assertion would violate Kaplan's principle (II): All indexicals are directly referential terms. If the indexical expression has as its content the referent itself as an F-type term but not as an S-type term, then the indexical as an S-type term cannot be directly referential.

The problem for Kaplan is that his formal semantics for indexicals cannot provide a semantics for S-type terms, even S-type indexical pronouns. His semantics only provides the character (and for demonstratives a demonstration) to determine the content of indexicals (and demonstratives). This

18. Kaplan, "Demonstratives," 524.

is the first functional representation of his principle (I). But we have just seen that the character alone, given a context of use, does not determine the content of S-type terms, thus violating the first part of his principle (I).

Kaplan cannot avoid this problem by claiming that S-type pronouns are not the kind of indexicals for which he attempted to provide a semantics since these terms should really be analyzed as bound variables in the familiar way. The problem with this claim is that many of the examples of S-type terms have their anaphoric background (i.e., their A-B sentence) in prior sentences than the sentence in which they occur. There is no ready-made semantics for intersentential binding. Consequently, Kaplan would have to develop a formal semantics for intersentential binding, similar to the semantics I provide in chapter 8.

Nor can he eliminate the problem by claiming that S-type pronouns are represented by free variables under a given assignment of a value. Again his semantics for indexicals would be inadequate. What, for example, in this semantics *determines* the assignment to the variable? It cannot be the character of S-type terms. For, as we have already observed, the character does not distinguish S-type occurrences of a term from F-type occurrences of the same term. The content of S-type terms is not merely a (character) function of the context of occurrences of these terms. In short, Kaplan cannot account for semantic differences between occurrences of a given term as F-type and occurrences of that term as S-type.

What is missing from Kaplan's account is the role of A-B sentences and anaphoric chains in the semantics and cognitive significance of S-type terms and of sentences containing these terms. In particular, it is the A-B sentence and anaphoric chain of an occurrence of an S-type term that is essential in determining its referent by determining its PSC. An assignment of a value to a free variable that represents the S-type pronoun must come from this class. The content of an S-type term is a function of its context, its A-B condition, and its anaphoric chain.[19]

3.4 Some New Puzzles about Identity Statements and Rigid Designation

I want next to discuss some puzzles about identity statements that arise in connection with rigid designator terms. The role of the A-B condition, anaphoric chain, and the semantics of an S-type term aid in a solution to

19. In chapter 5, I also criticize Kaplan's formal semantics for proper names.

these puzzles. First, let us consider a puzzle about the cognitive significance of certain identity sentences.

There seems to be something very different between the information conveyed by

(8)   Cicero = Tully

on the one hand, and

(9)   Water = H_2O

on the other. The discovery that (8) is true seems to be only the discovery that someone, Cicero, is the same person as Tully. Given that (8) makes use of the names 'Cicero' and 'Tully', we have the intuition that what we have discovered by this true identity sentence is that the two names are names for the same object. But the discovery that (9) is true (like the discovery of the truth of "Gold = Au_{79}" or "lightning = electricity") seems to give us more information. This scientific discovery seems to inform us about the essential properties (nature) of water. Such sentences we shall call *essentially informative*.

Indeed, defenders of the new theory of direct reference, such as Kripke, Kaplan, and Putnam, maintain that such scientific identifications convey information reflected in scientific discoveries of essential properties. But if 'water' and 'H_2O' are directly referential rigid designators, the sentence consisting of the identity sign flanked by these terms cannot convey discoveries of essential properties by means of what this identity sentence expresses. For if these terms are directly referential, then the sentence expresses the same proposition as the sentence of the form 'a = a' (where 'a' is one of the terms used in the scientific identification). It is then hard to see how such identification can be essentially informative. Rather, it would seem merely to express the truth that the object named by 'a', that is, the object named by 'b', is self-identical.

As we have previously discussed, Kaplan's notion of character is his solution to problems of how two sentences can express the same proposition and yet differ in informativeness, that is, cognitive significance. For although two sentences may express the same proposition, that is, have the same content, the terms in each of the sentences may differ in character. But we have seen that this account of the difference in the conveyed information of two sentences will not always be adequate to account for their different information. In particular, we argued that Kaplan's semantics as it stands cannot account for the new linguistic information that S-type terms acquire and contribute to sentences that contain them.

A second puzzle concerning identity statements is as follows: Since the identity relation is symmetrical, how can defenders of the new theory of reference maintain that, for example, being H_2O is an essential property of water, but being water is not an essential property of H_2O? Or for example, how can one maintain that being Au_{79} is an essential property of gold, but being gold is not an essential property of Au_{79}? It seems to me that anyone who holds that there are (directly referential) rigid designator terms is obliged to provide solutions for these puzzles.

That these new puzzles deserve attention gains further support from the following sort of linguistic intuition. While it seems that the name 'Cicero' is a name for Tully and the name 'Tully' is a name for Cicero, it seems that although the name 'water' is a name for H_2O, the name 'H_2O' is not a name for water. Now since water = H_2O, how can something be a name for water, that is, H_2O, be a name that refers to H_2O, and yet not be a name for H_2O as well, and vice versa?

Also, it is worth noting that Frege's solution to his (different) puzzle about the cognitive status of identity statements, although more general than these new puzzles, does not resolve them. For even if his solution could account for the informativeness of identity statements of the form 'a = b', there is nothing in his solution that explains, for example, why the discovery that water = H_2O is a discovery about the essence of water and not the other way around. Nor is there anything in the Fregean solution that suggests that the discovery that Cicero = Tully is merely the discovery of two names for the same object.

It should now be clear why certain identity sentences convey different semantic information from that conveyed by sentences of the form 'a = a' where both occurrences of the term are the same F-type or S-type term even though both identity sentences may well express the same proposition. This can happen when the term 'a' in the sentence 'a = a' is either a different type than the term 'b' or both terms are different S-type terms and 'a = b'. If, say, term 'a' is F-type and term 'b' is S-type, since each of these terms determine their referent in a different manner, they convey different information. Thus the fact that they each have a different manner of presentation of the same referent explains why they differ in cognitive significance and information they convey in sentences of the form 'a = b'. Such sentences cannot convey the same semantic information, or thus have the same cognitive significance, as sentences of the form 'a = a', where both occurrences of the term 'a' are the same F-type or S-type term. In the latter case, since both occurrences of the term are the same F-type or S-type term, they make the same contribution to the information conveyed by the sentence in which they occur. The semantic information conveyed by such an identity sentence is something like that conveyed either by the tautology "the thing focused on is the thing focused on"[20] or by the tautology "the object in question that satisfies the A-B condition is the object in question that satisfies the A-B condition." We shall say that such identity sentences are *trivially informative*.

But identity sentences in which one term occurring in it is S-type and the other either an F-type or a different S-type term may convey nontrivial *semantic* information, that is, they may be *semantically informative*. For example, consider an identity sentence of the form 'a = b' where one term is F-type and the other is S-type. What this sentence conveys is something like "the object focused on as the referent of the F-type term is the same as the object that in fact satisfies the A-B condition of the S-type term." Such information is obviously nontrivial. If we previously had no idea what object satisfies the A-B condition, being told this true identity sentence would inform us.

It is important to understand that when I talk about the semantic information conveyed by a given term, I am not talking about information that is part of the content or that is expressed by the proposition of the sentence containing that term. I simply mean part of the information that plays the semantic role in determining the referent of the term. Likewise, when I say that a sentence is semantically informative, I am not claiming that what is semantically informative about the sentence is part of its content or the proposition that the sentence expresses. I am also not claiming that information conveyed by an expression, semantic, essential, or otherwise, is the same as its cognitive significance, although such information is part of the expression's cognitive significance.

We are now in a position to take the first step in solving our puzzle, namely, to see why various theoretical identity sentences do not convey the same information as sentences of the form 'a = a'. Theoretical identifica-

---

20. Here we are assuming that the F-type term is not a demonstrative, such as 'this' or 'that', with different demonstrations.

tions, such as "gold = Au_{79}," "water = H_2O," and "lightning = electricity," are all sentences involving an identity sign between an F-type term and an S-type term. The term 'gold' is F-type, focusing on the substance that we take to be a yellowish metal, whereas the term 'Au_{79}' is S-type, rigidly referring to the substance, whatever it may be, that has the atomic number 79. The term 'water' is F-type, focusing on the substance that we take to be the clear liquid that we drink and that is in the lakes, and so forth, whereas 'H_2O' is S-type rigidly referring to the substance, whatever it may be, that consists of two hydrogen atoms and one oxygen atom.[21] 'Lightning' is F-type, focusing on a particular sort of flash of light, whereas 'electricity' is S-type, which in this context refers to streams of electrons discharged by the clouds.[22]

Now it might be objected that some of these S-type terms in these theoretical identifications are rigid definite descriptions, and hence are not directly referential. Terms for types of atoms and molecules are the most promising candidates for being rigid definite descriptions. But in such a case, no one would claim that these theoretical identifications express the same proposition as a sentence of the form 'a = a', and thus it would be trivial to account for the different information that the two sentences convey. It is only where there are identifications between directly referential terms that it is claimed that they express the same proposition as does a sentence of the form 'a = a'.

To this objection I would counter that it is only superficially plausible to think of the names of types of atoms and molecules as definite descriptions. The reason for this is that those names, based on a set of primitive directly referential names, encode a basis for "calculating" the atom or molecule to

21. I am not claiming that all the names of the elements are (or even were initially) S-type terms. In fact, most, such as 'hydrogen' and 'oxygen' are not and were not initially. Furthermore, in 1783, when Cavendish discovered that water was made up of hydrogen and oxygen, and shortly thereafter when Sir Humphrey Davey discovered that the molecular formula for water is H_2O, the formula 'H_2O' referred to the ratio of hydrogen to oxygen to form water. It was not until 1803, when Dalton hypothesized that matter is composed of atoms and that *all samples of any given compound consists of the same combination of these atoms,* that these structural names for molecular structures were introduced (by Dalton). It is these names, introduced as structural names of molecules, that I claim are S-type.

22. I do not consider the terms 'gold', 'water', and 'lightning' to be *pure* F-type terms, that is, F-type terms that do not also have characters, or "stereotypes" in Putnam's terminology, associated with their terms. But for our purposes here, we can ignore this point.

which it refers. Accordingly, I call these names *structural descriptive names*. The name 'H$_2$O', for example, refers to a substance the molecular structure of which consists of two hydrogen atoms and one oxygen atom. The name 'Au$_{79}$' refers to atoms with 79 protons. But this does not make these S-type names rigid definite descriptions any more than numerals, which are written with a given base, are rigid definite descriptions.[23]

The difference between definite descriptions and S-type terms regarding theoretical identity sentences is that such sentences with definite descriptions do not express genuine identity statements whereas they do with S-type terms. Sentences containing definite descriptions are analyzed à la Russell as existential statements. Even granting that when used in science, such sentences may express necessary truths, still, unlike identity sentences involving only S-type and/or F-type terms, they do not express genuine identity statements.

Moreover, we can trivially substitute for any rigid definite description an indexical or demonstrative that would thus be directly referential. For example we may refer to the square of two as "that number" or "it" and the substance the molecular structure of which consists of two hydrogen atoms and one oxygen atom as "that substance" or "it.". The pronoun 'it' or the demonstrative 'that' as used in "that number" or "that substance" is an indexical, the A-B sentence of which makes use of a definite description. Accordingly, the indexical is an S-type directly referential term. We may even introduce a proper name that would then directly refer to the thing referred to by the definite description. For example, for the thing rigidly referred to by "the substance the molecular structure of which consists of two hydrogen atoms and one oxygen atom," we may introduce the name 'H$_2$O'.

In any event, once we introduce these pronouns or proper names, they refer directly to whatever the rigid definite description refers to. We may then form theoretical identifications using these terms. For example, suppose we introduce the indexical 'it' as previously in the following anaphoric chain:

23. For, as Kripke has argued in his Harvard University Alfred North Whitehead Lectures, May 4–5, 1992, "Logicism, Wittgenstein, and *de re* Beliefs about Numbers," numerals have a certain structure. In base 10, for example, the numeral in the rightmost column tells us how many ones we have, the next column how many tens, and in general, the nth column how many 10^{n-1}'s. Nevertheless, this does not make numerals rigid definite descriptions. For details, see these lectures.

(10)   There is a substance (i.e., exactly one substance) the molecular structure of which consists of two hydrogen atoms and one oxygen atom.

(11)   It is identical to water.

Although both terms of this theoretical identification are directly referential, the semantic information conveyed, and thus the cognitive significance, by this identification would still be different from the semantic information conveyed by sentences of the form 'a = a'. The semantic information conveyed by the theoretical identity statement cannot be accounted for, contrary to Kaplan, by the character of the term 'it'. We can only account for the linguistic information conveyed by this identity sentence once we include the *acquired* linguistic information conveyed by the S-type term due to its A-B condition and its anaphoric chain.

We come now to solutions for our new puzzles concerning certain identity sentences. The first puzzle, recall, is that many identity sentences, such as the theoretical identifications above, are essentially informative. They seem to convey information about *essential* properties of objects. On the other hand, other identity sentences, such as "Hesperus = Phosphorus" or "Cicero = Tully," clearly do not. How can theoretical identifications convey anything but that the object named by 'a', that is, the object named by 'b', is self-identical?

Part of this puzzle has been resolved by noting that an identity sentence is semantically informative whenever at least one of its terms is S-type and the other term is either F-type or a different S-type term.[24] Since theoretical identifications, it seems, must contain at least one S-type term, such sentences are, therefore, semantically informative.

But not all semantically informative identity sentences are essentially informative. An identity sentence is essentially informative if it conveys an essential property of the object(s) referred to by its terms. What further condition, then, must be placed on a semantically informative identity sentence for it to be an essentially informative identity sentence? As the example below will help to make clear, it is not enough to require that the identity in question *express* a necessary truth, since all genuine identities express a necessary truth.

---

24. Notice that an identity sentence that contains two S-type terms is basically conveying in effect that the object that satisfies the A-B condition of one of the terms also satisfies the A-B condition of the other.

Suppose, for example, that in the year 2051, a woman, whose baptismal name is 'Sarah', is the first woman to land on Mars. The name 'Sarah' is an F-type term. Let us now return to our imaginary dialogue about the prediction of a woman landing on Mars in the year 2051. We can imagine someone saying, "Ah, so she is (identical to) Sarah," where the term 'she' is an S-type term pronominalizing on the A-B sentence

(12)   Some woman will be the first woman to land on Mars in the year 2051

in our earlier imaginary dialogue. But surely the identity sentence

(13)   She is identical to Sarah

does not convey essential information, even though (13) is a necessary truth. That is, given the relevant index, the S-type pronoun in (13) rigidly designates Sarah. What (13) does convey, and thus has as part of its cognitive significance, is equivalent to the following:

(14) $(\exists x)A(x$ is a woman who lands on Mars in the year 2051 & $x =$ Sarah).

Now (14) is not a necessary truth. It is not true in all possible worlds. Further, (14) clearly does not express an essential property of Sarah. For surely although Sarah *in fact* lands on Mars in the year 2051, under different circumstances she might not have.

Sentence (13) fails to be an essentially informative sentence because the A-B statement, (12), makes a claim about the actual domain, that is, the actual world (i.e., the world of the relevant index). That is, it is only claimed that the proposition expressed by (12) is true in the actual world. Thus the satisfier for the A-B condition of the S-type pronoun 'she' in (13) must come from the actual domain. But, as we will shortly see, in order for an identity sentence to be essentially informative, it must contain an S-type term the A-B statement of which makes a claim for all possible worlds— not merely the actual or one particular world. That is, it must be claimed that the A-B statement of the S-type term expresses a proposition true in all possible worlds.

Now we have claimed that the true identity sentence "Cicero = Tully" (or "Hesperus = Phosphorus") merely reflects the discovery that someone, Cicero, is the same person as Tully. Given that this identity sentence makes use of the names 'Cicero' and 'Tully', we said that we feel that we have merely discovered that the two names are names for the same object. Notice that the terms in identity sentences, such as 'Cicero = Tully' or 'Hesperus = Phosphorus', are only F-type. Unless these F-type terms have a different "character" in Kaplan's sense, F-type terms may not convey different semantic information in the sentences in which they occur. Thus if coreferential F-type terms do not have a character, they do not convey different semantic information in the sentences in which they occur. Thus an identity sentence formed with such terms cannot be essentially informative.

Identity sentences the terms of which are only F-type can be (nontrivially) informative from an epistemic point of view, however. Establishing the truth of these identifications requires a discovery, and such discoveries may even be of great importance. Accordingly, we call these identity sentences *epistemically informative.*

When we discover the truth of an epistemically informative identity sentence, we may then learn that the thing focused on at one occurrence is the same thing that is focused on at another occurrence. More generally, we may learn that two different focusings on an object may be focusings on the same object. This information may be very important for epistemic and psychological matters, such as analyzing psychological attitudes and clearing up puzzles about belief. With respect to our puzzle, when we discover that an identity sentence is only epistemically informative, such as "Cicero = Tully" is, it explains why the sentence merely reflects the discovery that someone, say, Cicero, is the same person as Tully. It also explains why we feel that we simply discovered that the two names, say, 'Cicero' and 'Tully', are names for the same person and that we have not discovered any essential property about the person. To be sure, since Cicero = Tully, necessarily Cicero = Tully, and thus in a manner of speaking one can say that "being Tully is an essential property of Cicero", that is, "being Cicero is an essential property of being Cicero." Now if this is a property at all, it is merely the property of being self-identical. Accordingly, we say that such identity sentences are trivially essentially informative.

The conclusions formed with the distinctions employed above may be summarized as follows. First, an identity sentence may be *epistemically informative* when formed with two (different) F-type terms; this accounts for the intuition that all we have discovered is that two names name the same thing. Second, an identity sentence is *semantically informative* if at least one of its terms has an A-B condition with different semantic content than that of the other term's A-B condition or one of its terms has a character different than that of the other term. Third, an identity sentence is trivially essentially informative if both its terms are F-type. Fourth, an identity sentence is essentially informative if its terms' A-B conditions differ and at least one of its terms has an A-B statement the claim of which has as its domain all possible worlds.

The second new puzzle about identity statements centers on the fact that the identity relation is symmetrical. How can it be maintained (as in the case of "H_2O = water") that being a is an essential property of b, but being b is not an essential property of a, where 'a' is a theoretical term and 'b' is not?

The solution to this puzzle is that, in general, we are interested in learning about things to which we bear an epistemic relation. We often develop science with an eye toward giving an account of the mechanisms, functions, properties, and essential properties of the things or phenomena with which we are in some sense acquainted. We bear an epistemic relation to these things, and thus we may focus on these things and refer to them with F-type terms. 'Gold' and 'water', say, are F-type terms. We are acquainted with their referents and focus on them. We later hypothesize that since they are both substances or kinds, it is their microstructure that makes them what they are. Accordingly, we develop a theory and a scientific program along the line of (15) to hypothesize various theoretical identifications.

(15)   All and only substances are essentially individuated by atomic or molecular structures.

Statement (15) is a guiding principle for establishing identities in chemistry. Chemistry, especially in the late eighteenth and nineteenth centuries, took (15) as a leading hypothesis for its scientific program of discovering the identity of specific substances with specific atomic or molecular structures. Further, the theory of chemistry states the following:

(16)   Atoms bond to form molecular structures by sharing valence (outermost shell) electrons and forming a full valence shell. With the exception of the first shell, which has two valence electrons, all shells have a valence of eight electrons.

Specifically, with regard to oxygen and hydrogen atoms, the theory states that hydrogen has one valence electron and oxygen has six valence electrons.

The A-B statement for the S-type term 'H_2O' is based on the molecular program expressed in (15), the theoretical statement of chemistry expressed in (16), and the specific claim regarding the valence electrons of hydrogen and oxygen. These statements applied to the case of a water molecule entail that one such molecular structure consists of two hydrogen atoms and one oxygen atom. That is to say,

(17)   Given the valence numbers of hydrogen and oxygen, any two hydrogen atoms may combine with an oxygen atom to form a molecular compound.

We call that molecular compound 'H_2O'.[25]

The anaphoric background for introducing this S-type term consists of statements (15), (16), and (17). These statements are not intended to be merely a claim made about the actual world. For example, the "all and only substances" and the "any two hydrogen atoms" of (15) and (17), respectively, are not intended to refer to all and only substances in the actual world or any two actual hydrogen atoms. These statements are intended to express laws of nature. As such, they are lawlike and support counterfactual conditionals. Thus the universal quantifiers in these statements are intended to range over substances, atoms, and molecules in any possible (i.e., counterfactual) circumstance, that is, to apply to all possible domains. Thus (15), (16), and (17)—the theoretical scientific statements that are the A-B statements of the term 'H_2O'—are claimed to be true in all possible worlds. Thus in order for an identity statement with at least one S-type term to be essentially informative, a condition is that the domain of the claim made with the A-B statement(s) must be the set of all possible worlds.

Now theoretical terms are often paradigms of S-type terms.[26] 'H_2O' and 'Au_{79}', mentioned earlier, are S-type terms. It is not in virtue of any

---

25. Of course, I do not mean that it is always technically possible to form the molecular compound consisting of two hydrogen atoms and one oxygen atom. The hydrogen atoms that are around in a given circumstance may be part of a compound that can't be decomposed to free its hydrogen atoms. I merely mean that in accordance with current molecular theory, we may form such a compound as opposed to, say, a compound consisting of three hydrogen atoms and one oxygen atom. There cannot be such a molecular compound; hence there cannot be a substance consisting in such a structure, since that combination has the wrong valence numbers. It is not merely that there is no such substance in the actual world; rather there is no such substance in any possible world.

26. For a view suggesting something along these lines, see Hilary Putnam, "Explanation and Reference," in *Conceptual Change,* ed. Glenn Pearce and Patrick Maynard (Dordrecht: D. Reidel, 1973), 199–221.

epistemic relation we may have to the objects denoted by these terms that the reference of these terms is fixed. Rather, these S-type terms denote whatever satisfies their respective A-B conditions. The anaphoric background for the term 'H$_2$O' is the hypothesis that there is a molecular compound the structure of which consists of two hydrogen atoms and one oxygen atom. The thing, whatever it is, that satisfies the condition of being the molecular compound the structure of which consists of two hydrogen atoms and one oxygen atom is the referent of the term 'H$_2$O'.

Suppose we have a theoretical identification between an F-type term and an S-type term, and that we further claim that this identity sentence is essentially informative. Our claim, then, is that the property in virtue of which something is a satisfier of the A-B condition of the S-type term is an essential property of the thing denoted by the F-type term. More precisely, we claim the following.

Being a is an essential property of b iff (i) 'a = b' is a genuine identity statement; (ii) the term 'a' has an A-B statement the domain of which is all possible worlds; (iii) the satisfier of its A-B condition satisfies this condition in all possible worlds; and (iv) no part of its A-B condition makes a reference to a specific context or world.

Condition (iii) and (iv) can never be conjointly met by F-type terms. The referent of an F-type term is the thing focused on (i.e., the satisfier of the focusing) in an initial context of introduction, that is, the context in which the F-type term is initially introduced. This is the baptismal step of naming. After this initial step, in any context of use, the F-type term refers to the thing focused on in this initial context of introduction. (See chapter 5 for further details.) The referent is not whatever in some possible world is phenomenally similar to, or in the same position or time as, the thing focused on in the context of introduction. The F-type term must only refer in all possible worlds to whatever is focused on in the context of introduction, even in possible worlds in which it wouldn't be the object focused on if the term were introduced in that world. Thus the satisfier of an F-type term's A-B condition will not in general satisfy this A-B condition in all possible worlds without the A-B condition's making a reference to satisfying this condition in the context of introduction.[27]

27. This is what I take to be the correct moral to draw from Hilary Putnam's Twin Earth examples in "The Meaning of 'Meaning'." I do not agree with him that this shows that these terms have an indexical element, however.

The property in virtue of which water satisfies the A-B condition of 'H$_2$O' is the property of being a molecular compound the structure of which consists of two hydrogen atoms and one oxygen atom. Thus it is an essential property of water to be a molecular compound the structure of which consists of two hydrogen atoms and one oxygen atom. The property in virtue of which lightning satisfies the A-B condition of the S-type term 'electricity' is the property of being a stream of electrons (discharged by clouds). Thus an essential property of lightning is the property of being a stream of electrons (discharged by clouds).

However, an essential property of H$_2$O is not being the thing initially focused on when introducing the term 'water', that is, being the thing focused on in the context of introduction for the F-type term 'water.' Although water = H$_2$O, being the property in virtue of which water satisfies the A-B condition of 'H$_2$O' is not the same as being the property in virtue of which H$_2$O satisfies the A-B condition of 'water'. This explains the asymmetry.

II

Propositional Attitudes and Vacuous Names

4

The Disquotational Principle, De Re and De Dicto Belief Attributions, and an Agent's Perspective

Thus far our discussion of proper names and pronouns used anaphorically has not treated their use in sentences that occur in intentional contexts, that is, in sentences within the context of a propositional attitude idiom to form a propositional attitude attribution. Considering just the belief attitude, we take the form of such attributions to be 'A believes that $\Phi\alpha$,' where α is a proper name or pronoun occurring at least once within the open sentence Φ.

In this chapter, I deal with two problems that involve such belief attributions. On the de dicto reading of a belief attribution, which is generally taken to be a relation between an agent and a proposition, it is usually assumed that the agent, A, will assent to the sentence '$\Phi\alpha$' (or its translation into the agent's language) that lies within the scope of the belief context. Indeed, Kripke has introduced customarily accepted principles of belief attribution that connect an agent's verbal behavior with a belief attribution. The de dicto reading of a belief attribution is supposed to express the *way* the agent thinks of or represents the content of the attributed belief. The attribution allegedly captures the "point of view" of the agent. Thus any principle of de dicto belief attribution must capture the agent's point of view or perspective. Kripke's principles, by connecting an agent's assent behavior with a belief attribution, appear, as we will see, to capture this point of view. Although I accept these principles as capturing central cases of belief attribution, I question requiring them for all cases.

Our first problem, then, is to specify under what conditions it is appropriate to make belief attributions for which the above principles fail. Our second problem is to specify in what sense such belief attributions (for which Kripke's proposed principles fail) still capture an agent's perspective or point of view. Here we intend to rule out an agent's beliefs that are based on mere "hunches" or on "feeling it in one's bones." Rather, we restrict ourselves to an idealized rational agent's beliefs that are formed in virtue of the agent being such an agent and having certain kinds of rational and semantic commitments (as explained in chapter 5).

I do not discuss the issue of whether such conditions constitute truth conditions or merely what our practice deems appropriate. Suffice it to say that on either view, we still need to account for these conditions in order to account for either the truth or the appropriateness of these attributions, since given our community practice, some of these attributions are accepted and others are rejected. I also do not deal with the well-known Kripkean puzzle about belief: I am neither trying to solve the puzzle nor claiming that my conditions avoid the puzzle about belief. In passing, however, some of my notions may help explain what happens when this phenomenon arises.

4.1 Principles of Belief Attribution

In this section, I argue that there are belief attributions deemed appropriate that violate Kripke's principles of belief attribution. I further argue that when we make such belief attributions, the agent cannot reflect upon his or her resources alone and assent to the sentence that expresses the attributed belief. We thus call a belief attribution that requires some extension or modification of Kripke's principles a *secondary belief attribution;* the sentence within the scope of the belief context of such an attribution we call a *secondary belief.* Ordinary belief attributions that are not secondary we call *primary belief attributions;* the sentence within the scope of the belief context of such an attribution we call a *primary belief.*

We begin with appropriate belief attributions that violate Kripke's proposed customary principles of belief attribution. In his article "A Puzzle about Belief," Kripke argues that Frege's puzzle about belief arises even in cases in which we don't apply the principle of substitutivity of coreferential proper names, salva veritate, within propositional attitudes.[1] Now with

---

1. Saul Kripke "A Puzzle about Belief," in *Meaning and Use,* ed. A. Margolit (Dordrecht: Reidel, 1979); also in *Propositions and Attitudes,* ed. Nathan Salmon and Scott Soames (New York: Oxford University Press, 1988); all page references given in this work are to the latter.

Kripke's central conclusion—that the puzzle about belief can arise without appeal to this substitutivity principle, and hence that this puzzle is not a problem for the new theory of reference for proper names—I have no quarrels, provided names are restricted to F-type (as, indeed, most uses of proper names are). But in so arguing, Kripke introduces the following two principles of belief attribution. Where 'P' is to be replaced, inside and outside all quotation marks, by any appropriate standard English sentence:

Principle 1 (the disquotational principle): If a normal English speaker, on reflection, sincerely assents to 'P', then he believes that P

and

Principle 2 (the strengthened biconditional disquotational principle): A normal English speaker who is not reticent will be disposed to sincere reflective assent to 'P' if and only if he believes that P.

The biconditional form of the disquotational principle strengthens the simple form of the principle by adding that failure to assent indicates lack of belief, just as assent indicates belief. It is only with the converse of principle 1 (what the strengthened biconditional disquotational principle 2 adds to principle 1) that we will presently be concerned. We refer to this part of the strengthened disquotational principle as *principle 2′,* or *the converse disquotational principle.* Principle 2, the strengthened biconditional disquotation principle, is the conjunction of principle 1 and principle 2′.

As a counterexample to principle 2′, let us suppose that I have a student, Mary, who writes a dissertation on Kripke's work on inadmissible ordinals. Suppose further that I do not know how to evaluate various technical claims made in her dissertation and that I decide to show the dissertation to Kripke for his evaluation. On some other occasion, let us say, Kripke hears me mention Mary by name, but he does not associate that name with the person whose dissertation I show him (her name is not on the copy I show him). Finally, suppose that Kripke, who has never met nor been otherwise acquainted with my student, reads the dissertation and concludes that my student is brilliant.

Under these conditions, it seems that I can correctly report to Mary,

(1)   Kripke believes that you are brilliant.

Moreover, let us suppose that my colleagues ask me what Kripke thinks of Mary. I can then correctly say the following:

(2)   Kripke believes that Mary is brilliant.

But Kripke will not assent to the sentence "Mary is brilliant" regardless of how much reflection he gives to this query, since he does not know that my student's name is 'Mary'. Yet principle 2′ requires his assent to this sentence upon reflection in order to correctly make attribution (2). We regard these attributions as correct, even though the agent cannot reflect upon his resources alone and assent to the sentence that expresses the attributed belief. Thus, in this example, (1) and (2) are illustrations of secondary belief attributions that violate principle 2′.

But are (1) and (2) genuine counterexamples to Kripke's principles of belief attribution? In order to be so, they must be de dicto belief attributions, since these principles are only designed to apply to such attributions. But are examples (1) and (2) really de dicto belief attributions?

Historically, a de dicto belief attribution is generally regarded as having the logical form of a dyadic relation between a believer and a proposition or a state of affairs.[2] Thus a de dicto belief attribution may be expressed in a sentence of the form

(i)   A believes that-P,

where 'A' stands in for the name of an agent and 'P' by a sentence expressing a proposition.

This formulation presents an immediate problem in arguing that (1) and (2) are de dicto belief attributions, however. For, as we noted earlier, a de dicto belief attribution is supposed to capture the *way* the agent thinks of or represents the content of the reported belief.[3] But the sentence within the belief context in (2) is generally regarded as expressing a singular proposition. A singular proposition is a structured proposition the constituents of which are individuals, rather than individual concepts, and an attribute or property. The individuals are referred to by directly referential singular terms in the sentence expressing the singular proposition; the attribute (or property) is expressed by the predicate of that sentence. Now

2. My characterization of a de dicto and de re belief is based on Lynne Rudder Baker's "De Re Belief in Action," *The Philosophical Review* 91, 3 (July 1982): 363–387.

3. I am considering only what the practice deems correct. I am not discussing whether or not the semantics of de dicto belief attributions requires capturing the way the agent thinks of or represents the content of the reported belief.

the problem with claiming that (2) (or (1)) is a de dicto belief report is not only that Kripke will not assent to the sentence "Mary is brilliant," and hence that sentence does not capture his way of thinking or representing the content of the reported belief. Kripke will not assent to *any* sentence that expresses the same content, that is, the same singular proposition, as expressed by that sentence. Thus on this analysis of a de dicto belief ascription, Kripke does not appear to have a de dicto belief relation to this singular proposition. Moreover, characterizing a proposition as a set of possible worlds does not help in arguing that (1) or (2) is a de dicto belief report. For Kripke will not assent to a sentence expressing that this is a world in which Mary is brilliant.[4]

Nor may (1) or (2) be interpreted as elliptical for some other specific de dicto belief ascription, where it attributes to Kripke having a (de dicto) belief relation to some other proposition. The problem is that since Kripke does not know that the student's name is 'Mary', he would refer to her by using any one of several other linguistic expressions. He might, for instance, point to the dissertation and use the referring expression 'the person who wrote this' or, while addressing me, use the linguistic expression 'your student who wrote the paper you just gave me'. We could then use, for example, the following sentence to express a certain de dicto belief ascription:

(3)   Kripke believes (the proposition) that Berger's student who wrote the dissertation that Berger showed Kripke is brilliant.

If (2) were to express a particular de dicto belief attribution, such as (3), then it would matter which of the above referring expressions I substitute

---

4. There is an alternative view of a de dicto belief report that analyses its logical form as a triadic rather than a dyadic relation, where the third relatum is the mode in which the object of the belief is accessible to the agent. (See, e.g., Mark Crimmins and John Perry, "The Prince and the Phone Booth: Reporting Puzzling Beliefs," *The Journal of Philosophy* 86, 12 (1989): 685–711; Mark Richard, *Propositional Attitudes* (Cambridge: Cambridge Press, 1990); and Stephen Schiffer, "Belief Ascription," *The Journal of Philosophy* 87 (1992): 602–614. On this view, Kripke would bear the relation to the singular proposition expressed by the sentence 'Mary is brilliant' where Mary is accessible to Kripke under the mode of presentation of 'the author of the dissertation' or some such mode of presentation. This view can thus analyze (10) and (11) as a de dicto belief attribution. But this view cannot handle the example in chapter 5 as either a de dicto or de re belief ascription.

(in the appropriate context) for 'Mary' in (2), since each substitution gives us a sentence that expresses a different proposition. But, in fact, there seems to be no basis to favor any of these substitutions over the others; Kripke could have used any one of them to express his belief. So it does not seem that (2) is an abbreviation for any of these resulting belief ascriptions. In fact, (2) does not imply that Kripke believes the proposition that is the object of the belief attributed to him in (3) or in any of the sentences resulting from substitution of one of the above referring expressions. Thus (2) does not seem to express or imply any of these specific de dicto belief attributions. And if this is the case, do we really have a counterexample to the converse disquotational principle?

Perhaps, then, (1) and (2) should more properly be considered de re belief attributions. A de re belief attribution is generally regarded as having the logical form of a triadic relation among a believer, an object or objects, and a property or relation that the believer ascribes to the object(s). A de re belief attribution may be expressed in a sentence of the form

(ii)   A believes that α is F,

where 'α' stands in for a singular term, where 'F' stands in place of a predicate, and where exportation of α from the belief context to the referential position must be permissible salva veritate. Accordingly, we may apply existential generalization to (ii) and obtain

(ii′) $\exists x$(A believes that x is F),

where x is the object that agent A believes has property F.

The conditions that must obtain in order for a reporter to make a true de re belief attribution are far from clear. The problem with establishing such conditions is that the notion of de re attribution is not a notion in ordinary language. It is a notion invented by philosophers. So we don't have intuitions of how we use this notion in ordinary language. If the notion is supposed to capture the notion of a belief's being *about* an object, then we do not have clear intuitions regarding the application of this notion. For the notion of being "about" something is a vague notion. Is the expression 'the president of the United States in 1972' about Richard Nixon? In some sense, the answer to this question is yes. But clearly, it does not follow that if someone has the de dicto belief that the president of the United States in 1972 is a Republican, that person has the de re belief of Nixon that he is a Republican. As a result of these considerations, that there is no notion of de re belief attribution in ordinary language and that the notion of aboutness is vague, I consider de re belief attribution to be vague and a matter of degree.

Consider a paradigm case, due to Quine,[5] in which we attribute to someone a de re belief: An agent, Ralph, believes, of the suspicious man in the raincoat whom he is looking at, that he is a spy. In such paradigm cases, three conditions seem to obtain. First, the constituent object of the belief is (or has been) in direct causal or cognitive contact with the agent. Second, as a result of this causal contact, the agent, Ralph, forms some justified belief (from his or her perspective), at the time of causal contact. For example, Ralph believes that the person appears in front of him and has a suspicious appearance of a spy. We call this justified belief *epistemic contact*. Third, the agent can recognize the object about which he has a de re belief. This is sometimes called the "knowing who" condition.

But these conditions for attributing a de re belief to someone, for the reasons stated above, are not clear and seem to be matters of degree. As for the first condition, although the agent may be (or may have been) in causal contact with the object of belief, the causal contact may not be *direct*. The agent may see a picture of the object or, perhaps, hear a singer's voice, say, that of Maria Callas, and identify the singer as the best soprano of the century. In still other cases, even weaker causal contact with the object may suffice in order to attribute a de re belief to the agent. For example, we might be willing to attribute a de re belief to the agent even though he is in causal contact with the object only on the basis of a report from some other person who is in direct causal contact with the object.

As for the second condition, the agent need not form the justified belief (i.e., establish epistemic contact) at the time of causal contact. Someone may mention something to the agent at a later date (say, "the person who we were talking to yesterday at the party is a spy").

As for the third condition, it is obvious that no agent can recognize the object under every circumstance. This is the source of Quine's point that in one circumstance (in which Ralph, say, is looking at Ortcutt, the suspicious man in the raincoat), Ralph believes that Ortcutt is a spy, while in another circumstance (say, in which Ralph sees his neighbor, who happens to be Ortcutt), Ralph believes that he is a respectable member of society.

5. W. V. O. Quine, "Quantifiers and Propositional Attitudes," in *The Ways of Paradox* (Cambridge, MA: Random House, 1966), 183–194.

Moreover, it does not suffice in order for an agent to have a de re belief about an object that the agent can recognize the object under *some* circumstance (e.g., when he or she is looking at a name tag on the object).

Now these three conditions are at best sufficient conditions for making a de re belief attribution. Nonetheless, based on these conditions and the problem of de re belief attribution stated above, there appears to be the following necessary condition for such an attribution. If we can attribute to an agent a de re belief toward a person or an entity, then the agent can more or less identify that person or entity again on the basis of those traits that figured in the agent's epistemic contact with the person or entity. There are, of course, obvious counterexamples to this condition, involving confusing the agent with an identical twin or other obvious skeptical predicaments. There is also the problem of distinguishing an entity's traits in the relevant sense from a product produced by the entity or from a trace of the entity. For example, can a person's singing figure in an agent's epistemic contact with the person? Can a person's photograph figure in this way? Granting that there are these problems for a precise formulation of a necessary condition for attributing a de re belief to an agent, nevertheless the above necessary condition still seems plausible.

The following two considerations can be raised against interpreting (2) as expressing a de re belief attribution. First, it is a fact that Kripke has neither met Mary nor otherwise become acquainted with her. If having a de re belief about someone requires having direct causal or cognitive contact with the person, then this alone makes it impossible to interpret (2) in the present context as a de re belief attribution. Second, having asserted (2), we can then correctly and consistently assert

(4)   But Kripke doesn't know who Mary is.

Now, suppose that the third condition (knowing who) is required in order to make a true de re belief attribution, that is, that the agent must recognize the person about whom the agent has the belief. This is the condition of knowing who the person is. But then the fact that we can assert (4) consistently with (2) is further evidence that (2) does not express a de re belief attribution.

Nevertheless, despite these considerations, we still might say that in some sense (2) is a de re belief attribution. For it seems that despite the considerations above—namely, that Kripke fails to have direct causal or cognitive contact with Mary and that in some sense he does not know who she is—Kripke has a belief *about Mary*, namely, that *she* is brilliant. We have this intuition because (i) Kripke has direct causal or cognitive contact with the product of Mary's that is his basis for attributing the property of brilliance to her and (ii) in some sense Kripke believes that only a brilliant person could have produced such a product, or that to produce this product essentially, that is, necessarily in some sense (to be elaborated later), requires that the producer is brilliant.

It seems plausible, then, that we may consider, perhaps in some loose or extended way, (2) as a de re belief ascription. For I consider such secondary belief attributions analogous to (or attempts at) making de re belief attributions: Such secondary beliefs are "about an object," and such secondary beliefs require that the agent (here, Kripke) has direct causal or cognitive contact with a product of the person whom the belief is about and, reasoning from this product, the agent attributes a property (here, being brilliant) to its producer. Accordingly, we may think of this kind of secondary belief attribution as a secondary de re belief attribution, as it is a secondary direct causal or cognitive contact, through direct contact with the product, that the agent has with the object of the belief and that forms his or her basis for attributing a property to the producer of that product.

Once we thus liberalize the criteria of direct causal or cognitive contact, however, we must be careful in presenting criteria for this liberalization. Otherwise, the required kind of direct causal or cognitive contact can be made implausibly loose. For example, suppose that we let merely being on the chain of an F-type proper name count as having a de re attitude towards the referent of the F-type name, perhaps by making direct causal or cognitive contact a transitive relation for members on the chain. Thus, for example, suppose John overhears his friends discussing Feynman, but hears only that he is a physicist. Suppose further that John believes them and thus he forms the belief that Feynman is a physicist. Since John has acquired the name in a normal way that places him on the chain of reference for the name 'Feynman', the above liberalization, on the basis of this alone, deems the sentence "John believes that Feynman is a physicist" a de re belief ascription.[6] I find this implausible.

---

6. But Nathan Salmon in personal communication has taken and defends such a position.

So it seems that (1) and (2) are, indeed, de re belief attributions. If so, then why should they be considered counterexamples to principle 2'? The answer lies in the following *principle of restricted universal importation:*

If X believes of α that ϕ, and if X does not dissent from 'ϕ_β', where $\ulcorner\beta\urcorner$ is a name (or directly referential term) designating α for the agent (i.e., an expression in the agent's language or a grunt, gesture, demonstration, or the like) then X believes that β is ϕ (i.e., ϕ_β).

This principle seems very plausible, especially since we don't require the language to contain $\ulcorner\beta\urcorner$, so that $\ulcorner\beta\urcorner$ could be a demonstrative (together with a demonstration). Accordingly, if an agent believes de re of an object α that it has a property ϕ, it seems prima facie plausible to attribute to the agent the de dicto belief that-$\phi\alpha$, even if he or she is unable to express it for want of the term 'α' or because he or she fails to realize that 'α' (rigidly) designates the object of his or her belief. Such an attribution would be defeated by the agent's having a contrary belief such as ~ϕ_β, where 'β' rigidly designates α; this is what generates the puzzle cases, and I am offering only a diagnosis, not a solution, of these. But, when the agent does not dissent from any sentence expressing the (singular proposition) belief in question, it seems reasonable to attribute this belief to the agent.

Now from the principle of restricted universal importation and from the fact that (1) and (2) are true de re belief attributions, it follows that we may also read (1) and (2) as true de dicto belief attributions. For in this example, Kripke never dissents from the sentence "Mary is brilliant." Thus accepting the above plausible principle of restricted importation leads to viewing (1) and (2) as counterexamples to Kripke's principle 2'.

The problem with principle 2' is that although it accounts for a speaker's assent upon reflection, there are two different sorts of considerations that we allow an agent to reflect upon when we attribute a belief to the agent. But principle 2' cannot account for both sorts. First, there is reflection that often requires coaxing the agent so that he or she may reflect upon his or her own resources. For example, an agent may mistakenly not say something that he or she "really" believes or may mistakenly say something that goes against what the agent is committed to believing. We may then remind the agent of various beliefs that he or she already strongly accepts but did not consider and that imply that the agent should revise his or her verbal behavior upon reflection on these beliefs. When a baseball fan says that the Yankees will win the game today, we may remind the fan that (he or she believes that) the Yankee pitcher injured his arm and that the star player for the Yankees is in the hospital. We thus remind the fan of various beliefs he or she already strongly holds, or of norms the agent has toward beliefs, that is, that they should be consistent, based upon evidence, and the like. Now such a case is an instance of aiding the agent so that he or she may reflect upon his or her own resources; this is what is meant in the literature by "reflective assent."

But not all coaxing aids the agent in reflecting upon his or her resources alone. We may also consider what the agent would, or should, say were we to present the agent with a name (or directly referential term) designating the object to which the agent bears the appropriate epistemic relation in the corresponding de re belief attribution. In our example above involving my student and Kripke, we considered what Kripke would or should say were he given the fact that the name of the student about whom he was talking is 'Mary'.[7] We would then feel that upon reflection on this fact, as well as his own resources, Kripke would assent to the sentence "Mary is brilliant," or at least that he should assent to it. We feel justified in attributing to him the (de dicto) belief that Mary is brilliant because we believe that Kripke satisfies the following conditions. First, that Kripke has some general view (to be elaborated in chapter 6) that people have names; second, that Kripke has expertise in the domain of inadmissible ordinals; and third, that if asked, Kripke would sincerely assent to the following:

(5) 'α is brilliant', where 'α' stands for the name of my student that wrote the paper.

But why should we accept (5) as a basis for attributing to Kripke the (de dicto) belief that Mary is brilliant? For surely we would not attribute to an agent the belief that, say, John Doe is a spy, if John Doe is the shortest spy, simply because the agent may assent to the sentence "'α is a spy', where 'α' stands for the name of the shortest spy." The difference is that in the former case, Kripke satisfies the epistemic condition required to have the

---

7. By supplementing an agent's knowledge with this additional fact of which the agent may not be aware, I am not suggesting that the relation between a name and what or whom it denotes is analytic in a given language. Rather, I am invoking the attributer's view of what the agent would use as a name for the object of the agent's belief if the agent had the resources available to express his or her belief.

belief about Mary that she is brilliant. In particular, Kripke is in epistemic or cognitive contact with her, or a product produced by her, which is his basis for attributing brilliance to her. In the John Doe case, what is missing is the agent's having the right kind of epistemic contact with John Doe.

We conclude, then, that the principle of restricted universal importation is incompatible with the converse disquotational principle 2′. If we accept the principle of restricted universal importation, which I have been defending, we must conclude that (1) and (2) can have a de dicto reading and are thus counterexamples to principle 2′.

4.2   Conditions for Secondary Belief Attributions

Since we have seen that there are secondary belief attributions, that is, true belief attributions that violate Kripke's principle 2′, what then are the conditions for accepting these attributions? In order to state these conditions, we must introduce the notion of *a product for a given agent.*

An agent may be in "direct contact" with or have "direct cognitive access" to a certain product, process, or trace that is the agent's basis for believing that the producer of this product, process, or trace has a certain trait. For example, the written dissertation is the product that is Kripke's basis for believing that the producer of this product is brilliant. In other cases, a political office may be thought of as the product or process that is an agent's basis for believing something about the person who holds that office. A certain trace, such as a fingerprint on a gun, may be the detective's basis for believing that the producer of this trace is a criminal. The product, process, or trace with which the agent is in direct cognitive contact or to which the agent has direct cognitive access that is the agent's basis for attributing a given trait to the producer we call *the product for the given agent.*

Accordingly, we formulate the following condition for forming true secondary belief attributions.

Condition 1: (a) an agent, X, attributes a trait ϕ to the producer of the product for the agent and believes that it is "essential" that the producer have this trait in order to produce this product; further, agent X satisfies the weak disquotational principle for a sentence 'ϕ_t,' where 't' designates the producer of the product for the agent, and (b) the attributer's referring expression is a name (or directly referential term) 'α' that designates this producer, and X does not dissent from the sentence 'ϕ_α.'

If this condition is satisfied, we may substitute the attributer's name (or directly referential term) 'α' for the term 't' within the belief context of the belief attribution 'X believes that ϕ_t'.

Thus in the secondary belief attribution "Kripke believes that Mary is brilliant," Kripke is the agent and 'Mary' is the attributer's name for the producer of the product (the dissertation) for Kripke. We formed the attribution by substituting the name 'Mary' for, say, "the author of this dissertation" (while pointing to the dissertation) in the belief attribution "Kripke believes that the author of this dissertation is brilliant." Condition 1 may be thought of as an epistemic condition for a de re belief attribution, especially if we consider true de re belief attributions a matter of degree.

It remains to explain the sense in which having a given trait is "essential" in order for the producer to produce the given product. Now the sense in which such a trait is essential needs to be qualified in two important respects.

First, we are not in general talking about necessity in the deepest sense. We may, for example, only mean that given current biology and psychology or given a community-shared worldview (see chapter 6 for details), the trait is necessary in order to produce the given product. In the above example, given Kripke's generally shared community-wide beliefs and given his special expertise[8] in the domain that the dissertation topic is in, Kripke believes that *only* a brilliant person *could have* written the dissertation. Among Kripke's generally shared community-wide beliefs are that the dissertation was not written by typing randomly into a computer, that it did not just fall from the sky, that the author was trying to do his or her best work, and various beliefs concerning the average intelligence of rational human beings. Among his beliefs due to his special competence is that in the domain that he has expertise, the dissertation contributes something that *must* be the contribution of a brilliant person. Contexts and interests will in general determine in what sense or how loosely we may be speaking of an essential trait, or even which essential trait is relevant.

Second, in calling a trait essential, we do not merely mean that the product could not have been produced unless the producer has this trait. For in

---

8. Again, see chapter 6 for details of a notion I call "institutional competence," based on Hilary Putnam's famous use of the role of "experts" in formulating his notion of the linguistic division of labor in "The Meaning of 'Meaning'" and "Meaning and Reference."

our example above, had Kripke said only that the author of this dissertation was breathing when writing it, we would not be justified in making
the secondary belief attribution

(6)   Kripke believes that Mary was breathing when this dissertation was
written.

The reason that we cannot make the above secondary belief attribution
is that this essential trait (given our community-wide generally shared beliefs) applies to *any* author of a dissertation. Thus suppose it is part of, say,
our community-wide generally shared beliefs or special competence or expertise that the trait the agent attributes to the producer of the product applies to *any* producer of a product that is a member of the domain of such
products. Then this trait cannot serve as one that will permit us to substitute a name or pronoun for the agent's referring expression in the sentence
that expresses the agent's primary belief attribution (in the sense of a belief attribution that does not require some modification of Kripke's principle of belief attribution).

For our guiding intuition regarding such substitution is that it is *as if*
one's community-wide generally shared beliefs and expertise in a given
domain enables one to pick out the special type of producer of a given
product in that domain by means of a deferred ostension through one's acquaintance with the product and one's knowledge of the "essential trait"
that the producer must have in order to produce that product. That is,
given the expert's cognitive contact with the product for the expert, an expert has the right kind of epistemic relation with the producer of the product to be able to attribute a relevant (cognitive) property to the producer
to distinguish the producer from many other members of the domain (pro-
ducers of such a product). Consequently, we attribute to the agent a de re
belief attitude toward the producer of the product. This intuition is clearly
violated when the trait attributed to the producer of the product applies
to *any* producer of any product that is a member of the domain of such
products. The domain of a given product (in this example, the class of dis-
sertations) is relative to a description of the product. And as noted above,
such a description is relative to the purpose, context, or interest in the
product.

In our example above, Kripke shares with us various community-wide
generally shared beliefs, and he has the appropriate expertise in the domain in question. That is, he is a member of a certain subgroup within the

community that has special competence, or expertise, in the domain of the dissertation topic. Moreover, Kripke is in direct cognitive contact with the dissertation, which is his basis for forming the belief that the author is brilliant. Given these factors, Kripke believes that anyone who has produced such a dissertation *must* have the property of being brilliant. Our intuition that Kripke has the right kind of epistemic relation with the producer of the product is satisfied, and we feel justified in substituting the name 'Mary' for Kripke's referring expression in the sentence that expresses his primary belief in order to form a true secondary belief attribution.

It should be clear that the notion of a trait essential in order for the producer to produce the given product (as well as the degree to which one would be required to have competence in a given domain) is not meant to have precise sharp criteria. If, for example, Kripke guessed that the author of the dissertation was a woman with blue eyes, and even if that correctly describes Mary, the author of the dissertation, we would feel somewhat reluctant to make the following attribution:

(7)   Kripke believes that Mary is a woman who has blue eyes.

This reluctance seems to come from the lack of any special institutional competence or community-wide generally shared beliefs relating gender, eye color, and a certain kind of dissertation. First, Kripke does *not* have any special competence regarding the trait of the gender and eye color of an author of a dissertation. There is no institutionally accepted theory regarding such a connection. Thus neither Kripke nor anyone else can be a member of the relevant subgroup that has special competence in this domain. Second, there aren't any community-wide shared beliefs or presuppositions linking gender and eye color to dissertation writing. For these reasons, we feel reluctant to assert (7).

Now suppose that there were a strongly institutionally accepted theory (i.e., a scientific theory) linking gender and eye color to a certain kind or style of dissertation and that Kripke were one of the leading experts having special competence in this domain. Then our intuitions regarding the truth of (7) would change.

My notion of secondary belief attribution is intended to rule out cases of an agent's beliefs based solely upon a "hunch" or a random guess. But to what extent a belief is the product of a hunch (or of rational justification) is often a matter of degree. The less the agent's primary belief is based on a hunch, and the more it is rationally justified, the more inclined we are to say that the agent has the right epistemic relation to the producer of the product, and thus has a de re belief attitude toward the producer. That is, the more the agent's primary belief is based upon the agent's approaching an idealized rational agent, the more we are inclined to make a secondary belief attribution.[9]

Now sometimes, due to the pragmatics in a given situation, we place stronger requirements than condition 1 in order to form a secondary belief attribution by substituting a proper name for the agent's referring expression in the sentence that expresses his or her primary belief attribution. For example, suppose that a detective believes that Smith's murderer is insane solely on the basis of examining Smith's mangled body. Let us grant that the detective has the appropriate expertise to have the right epistemic relation to the producer of this product, that is, to Smith's murderer. Even so, we would not, in this situation, apply the principle of restricted importation to substitute a proper name, say 'Jones', for the referring expression 'Smith's murderer' in the primary belief attribution

(8)   The detective believes that Smith's murderer is criminally insane

to form the secondary belief attribution

(9)   The detective believes that Jones is criminally insane.

Since the job of a detective is to find out who the murderer is, the pragmatics gives rise to the presupposition that such substitution is permissible only when the detective believes he or she knows who the murderer is. For that reason, in the situation described above, we do not permit such substitution.

This situation is not, however, a counterexample to our claim that condition 1 in general suffices to permit such secondary belief attributions. For in general, in order to permit such substitutions to form secondary belief attributions, there are no presuppositions to the effect that an agent, even if an expert, must believe he or she knows who the producer of a given product is.

Consider, for example, the situation in which we already know that Jones committed the murder, and he is about to stand trial. Suppose further that the detective, neither having met Jones nor knowing his name or

---

9. In chapter 6, I make explicit the basic assumptions we are here implicitly assuming regarding an idealized rational agent.

even having a clue as to who he is, is given Smith's body to determine whether the murderer is criminally insane. Finally, suppose that on this basis alone the detective announces that Smith's murderer is criminally insane. In such a situation, Jones's defense attorney can say at Jones's trial that the detective believes that *Jones* is criminally insane. In order to make such an attribution, the presupposition that the detective must believe that he or she knows who Smith's murderer is does not hold, since the pragmatic situation is no longer one in which we are turning to the detective's beliefs to find out who Smith's murderer is. What justifies making this attribution are the detective's expertise in determining whether a murderer is criminally insane on the sole basis of examining the victim's body, that is, the detective's special institutionally recognized competence in this domain, and the detective's belief that this trait, criminal insanity, is essential in order for the murderer, the producer of the product for the detective, to commit *this* crime. Thus condition 1 obtains.

Violations of other presuppositions place further constraints on our conditions for forming secondary belief attributions by substituting a proper name for the expert's referring expression in the primary belief attribution.

In chapter 6, I develop further some of the notions in this chapter as well as others and apply them to the problem of intentional identity.

5

Propositions and Belief Attributions Containing Vacuous Names

It is a generally held view that a proposition is the bearer of truth, the "thought" or "content" of what a declarative sentence expresses,[1] and the object of a propositional attitude (perhaps under a description or mode of presentation). The latter role, being an object of a propositional attitude, presents the greatest challenge to the view that propositions play all three roles. In addition to the puzzle about belief, there is the problem of belief attributions involving vacuous names, which arises when the sentence $\Phi\alpha$ occurs within a belief context and the proper name α fails to refer. In the ordinary case, the de dicto reading of a belief attribution is generally taken to be a relation between an agent and a proposition denoted by 'that-$\Phi\alpha$'. But since α fails to refer, what, if anything, can this proposition be?

Thus one question is what, if anything, is the object of belief expressed in belief attributions of the form 'A believes that-$\Phi\alpha$', where α is a nondenoting proper name or pronoun that fails to refer; another is under what conditions is it appropriate to make such a belief report. I intend to deal with both these problems. One consequence of my view is that the generally held view regarding propositions is false; there is no entity that can always satisfy the three conditions: being a truth bearer, being the thought or content of a declarative sentence, and being the object of a propositional attitude every time we rationally attribute a belief to an agent.

---

1. Not every declarative sentence expresses a proposition. For example, some declarative sentences contain category mistakes, and others lead to paradox. This is merely a rough approximation.

5.1   Belief Attribution with Vacuous Names

We begin with a note from the history of science. In 1846, the French as-
tronomer, Babinet, believing that the irregular perihelion of Mercury was
produced by the perturbing effect of one and only one intra-Mercurial
planet, proposed to call it 'Vulcan'. Although Leverrier at first rejected the
hypothesis of an intra-Mercurial planet, later he endorsed it.[2]

Now suppose, contrary to fact, that Babinet originally introduced the
name 'Vulcan' only to designate the one and only one intra-Mercurial
planet. When he originally introduced the name, neither he nor anyone
else believed that Vulcan produces the perturbing effect on Mercury that
accounts for its irregular perihelion. Only much later did he and others
come to believe that Vulcan produces the perturbing effect on Mercury.
Let us suppose further that Leverrier had never heard of the name 'Vulcan',
but did hypothesize that there is one and only one planet that produces the
perturbing effect on Mercury. He entertained no hypothesis at first, let us
say, about whether this planet is intra-Mercurial. Much later on, based
on his scientific calculations, he came to believe that this planet is intra-
Mercurial. Finally, let us suppose that Leverrier believed, again based on
his scientific calculations, that this planet is small.

It seems that under these suppositions we can correctly report the
following:

(1)   Leverrier believes that Vulcan is a small planet.

The belief attribution, (1), cannot be reporting one of Leverrier's *de re*
beliefs, since the planet Vulcan does not exist, and under any analysis of a
de re belief, there has to exist an object about which the agent has a belief.
In the absence of such an object, (1) clearly does not express a *de re* belief
attribution.

Can (1) express a *de dicto* belief attribution, where the object of belief
is a proposition? It is a tenet of direct-reference theorists that the thought
or content of a declarative sentence containing proper names, demonstratives, and other directly referential expressions is a singular proposition,
where the constituents of such a proposition are both the referents of these
directly referential expressions and the property or relation expressed by

2. N. T. Roseveau, *Mercury's Perihelion: From Le Verrier To Einstein* (Oxford:
The Clarendon Press, 1982).

the open sentence formed when we replace the directly referring expressions in these sentences with free variables.

The sentence within the belief context of (1) contains the nondenoting proper name 'Vulcan'. Since Vulcan does not exist, the object of Leverrier's belief cannot be a singular proposition. In fact, it is not at all clear that the object of Leverrier's belief can be any genuine proposition. Since the object of Leverrier's belief is not a singular proposition, in order for (1) to be interpreted as a de dicto belief attribution, that is, a belief relation between Leverrier and a proposition, a neo-Fregean would analyze the name 'Vulcan' in the sentence expressing this proposition as an abbreviation for some definite description, or as a uniquely specifying set of conditions.

Now Leverrier, according to our supposition, has not heard the name 'Vulcan'. The basis on which we report (1) is that Leverrier, by supposition, hypothesized that the one and only one planet that produces the perturbing effect on Mercury is intra-Mercurial and further that this planet is small. But the name 'Vulcan' does not mean "the one and only one planet that produces the perturbing effect on Mercury," and, therefore, cannot be an abbreviation for this expression. In fact, according to our supposition, no one originally believed that Vulcan produced this effect when the name 'Vulcan' was originally introduced. Hence no one at that time held that the sentence "Vulcan is the one and only one planet that produces the perturbing effect on Mercury" is true, let alone an a priori or necessary truth.

Moreover, the name 'Vulcan' does not even simply mean "the intra-Mercurial planet," even though this description is what fixes the reference of the name 'Vulcan'. Thus the sentence "If Vulcan exists, then it is the intra-Mercurial planet" (translated into French) is an a priori truth as expressed by Babinet, whether he realizes it or not. But it is not a necessary truth. Hence, 'Vulcan' does not abbreviate this description either.

Now the neo-Fregean analysis that we are considering of a (de dicto) belief attribution in which the sentence 'Fα' within the scope of its belief context contains a nondenoting proper name α is as follows:

(2) $(\exists \Phi)(X$ believes that the Φ is F),

where 'Φ' is a property or condition, such as 'is an intra-Mercurial planet', and 'F' is a predicate, such as 'is a small planet'. In this way, we can still preserve the standard view that whenever we make correct belief attributions, we are expressing a relation between an agent and a proposition.

There are problems with such an analysis. First, not everyone in the community will associate with α the same property or condition Φ, and thus not everyone will have the same belief when they believe that Fα. Second, it seems unlikely that the logical form of a belief attribution, 'X believes that Fα', should vary depending upon whether the world cooperates to secure a referent for the proper name α. Last, Kripke has already shown the problems with analyzing a proper name as a description or a cluster of descriptions. One such problem is that although the proper name is a rigid designator, the descriptive phrase is not. Thus different objects in different possible worlds may satisfy the description, whereas that is not true for the proper name.

To rectify this problem, the neo-Fregean might consider modifying (2) as

(3) $(\exists \Phi)$(X believes that the AΦ is F),

where 'A' is the actuality operator. Thus (3) in effect says that X believes that whatever is the Φ in the actual world is F. But what this means is that in order for someone in some possible world w to believe that 'Fα' is true in w, that person in w would have to believe that in the actual world (not the world w that the person is in) the Φ is F. This seems extremely implausible as an analysis of a belief attribution in which the sentence 'Fα' within the scope of the belief context contains a nondenoting proper name α. For why should someone's belief about what is the case in the world they are in be analyzed as that person's belief about what is the case in some other world? And what could it mean for such a person to believe that he or she is not in the actual world?

5.2   Naming Conditions and Expressing a Definite Proposition

Now we have said that a term the reference of which is fixed by description refers rigidly to whatever satisfies this description in the context of introduction of its A-B statement. Accordingly, we have called such a term *S-type* and the condition that the referent of this term must satisfy the *A-B (anaphoric background) condition* for this term. The existential sentence $\exists x \Phi$, where Φ is the reference fixing description, we have called the *A-B sentence for the given term*. It is a presupposition of the truth of the sentence 'N exists', where 'N' is an S-type term, that its A-B sentence be true, and it is a presupposition of all other sentences containing this term to have a truth value that its A-B sentence is true.

In our example, the condition of uniquely being the intra-Mercurial planet is the A-B condition for the name 'Vulcan', and the sentence "There is a unique intra-Mercurial planet" is the name's A-B sentence. Babinet knows a priori that if Vulcan exists then it satisfies this A-B condition and its A-B sentence is true.

Now the reason that we feel justified in asserting (1) is that it deductively follows from Leverrier's scientific theory that there is a small planet that satisfies the A-B condition for the name 'Vulcan'. Nevertheless, the sentence expressing the object of Leverrier's belief in (1), "Vulcan is a small planet," cannot have a truth value and thus cannot express a definite proposition.

Still, this sentence strikes us as meaningful even if in this case it does not appear that it can have a truth value. For we seem to have a clear understanding of what Leverrier believes, at least clear enough that we can attribute the belief to him, and we seem to know what would have to be the case to discover that, in fact, Leverrier's belief is true. That is, we seem to know what would have to be the case for the object of this belief to be a genuine singular proposition that is true. It does not strike us either as a nonsensical or incoherent belief or as some sort of confusion on his part. Indeed, for the reason stated above, the belief attribution expressed in (1) seems true, given our supposition, even though Leverrier's belief itself may fail to have a truth value.

Now Strawson remarked that the sentence

(4)   The present king of France is bald

lacks a truth value as long as its presupposition, that there is a present king of France, is false. Moreover, he remarked that the sentence could be used on different occasions to make different statements. Kaplan, commenting on this, notes that Strawson used "statement" in a way similar to Kaplan's own use of "content," or what has traditionally been called "proposition."

Thus, (4) alone, in the absence of what Kaplan calls a context of use, fails to express a definite proposition. Nevertheless we understand (4), so that if the presupposition that there is a present king of France is satisfied, it expresses a definite proposition. For this reason, we say that a given instance (i.e., utterance) may express a possible proposition in the sense that such an instance uttered in a given context in which the presupposition is satisfied expresses a definite proposition regardless of what such an instance in the actual context expresses.

Now a sentence containing a vacuous proper name, such as "Vulcan is a small planet," also lacks a truth value and thus fails to express a definite proposition. The presupposition for this sentence is the A-B sentence for the name occurring in this sentence. As with (4), its presupposition, "there is a unique intra-Mercurial planet," is, in fact, false. Nevertheless, as with (4), we understand this sentence so that if its presupposition, or A-B sentence, is true, (4) expresses a definite proposition. Again, as with (4), such a sentence may make different statements on different occasions, if the name and its A-B sentence had been introduced in different contexts (where the A-B sentence is true) than the context in which they were in fact introduced. It is thus reasonable, analogous to (4), to say that a given utterance may express a possible proposition in the sense that the proposition such an utterance expresses is dependent upon what satisfies its A-B condition in a given context in which the name and its A-B sentence is introduced. When the A-B sentence is true had it been introduced in this initial context, then the utterance expresses a definite proposition regardless of what such an utterance expresses in the actual context in which the name and it's A-B sentence are in fact introduced. Accordingly, sentences with names that fail to denote can be linguistically meaningful.

Names, we have said, are introduced into the language by means of some anaphoric background conditions. When a proper name is introduced into a language with the intention of its succeeding in naming, it must be introduced in a standard legitimate way. Accordingly, we say that the semantic A-B conditions for introducing a name into the community must be *authentic*. These conditions are authentic if, in introducing the name, all the conceptual apparatus for uniquely specifying the name's reference is in place, even though the world may not cooperate—that is, either the right causal connection between the name and an object does not in fact obtain, so the A-B condition for an F-type term is not met, or some descriptions used in fixing the reference when introducing the name may be false, so the A-B condition for an S-type term is not met. The former failure occurs, for example, when someone is either hallucinating or having an illusion and introduces a name for what is wrongly taken to be an object. The latter failure is exactly what happened in the case of the name 'Vulcan'. Yet, despite the failure, the name was introduced in a standard legitimate way as naming whatever is uniquely specified by the description 'the planet that is intra-Mercurial'. Thus the semantic A-B condition for the name's introduction into the community was authentic.

When a name's A-B conditions are authentic, we know exactly what would have to be the case in order for the name to denote. For example, we know exactly what would have to be the case in order for the name 'Vulcan' to denote, namely, that there be a unique satisfier of the A-B condition for the name 'Vulcan' in its context of introduction. But in fact, that is, in the actual world where the name was introduced, this condition is not satisfied. Therefore, Vulcan fails to exist. Even in possible worlds representing *circumstances of evaluation* in which there is one and only one intra-Mercurial planet, Vulcan does not exist, due to the name's failure to denote in the actual context in which the name and its A-B condition were introduced. Thus Vulcan necessarily fails to exist.

Nevertheless, the name's semantic A-B condition, that is, the condition that an entity must uniquely satisfy in order to be the denotation of the name 'Vulcan', is perfectly clear. It is the condition of being the unique intra-Mercurial planet, even though as a matter of fact nothing satisfies this condition in the name's context of introduction. Thus when a name's conceptual apparatus is in place, sentences making use of the name are meaningful even though the world may fail to cooperate by providing anything for the name to denote.

As a test that the A-B conditions for the introduction of a name are authentic, we use the notion of a possible context of introduction. We call a context where a name is introduced but some of the parameters, such as the world, place, time, and so on, of the context are not assigned the same values as what, in fact, is assigned to the parameters of a name's context of introduction, *a possible context of introduction;* and the world of such a context we call *a possible context world.*[3] Now suppose that there is a possible context of introduction for a given name in which this name is introduced in the same way that it in fact is introduced in its context of introduction. Suppose further that in the possible context of introduction, the A-B condition of the name is satisfied. That is, in this possible context, either there is the right causal connection between the name and an entity

---

3. According to Kaplan's terminology, by definition, the world of the context is called the actual world. But I restrict my use of the term 'actual world' to what indeed is the actual world, that is, the real world that we live in. Thus in my terminology, contexts can contain possible worlds that are not actual.

or there is a unique satisfier of the descriptions used to fix the reference of the name. Then the A-B condition for the name is authentic.

Suppose the name 'Vulcan' is introduced in a possible context in which the possible world of that context has one and only one planet that is intra-Mercurial. Then in that context, that planet is the unique satisfier of the A-B condition for the name 'Vulcan', and the name rigidly denotes that planet. Sentences containing the name 'Vulcan' would then express definite propositions.

But even that possible context is not a context in which Vulcan could have existed (as we use the name, given the context of introduction in which the name in fact is introduced). In the possible context in which the A-B condition for the name is uniquely satisfied, the name 'Vulcan' does not, indeed cannot, denote the same thing as it denotes when introduced in the context of introduction in which it in fact was introduced. When introduced in that possible context, sentences containing the name 'Vulcan' do not express the same proposition as they do when the name is introduced in the context in which it in fact was introduced. For in the latter context, the name fails to denote, and thus sentences containing the name 'Vulcan' fail to express any definite proposition.

In his John Locke Lectures, Saul Kripke develops his view that a name occurring in fictional discourse is, in its primordial sense, merely a pretended name and that sentences containing such a name "pretend to express a proposition rather than really doing so."[4] If Kripke's view is correct, as I believe it is, then the A-B conditions for introducing a name in fiction are not authentic. It is not a case in which the conceptual apparatus for uniquely specifying the name's reference is in place but the world does not cooperate. Nor is there a context in which the name is introduced in the same way yet in which the A-B conditions of the name are satisfied. For in introducing a name solely as pretense, there are no A-B conditions to be satisfied. Indeed, that is part of the pretense—that there are such conditions and that they are, in fact, satisfied.

Still, someone could mistake Sir Arthur Conan Doyle's novels and stories for nonfiction. Someone, for example, may believe that Sherlock

4. "Reference and Existence" (The John Locke Lectures, presented at Oxford University, 1973). Kripke also holds that there is a secondary sense in which names from fiction denote fictional characters. It is clear from context that when Kripke is talking about the "primary" sense of a name introduced in fictional discourse, he means the primordial sense.

Holmes is a brilliant detective who smokes a pipe. We thus have a belief attribution in which the sentence within its belief context is merely a pretense for expressing a proposition. But the sentence as pretense fails even to express a possible proposition.

To be sure, there was no intent on Conan Doyle's part to deceive when writing his novels. Nevertheless, the fiction purports to be a recounting of actual events, and in that sense there is a pretense that the sentences within the Sherlock Holmes novels and stories express propositions.

5.3 The Representation of Authentic Naming Conditions and A-B Conditions

I have been arguing that there are belief attributions that we accept for which there need not be any object of belief, at least if that object is supposed to be a definite proposition. There may be a pretense that there is a proposition, and an agent may, failing to recognize the pretense, believe that there is a true proposition. This is the case where someone believes a piece of fictional discourse, such as the claim that Sherlock Holmes is a real person who smokes a pipe.

I have also argued that in the case of a vacuous name introduced in a false hypothesis, someone may fail to have a belief relation to a proposition. The agent, of course, believes himself or herself to be in a relation to a true proposition. Such is the case in my Leverrier example, in which he believes that Vulcan is a small planet. Moreover, I have maintained that in the case of a false hypothesis, further conditions on the introduction of the name must be met in order for us to speak as if sentences in which the name occurs are expressing possible propositions. What then is the object of the agent's belief in those cases in which a correct belief attribution contains a sentence with a vacuous name within the belief context? Before answering this question, we must first develop the formal semantics of proper names.

In chapter 1, I noted that Kripke's account of reference determination of proper names has two parts. First, there is an initial baptismal step, where a name is introduced into the language; second, there is a reference transmission step, where there is a historical chain of speakers of the community intending to use the name with the same reference that it had for the speaker from whom they acquired the name.

In chapter 3, I observed that in his article "Demonstratives," David Kaplan argues that a meaningful linguistic expression has two semantic features: its character and its content. Recall from that chapter that character plays an analogous role to the dictionary meaning of the expression. Content is "what is said" by a speaker in using the expression in a given context of use and what is evaluated in possible circumstances to determine the extension of the expression in the given possible circumstance of evaluation. Carnap represented this latter notion by a function mapping possible circumstances to extensions; he called such functions the intension of an expression. We also observed that Kaplan has extended Carnap's project by representing the character of an expression by a function that maps contexts of use into contents.

In "Demonstratives," Kaplan offers a formal semantics for proper names. A proper name lacks a character or trivially has a stable character, that is, the name may be represented by a constant function mapping any context of use into the name's referent. For as Kripke has shown, a proper name does not have a Fregean sense or dictionary meaning that determines its content, that is, its referent. Proper names are thus context-insensitive.

But Kaplan's notion of a character for a proper name, which maps a context of use into the name's referent, formalizes only part of Kripke's account of reference determination of proper names. It formalizes the second step, reference transmission, where once the name is introduced into the language, in any context of use the name's referent remains the same. What is missing is a formal semantics for the first step, initial baptism.

We develop a natural extension of Kaplan's formal semantics for proper names, within which we make an analogous distinction to that found in Kripke's account of reference determination of proper names. In particular, we make use of our distinction between two kinds of contexts. First, there is the context of introduction. In this case, it is the context in which a name is introduced into the community by means of A-B conditions. The context of name introduction is the context in which the initial baptismal step takes place. Second, there is the context of use. It is the context in which the name and its reference are passed on in a given link of the transmission step.

Now I have argued in section 5.1 for the importance of a vacuous name's A-B condition (when this condition is authentic) in determining a possible proposition that a sentence containing such a name might express. In light of this, we use the A-B condition for a name to introduce a natural extension to Kaplan's notion of the character for a name. Suppose that a name is introduced in a given possible context of name introduction in the same way in which it is, in fact, introduced, that is, with the same A-B condition as in the context of name introduction in which the name in fact is introduced. Then that A-B condition for the name, given a possible context of name introduction, determines a possible (stable) character for the name. The possible character for the name, in turn, determines a possible referent for it.

Accordingly, we represent the *A-B condition for a name* by a function, f_{A-B}, that maps *possible contexts of name introduction, c_i,* into possible (stable) characters for that name. We call this function, f_{A-B}, the *A-B function*.

The A-B function for a name determines a possible character for that name by being context-sensitive, that is, sensitive to the possible context of name introduction. Given such a context, the name is then insensitive to a context of use. That is, the name is then given a stable character that maps any context of use into a given referent, namely, the possible referent that the name would rigidly denote had it and its A-B condition been introduced in the given possible context of name introduction.

Similarly, the A-B function for a name partially determines a possible character for linguistic expressions containing that name. For we accept the Frege/Kaplan principle that the character of the whole is a function of the character of its parts. Thus consider, for example, a sentence S containing a name n introduced in a given possible context of name introduction, c_i. Then, given c_i, the A-B function for n determines its possible character for n. Hence given c_i and the Frege/Kaplan principle, the possible character of S is a function of this possible character of n. So just as the possible characters of n are a function of possible contexts of introduction, so are the possible characters of S. Thus, for each possible context of name introduction, there is a corresponding possible character of S, where S contains n.

Now each such possible character of S maps contexts of use into a possible content, or proposition. The possible proposition is what S would have expressed had the name occurring in it been introduced in the given possible context of name introduction to which the possible character of S corresponds. The range of the class of possible character functions for S is the class of possible propositions that S could have expressed, given the A-B condition for the name occurring in S. Thus the A-B condition for a given name is crucial for determining whether a sentence containing the name expresses (or could have expressed, had the name been introduced in a given context of introduction) a definite proposition.

There are three cases regarding an A-B condition for a name to consider. First, if the introduction of a name n into a language is by means of an A-B condition that is not an authentic naming condition, the value of the A-B function for n is always undefined.[5] Consequently, there is no possible (or actual) character function for the name n. Hence any possible (or actual) character of S, where S contains n, only partially determines a definite proposition, namely, whatever the character of S determines for the rest of the sentence.

Second is the case in which a name is introduced into the language by means of an A-B condition that is an authentic naming condition, but there is no entity that satisfies this condition with respect to the context of introduction. Here the value of the A-B function is undefined for the context of introduction in which the name in fact is introduced. Consequently, there is no character that the name in fact has. Accordingly, the character that S in fact has, where S contains n, only partially determines a definite proposition, namely, whatever the character of S determines for the rest of the sentence. But, unlike the first case, the A-B function for n may be defined for various possible contexts of introduction. Where this is the case, the A-B function for n determines a possible character for n. Accordingly, in such cases, there are possible characters for S, which determine possible propositions that S could have expressed.

Last is the case in which a name is introduced by means of an A-B condition that is an authentic naming condition, and there is an entity satisfying this condition with respect to the context of introduction. In this

---

5. I am thinking of a totally undefined function as the limiting case of a partially defined function, that is, although the function has a specific domain, there is no value for any member of the domain. If one doesn't like to think of the existence of functions that are totally undefined, there are technical ways around this. Two obvious ways are as follows: (1) in contexts of introduction where the original function is undefined, assign to it the empty set; (2) define the function that maps ordered triples of A-B conditions, names introduced in the language at a given time and place, and contexts of introduction into content, that is, a referent. We then have the existence of a partially defined function.

case, the A-B function determines the character that the name in fact has. Consequently, the value of this character is completely defined for any context of use, and the character that S in fact has maps any context of use into a definite proposition (assuming that everything else in S is in order). As in the previous case, there may be possible characters for S, which, in turn, determine possible propositions that S could have expressed.

The first case may be illustrated by cases in which someone wrongly believes a piece from fictional discourse. There is no authentic naming condition for a name introduced in a piece of fiction. The only anaphoric background to such a name, as Kripke has argued, is simply a pretense that the name n denotes and that sentences in the fictional discourse containing the name express a definite proposition. Thus, unlike the case where a name has authentic naming conditions, we couldn't even state what would have to be the case for us to discover, say, that Sherlock Holmes smokes a pipe or that unicorns exist. For in the absence of authentic naming conditions for 'Sherlock Holmes' and 'unicorn', there is nothing that counts as a satisfying condition for an object to be the denotation of these terms.

For our first case, then, the value of the A-B function for a name n introduced into the language by means of a nonauthentic (naming) A-B condition, such as a fictitious name, is undefined. Consequently, there is no character function for n. Here there cannot be a *class of possible propositions* that might have been expressed by a given sentence containing such a name, and thus it is incoherent to attribute to the agent belief in a member of such a class.

Nevertheless, such a sentence is meaningful in that there is a syntactically well-formed declarative sentence for which all but the semantics of the proper name is semantically fulfilled. And I have been urging that a sentence containing a vacuous name is meaningful since we understand the sentence, even though an agent is mistaken in thinking that the sentence expresses one of his or her beliefs. Further, if we assume that for any proper name n that denotes, n denotes n, then the sentence has the propositional form of what the agent thinks he or she is believing, even though the object of the belief is not a definite proposition.

Recall from chapter 1 that an A-B statement for a name n states, in effect, that there is an object uniquely satisfying the A-B condition for n. The truth of an A-B statement for n is a precondition for any statement n expressed by a sentence containing n to have a truth value. In Strawson's terminology, we say that any such statement S *presupposes* the truth of the A-B statement for n. Again following Strawson, we say that in using a sentence containing a name 'n' to make an assertion or denial, express a belief, and so on, an agent *is committed to* the truth of the A-B statement for n.

Accordingly, when we attribute to an agent a belief expressed by a sentence containing a name from fiction, say, that Sherlock Holmes smokes a pipe, we may say that the agent is committed to the truth of the A-B statement for the name 'Sherlock Holmes'. That is, the agent is committed to there being an authentic naming condition for the name 'Sherlock Holmes' that is satisfied uniquely. But since the A-B statement for the name is false, the best it seems we can attribute to the agent is that "A believes that there is a true proposition that Sherlock Holmes smokes a pipe."

In the second case, the A-B condition is an authentic naming condition, but there is no object satisfying this condition with respect to the context of introduction. The Leverrier example illustrates this case. Here we said that although Leverrier has never heard the name 'Vulcan', we feel justified in attributing to him the belief that Vulcan is a small planet. For Leverrier believes that his theory is true of the actual world; indeed, he developed it in order to explain certain phenomena in it. Moreover, it deductively follows from his theory that there is a unique satisfier of the A-B condition for the name 'Vulcan' and that this satisfier is a small planet. Also, it follows from the A-B condition for the name 'Vulcan' that something is the unique satisfier of this condition in the actual world if and only if it is Vulcan.[6] Thus there is a clear sense in which Leverrier, believing his theory, is *committed* to the A-B condition for the name 'Vulcan' being uniquely satisfied and to the claim that Vulcan is a small planet.

For these reasons we attribute to Leverrier the belief that Vulcan is a small planet. Were he given the name 'Vulcan' and told its A-B condition, he would unhesitatingly assent to the sentence "Vulcan is a small planet" (translated into French). From his perspective, the object of his belief is a true truth bearer, that is, in our terminology, is a true definite proposition. Leverrier would thus claim, again in our terminology, that he believes the true definite proposition that Vulcan is a small planet.

But, in fact, Leverrier's theory is false; it is not true of the actual world. There is no definite proposition, true or otherwise, that he believes.

6. That is, it follows assuming the correctness of my view of names like 'Vulcan' that they are not abbreviated definite descriptions.

Unlike the A-B condition for a fictional name, the A-B condition for the name 'Vulcan' is an authentic naming condition. This allows us to say more than that Leverrier believes that there is a true proposition that-P, (where 'P' is the sentence "Vulcan is a small planet"). We can add that there is a class of logically, or epistemically,[7] possible context-of-introduction worlds that contain a unique satisfier of this A-B condition. Now, Leverrier's theory commits him to the view that the actual world is a member of this class. Further, corresponding to each such world in this class is a logically possible proposition about that world's unique satisfier of the A-B condition for 'Vulcan'. Leverrier's theory thus also commits him to the view that this class of possible propositions contains a true definite proposition that Vulcan is a small planet.

Since we do not accept Leverrier's theory, we do not share Leverrier's commitments. Rather, what we say is that he is taking the actual world to be among the possible context-of-introduction worlds that contain a small planet as the unique satisfier of the A-B condition for the name 'Vulcan'.

But since the actual world is not among such possible worlds, which one of these possible worlds does Leverrier believe to be the actual world? In each of these possible worlds, there may well be a different unique satisfier of the A-B condition for the name 'Vulcan'. So which one is it that Leverrier believes to be Vulcan? And, considering that to each satisfier there corresponds a different logically possible proposition, which one can we say he believes?

It seems to me that short of simply saying 'none', there can be no coherent answer to these questions. For presumably Leverrier's beliefs were not so detailed that only one possible world could satisfy them. So even on the assumption that he takes the actual world to be among the logically possible context-of-introduction worlds that uniquely satisfies the A-B condition for the name 'Vulcan', we still could not attribute to him a belief even in a definite *possible proposition*. A belief in a definite possible proposition requires greater specificity, and he seems not to believe any one of these possible propositions specifically.

We see now what the authentic naming condition for the name 'Vulcan' allows us to say. We can say that Leverrier is taking the actual context-of-introduction world to be among the class of logically possible worlds that contain a unique satisfier of this condition. We can also say that Leverrier

7. We use "epistemically possible" to mean the same as "logically possible."

is committed to the view that the class of logically, or epistemically, possible propositions (mentioned above) corresponding to such possible worlds contains the true definite proposition that Vulcan is a small planet. We can say this, even though there may be no specific logically possible proposition from this class that he believes. Leverrier, of course, would not report his belief this way, since he thinks he believes a definite proposition. But there is nothing more definite that Leverrier believes.

Last, we consider the case in which there is an authentic naming condition and an object satisfying this condition in the actual context of introduction. Here the name occurring within the sentence expressing the agent's belief is nonvacuous, and the A-B function determines the value of the actual character for the name. Thus the agent's commitment to the truth of the A-B statement for the name is satisfied, and hence the object of the agent's belief is indeed a definite proposition with a definite truth value.

Now, in all three cases, we have been attributing a "belief" to the agent, even though in two of these cases the sentence within the belief context contains a vacuous name. (I put the phrase "belief" in scare quotes because we may not want to say that there is a genuine belief in the first two cases since the singular term 'that-S' occurring within their respective belief contexts fail to denote a proposition.) Thus such a sentence fails to express a definite proposition. Nevertheless, we consider the agent rational, and we do not interpret the agent as saying or believing nonsense.[8] On the contrary, we have been arguing that, under the circumstances described in these cases, the agent is warranted in forming such an alleged "belief." That is, although literally speaking there may well be no belief, the agent is *entitled* to express his "belief" in these or similar terms in his or her language. Moreover, we can interpret the agent by applying our semantics in

---

8. There are two other cases in which we attribute a belief to an agent. In one, the agent does not have a coherent belief, as in Heidegger's "The nothing nots." When we say "Heidegger believes that the nothing nots," we say that he holds that the following sentence expresses a truth: "The nothing nots." In the second, a rational agent believes something that we accept as expressing a true proposition, but we don't believe the agent understands what he is saying or believing. For example, the agent may state Gödel's Incompleteness Theorem without understanding it, but believe it is true, having seen it in a textbook. In that case, we say that he or she believes that the sentence "Peano Arithmetic is incomplete" expresses a true proposition.

a manner that makes sense of the agent even though we deny that there is an object of the agent's belief. That is, we are *enabled* to attribute to the agent this "belief" in our terms in our language.

When we talk about an agent being warranted in forming a "belief," we are not talking about the agent's justification for such a "belief." Rather, we are talking about something more akin to what Tyler Burge calls an agent's "entitlement" to a "belief."[9] To explain his distinction between two different kinds of epistemic warrant, that of "entitlement" and that of justification, Burge draws on an analogy from the epistemology of perception. There he points out that one normally justifies a perceptual belief by reference to (perceptual) "experiences, seemings (appearances), stimulations, ordinary conditions, possible sources of error, or the like."[10] But to be warranted in one's perceptual belief, we normally need not refer to these things; that is, we "need not be able to *justify* [our] perceptual belief at all."[11] Burge rightly points out that we are normally warranted in our perceptual beliefs "straightway, without reason, evidence, or justification." In his terminology,

one is *entitled* to the belief without raising questions about it, unless specific contextual grounds for doubting it arise. Entitlement is an epistemic warrant that need not be fully available to the warranted individual. The individual need not even have the concepts to explain the warrant. Entitlement thus contrasts with justification . . . One can be warranted in one's perceptual beliefs without being able to justify these beliefs, and even without having the concepts to do so. Such warrant requires having perceptual experience, but it requires no reference to it.[12]

Burge then goes on to claim that ordinary understanding of certain aspects of words used by another person is in this way analogous to ordinary perception. In both cases, warrant does not require evidence or justification.

Now it is my claim that there is an analogous use of the notion of entitlement that applies to a rational agent's forming a belief. A rational agent is warranted in forming a belief without being required to be able to justify the belief or even to possess the concepts to do so. Such warrant

9. Tyler Burge, "Comprehension and Interpretation," in *The Philosophy of Donald Davidson*, ed. Lewis Hahn (Peru: Open Court, 1999), 232–234.

10. Burge, "Comprehension and Interpretation," 232.

11. Burge, "Comprehension and Interpretation," 232.

12. Burge, "Comprehension and Interpretation," 233.

does not require the agent to have the semantic concepts and machinery necessary to explain and justify the warrant.

Two immediate questions arise: What *entitles* a rational agent to form "a belief" and express it in these or similar terms in his or her language where the object of belief fails to be a proposition, and what *enables* us to interpret the agent and to apply our semantics in a manner that makes sense of the agent so as to attribute to the agent "this belief" in our terms in our language, even in cases in which we may deny that the agent is, indeed, expressing a belief, or proposition? The answer to both questions lies in the fact that all three cases are instances of the following schema, which we call the *Belief Commitment Schema*:

(BCS) $\exists f_{A\text{-}B} \exists c_i \exists C_s \exists c_u (A$ is committed to the claim that $\exists o((f_{A\text{-}B}(c_i) = o) \wedge C_s(c_u) = $ that-S $\wedge$ S),

where 'S' stands in for a sentence, o is an object, C_s is the character of 'S', c_i is the context of introduction, c_u is a context of use, A is the agent of c_i and c_u, and $f_{A\text{-}B}$ is the anaphoric background function for the name 'n' that A is committed to use to denote o.

Each instance of this schema corresponds to a singular term ⌜that-S⌝, putatively denoting a definite proposition. Each instance also corresponds to the belief report ⌜A believes that-S⌝ and to the A-B condition for the name contained in the sentence 'S'. When a rational agent believes that there is a true proposition ⌜that-S⌝, even in cases where the term ⌜that-S⌝ fails to denote, the agent must satisfy an instance of the BCS that corresponds to a term that purportedly denotes the same proposition as does ⌜that-S⌝. For a necessary restriction on rational belief, that is, on the agent's not believing nonsense even though there is nothing that is the object of the agent's belief, is that the agent satisfy the commitment of one of these corresponding instances. Accordingly, we call such a corresponding instance *a commitment to the belief* ⌜that-S⌝, where the term ⌜that-S⌝ may be thought of as forming an equivalence class, each member of which is one of these corresponding instances. The agent, of course, need neither be aware of this commitment nor have the concepts of A-B function, context of use, context of introduction, and the like. Nevertheless, the agent may still have such a commitment. For now, we shall say that an agent satisfies an instance of the BCS if it deductively follows from the agent's beliefs together with his or her semantic and rational commitments (to be discussed in this chapter and in detail in chapter 6).

In considering the first case, where the A-B condition is not an authentic naming condition, our formal semantics for the reference of proper names permits us to represent these commitments as follows:

(5) $\exists f_{A-B} \exists c_i \exists C_s \exists c_u$(A is committed to the belief that $\exists h((f_{A-B}(c_i)=h) \wedge C_s(c_u) =$ that-S $\wedge$ S),

where 'S' stands in for the sentence "Sherlock Holmes smokes a pipe," 'h' denotes Sherlock Holmes, C_s is the character of the sentence "Sherlock Holmes smokes a pipe," c_i is the context of introduction, c_u is a context of use, A is the agent of c_i and c_u, and f_{A-B} is the anaphoric background function for the name 'Sherlock Holmes'. (In section 5.4, I say more about an agent's commitments to a belief.) This formalization says that there is an A-B function and context of introduction such that the agent is committed to the following: (1) the existence of a value for this function with c_i as argument, and (consequently) (2) that the character function of 'S', for any context of use, has a value, that-S, and (3) that the truth value of that-S is true.

In our second case, in order to represent Leverrier's commitments, we may once again appeal to our formal semantics for the reference of proper names.

(6) $\exists f_{A-B} \exists c_i \exists C_s \exists c_u$(A is committed to the belief that $\exists v((f_{A-B}(c_i) = v) \wedge C_s(c_u) =$ that-S $\wedge$ S),

where 'S' stands if for the sentence "Vulcan is a small planet," 'v' denotes Vulcan, C_s is the character of the sentence "Vulcan is a small planet," c_i is the context of introduction, c_u is a context of use, A is the agent of c_i and c_u, and f_{A-B} is the anaphoric background function for the name 'Vulcan'. (We may substitute the A-B function for any other name or directly referring device that Leverrier may use (or try to use) to denote Vulcan and substitute that name or referring device for 'Vulcan' in 'S'.)

Last, we consider the case in which there is an authentic naming condition and an object satisfying this condition from the actual context of introduction, for example, where an agent believes that Beethoven is a great composer. As with the previous two cases, we may formalize the agent's commitments.

(7) $\exists f_{A-B} \exists c_i \exists C_s \exists c_u$(A is committed to the claim that $\exists b((f_{A-B}(c_i)=b) \wedge C_s(c_u) =$ that-S $\wedge$ S),

where 'S' stands in for the sentence "Beethoven is a great composer," 'b' denotes Beethoven, C_s is the character of the sentence "Beethoven is a great composer," c_i is the context of introduction, c_u is a context of use, A is the agent of c_i and c_u, and $f_{A\text{-}B}$ is the anaphoric background function for the name 'Beethoven'.

The A-B condition for the name 'Beethoven' is an authentic naming condition satisfied by an object in the actual context of introduction. This allows us to say still more than in the previous two cases. In this case, the agent's commitments regarding the name 'Beethoven' are correct. Thus in this case we may also say that the object of the agent's belief is indeed a definite proposition, and hence it has a definite truth value.

Thus the answer to our first question is that *an agent is entitled to "believe that-S," even when 'that-S' fails to denote a definite proposition, if and only if the agent satisfies a corresponding instance of the BCS that is a commitment to believe that-S.* Accordingly, each such corresponding instance counts as satisfying *the same entitlement condition* to believe that-S. Again, the agent need not be aware of the entitlement condition. The agent need not even have the requisite concepts employed in this notion to explain or justify the agent's "belief that-S." Nevertheless, the agent may still satisfy one of the corresponding instances of the BCS that is a commitment to believe that-S, and thus be entitled to "believe that-S."

Before answering our second question, what *enables* us to interpret the agent and to apply our semantics in a manner that makes sense of the agent, it is natural to ask here what the logical form is of a belief attribution. The received view is that the de dicto reading of 'believes' is a two-place predicate, where an agent bears a relation to the denotation of the singular term 'that-S', which is normally taken to be a proposition. It is my view that the de dicto reading of 'believes' is, indeed, a two-place predicate. But since the singular term 'that-S' may fail to denote, what, in such cases, could this relatum be?

The ordinary person's intuition is that when we attribute a belief to someone, there is something that the person's belief is about. For example, if John believes that Mary is going to the movies, his belief is about Mary or the state of affairs, that is, Mary's going to the movies; either way, the object of belief is a proposition. But this intuition has to be modified somewhat when we say that A believes that Cicero is a Roman orator but does not believe that Tully is a Roman orator. Here the ordinary person's intuition falters, for the object of A's belief (Cicero, or Cicero's being a Roman orator) is paradoxically the object of A's disbelief as well. In order to preserve the ordinary person's intuition that a belief is about something, we add that beliefs are about something *under a description or guise,* thus resolving the paradox.

Now I am claiming that there is a third case, namely, that in which we attribute to someone a belief the expression of which contains vacuous names and terms for "non-existing" objects and uninstantiated properties. This third case requires still further modifications of the ordinary person's intuitions in order to preserve the general intuition that a belief is about something. In particular, we must add semantic machinery representing authentic naming conditions such that the agent is committed to its being the case that these vacuous names and uninstantiated properties in fact denote and instantiate.

Thus if my previous semantical analysis is correct, then the answer to our second question lies in the fact that whenever we attribute a de dicto "belief" to an agent, there is a corresponding belief commitment that we can correctly attribute to the agent, namely,

$\exists C_s \exists c_u$(A is committed to the belief that the value of $C_s(c_u)$ is true).

For when the agent believes that-S, the agent must at least be committed to the belief (if not tacitly believe) that all the semantic machinery is in place, whatever that machinery is or is believed to be, such that the singular term 'that-S' succeeds in denoting. Then one can have a de re belief (or commitment) toward this machinery, that is, toward the function C_s, that the truth value of $C_s(c_u)$ is true. This in effect restates what it is for an agent to satisfy one of the corresponding instances of the BCS that is a commitment to the belief that-S.

In the case in which the value of the character function for S in a context of use is a definite proposition p, that is, $\exists p(C_s(c_u) = p = $ that-S$)$ (and the agent believes that-S), the agent is literally committed to believing of the character function, given the context of use, that its value is a true definite proposition. Moreover, the term 'that-S' within the corresponding de dicto belief attribution denotes, and thus this de dicto attribution is also literally true.

But in the case where the value of this function is not a definite proposition, we only have enabling conditions for an attributer to attribute a corresponding de dicto "belief" to an agent. And in such cases, the best we can say is that *we deem it appropriate to attribute such a de dicto belief to the agent,* even though it is literally true that the agent has the corresponding de re belief (or belief commitment). Indeed, the agent's belief commitment is the basis for making the corresponding de dicto belief attribution, even though such an attribution cannot be viewed as literally true. For what could it literally mean to believe that Vulcan is a small planet when Vulcan does not exist? What is it that one is literally believing to be a small planet?

5.4   Conditions for Belief Attributions Containing Vacuous Names

What are the enabling conditions for belief attributions for which the sentence within the belief context contains a vacuous name? And when we do make such attributions, under what conditions can we say that two agents have a belief about the "same object"? These questions take on great significance if we claim that in such cases there is no object of the agent's belief. For then we need a basis for attributing to A the belief that-S yet not the belief that-S', where 'that-S' and 'that-S'' both fail to denote. For we do not want to attribute to the ancient Greeks a belief in the same gods as the ancient Norse on the grounds that the names of these gods all fail to denote. Further, what sense, if any, can we make of saying that if two agents both believe that-S, where 'that-S' fails to denote, there is, nevertheless, something that they both believe?

Our entitlement condition, that the agent satisfy one of the relevant corresponding instances of the BCS, answers some of the questions stated above. Entitlement conditions are necessary, but by no means sufficient, conditions for having a certain belief, since satisfying an instance of the BCS only implies that the agent is committed to believing that there is a proposition, that-S, and that that-S is true. Thus we have a partial answer to our question regarding enabling conditions. *A necessary, but not sufficient, condition for attributing a certain belief to an agent is that the agent satisfy the corresponding entitlement condition.* With this condition, if an attributer correctly attributes the same belief to two agents, then both agents must satisfy the same entitlement condition for this belief. If, for example, both Leverrier and Babinet believe that Vulcan is a small planet, then they both must satisfy a corresponding instance of the BCS that satisfies the same entitlement condition, namely,

(8) $\exists f_{A\text{-}B} \exists c_i \exists C_s \exists c_u$(A is committed to the belief that $\exists v((f_{A\text{-}B}(c_i) = v) \wedge C_s(c_u) = \text{that-S} \wedge S)$,

where 'S' stands in for the sentence "Vulcan is a small planet" (or the substitution in this sentence of some other name used for purportedly denoting Vulcan; see below and chapter 6 for conditions in which two names puportedly denote the same thing), 'v' denotes Vulcan, C_s is the character of 'S', c_i is the context of introduction, c_u is a context of use, f_{A-B} is the anaphoric background function for the name 'Vulcan' (or some other name purportedly denoting Vulcan), and A is instantiated by both Leverrier and Babinet. There is no proposition that Leverrier and Babinet both believe which enables an attributer to attribute the same belief to them. Nevertheless, there is an entitlement condition that they both must satisfy to enable the attributer to make this attribution to them.

Equivalently, suppose two agents do not satisfy the same entitlement condition. Then the same belief cannot be attributed to both agents even though in both cases there may not be anything that the attributer attributes to them as the object of their respective beliefs. If Johannes believes that Wotan is the most powerful god and Achilles believes that Zeus is the most powerful god, then a reporter cannot attribute to them the same belief on the grounds that there is no object of their respective beliefs. There are different entitlement conditions that these agents satisfy.

Accordingly, we say that we deem it appropriate for an attributer to attribute the same "belief" to two agents only if both agents satisfy the same entitlement conditions.

In order to answer the various questions relating to enabling conditions and to satisfying an instance of the BCS more fully, we first must introduce two kinds of commitments that we normally attribute to a rational agent and that impose constraints upon an agent's beliefs. Indeed, in my view, these constraints are generally tacitly assumed when we attribute a belief to an agent.

The first kind of constraint is due to the agent's language, and we call these constraints the agent's *semantic commitments*. Agents express beliefs in a language. If the agent uses language in a normal way, that is, has a general intention to use language in the normal way, then he or she is semantically committed to certain beliefs in virtue of what follows from his or her discourse, whether the agent realizes it or not. For example, when the agent uses a proper name, the agent is committed to believing in the existence of the object to which the name refers, whether or not the agent is able to identify the object to which he or she is referring. *An agent is se-*

mantically committed to an S-type term's referring to the unique satisfier of its A-B condition even if the agent is unaware of this condition or its unique satisfier.

Also, an agent may have a belief about a particular person or object, but may not be in a position to express this belief with the name of the person or object, due to ignorance of this name. Nevertheless, the agent is semantically committed to accepting the belief, even when it is expressed by means of using the correct name of the person or thing that the agent's belief is about. Accordingly, we are justified in attributing such a belief expressed by means of this name to the agent, even though the agent may not realize that his or her belief is about this name's referent.

The second kind of constraint is what we call *rational commitments.* These are due not to the language that the agent uses but to the rational implications of the agent's beliefs. As an example, if the agent realizes that Q follows from P, and the agent believes P, then he or she *should* either accept Q or reject or suspend judgment on P. The agent is *rationally committed in this case to accept Q or reject or suspend judgment on P.* When attributing a belief to an agent, we are justified in taking into account the rational commitments of the agent.

Of course, when we attribute a belief to an agent, we do not attribute to the agent every belief that is in the deductive closure of an agent's beliefs. That would be too strong a requirement. Often an agent has contradictory theories, and we do not want to attribute to the agent any arbitrary belief on the grounds that any belief is a consequence of a contradiction. Moreover, we could not always make sense of the activity or enterprise of an agent if we were to attribute to the agent the deductive closure of his or her beliefs. Mathematicians strive to prove theorems in part because they may not already believe all the consequences of their axioms. Also, many mathematicians tried to trisect an angle with compass and straightedge alone, even though it is a consequence of their axioms that it is impossible.

In practice, various factors, such as the agent's verbal dispositions and dispositions to act in certain ways, together with what we would regard as "reasonable" for the agent in a given activity or enterprise to realize are deductive consequences of his or her beliefs, restrict what we attribute to an agent. (Tension among these factors and an agent's semantic and rational commitments give rise to puzzles about belief.)

We are now ready to consider the conditions under which we attribute to an agent "a belief" using a sentence that contains a vacuous name. We have been suggesting that there is an important difference between vacuous names introduced in fiction and vacuous names introduced in mistaken hypotheses.

We consider, first, a name introduced in fiction, where the A-B condition for the name, 'n', in the fictional discourse does not contain any uniquely specifying conditions of the object. In this case, we are enabled to report that 'A believes that-Φn' only when the name n is on the historic chain that is linked to and terminates in the fiction, and A believes that there is an object n that instantiates Φ. We may attribute to two agents the "same belief" that-Φn if and only if 'n', as used by both agents, comes from the same chain linked to and terminating in the fiction, and both agents believe that there is an object, n, that instantiates Φ. Although both agents believe that Φn expresses a true proposition, they are both *semantically committed* to that-Φn's merely having the pretense of expressing a proposition.

Likewise, consider the case where two pieces of fiction that are truly independent of one another, in the strong sense that all the pretense names and pretense propositions are on different historic chains and that we cannot even say that one author took or modified any ideas from the other. In that case, we cannot even say that two agents, one linked to only one of these pieces of fiction, the other linked to only the other, believe the same pretense propositions, even if the two works of fiction are word-for-word identical.

Of course, such an astounding coincidence is more than likely to end up in litigation. The situation I just described is, indeed, incredible. Nevertheless, it is a possible situation, and in that situation the two agents would have a relation to different pretenses, that is, to different A-B conditions. Consequently, they do not share the "same beliefs," even though their beliefs are expressed with syntactically the same sentence.

We now consider vacuous names introduced in mistaken hypotheses. Here the situation is quite different. As we have already seen from our hypothetical example, Leverrier does not have a term that is on the same chain as Babinet's term 'Vulcan'. Nevertheless, we can attribute to them "a belief" in the existence of the same object. The same class of circumstances would have to obtain in order for this object to exist, and both of them believe that these circumstances do, in fact, obtain.

In Leverrier's case, we say this because it deductively follows from his theory that there is a unique satisfier of the A-B condition for the name 'Vulcan'. From each member of the class of context worlds that will make his theory true, there is a unique satisfier of the A-B condition for the name

'Vulcan'. Thus Leverrier is rationally committed to the existence of Vulcan. He also is rationally committed to the belief that there is a true proposition that Vulcan is a small planet.

In Babinet's case, since he introduced the name 'Vulcan', he perforce believes that there is a unique satisfier of the A-B condition for the name 'Vulcan'. Since he uses the name 'Vulcan' in expressing his theory, Babinet is both rationally and semantically committed to the existence of Vulcan. Thus Babinet and Leverrier are both committed to believing the same planet exists, and we are justified in attributing this belief to both of them even though there is no such planet as Vulcan.

There are several intermediaries between what I am calling pure fiction and outright hypotheses or theories of the world, and thus the distinction between fiction and false belief may be a matter of degree. Certain myths may well contain elements of both. The ancient Greeks used myth to account for certain human psychological traits. A legend often involves a mixture of fact and exaggeration of an actual person, place, or thing, and often attributes uninstantiated properties to the actual object, such as when it is claimed that this bush can burn eternally or this person can fly. And what about the person who adds his or her own hypotheses to fiction that he or she mistakes for fact? The closer we get to authentic naming conditions, the more we can say about the agent's beliefs. Nevertheless, in all these cases, it seems perfectly coherent and reasonable to attribute "a belief" to an agent, even though there is no proposition that is the object of the agent's belief.

Thus far, I have discussed necessary conditions for enabling an attributer to attribute a belief to an agent. We are enabled to attribute a belief to an agent only if the agent has certain kinds of rational or semantic commitments. These commitments do not, however, suffice to enable an attributer to make such an attribution. Sometimes when an agent is unaware of some of his or her commitments, he or she may fail to believe something that he or she is committed to or may even believe something that contradicts some of his or her own commitments. Should an agent's unawareness of his or her commitments be a constraint on enabling conditions, as in the examples above involving the rational commitments of the mathematician?

It seems that sometimes we may justifiably attribute a belief to an agent on the sole basis of what an agent is committed to either semantically or rationally even though the agent is not aware of this commitment. This is what often gives rise to the puzzle about belief. We are justified in attributing contradictory beliefs to an agent despite the agent's flawless logical acumen, as in the Pierre example, in Kripke's article "A Puzzle about Belief."[13] In that example, as I analyze it, Pierre is rationally committed to the belief that 'Londre' and 'London' name different cities. But even though he doesn't realize it, semantically he is committed to their naming the same place. So sometimes we are justified in attributing a belief to an agent based on the agent's semantic or rational commitments even if the agent is unaware of these commitments. People who fail to appreciate the subtlety of Kripke's puzzle about belief usually ignore the significance of one or the other kind of commitments in attributing a belief to the agent.[14]

What, then, are the sufficient conditions that enable an attributer to attribute a belief to an agent? As we have said earlier when discussing rational commitments, in practice, various factors play a role in determining what we may attribute to an agent. Among them are the agent's dispositions to verbal behavior and to act in certain ways. Also relevant is what we would regard as "reasonable" for an agent in a given activity or enterprise to realize are deductive consequences of his or her beliefs. Similar remarks apply to semantic commitments. But it is unlikely that there are sharp boundaries that delineate cases in which these commitments justify attributing a belief to an agent from cases in which they do not.

In his article "A Puzzle about Belief," Kripke concludes from his puzzle that "our normal practices of interpretation and attribution of belief are subjected to the greatest possible strain, perhaps to the point of breakdown. So is the notion of the *content* of someone's assertion, the *proposition* it expresses."[15] The fact that there are no sharp sufficient conditions enabling an attributer to attribute a belief to an agent in cases that involve sentences containing vacuous names points in a similar direction. Nevertheless, anaphoric background conditions and presuppositions in the introduction of a name and an agent's semantic and rational commitments play a central role in clarifying what an agent is trying to express, and thus in clarifying what we attribute to an agent.

13. See Kripke, "A Puzzle about Belief."

14. See, for example, Schiffer, "Belief Ascription," which ignores the significance of semantic commitments in attributing a belief to an agent, and Nathan Salmon, *Frege's Puzzle* (Cambridge: MIT Press, 1986), which underestimates the significance of rational commitments in attributing a belief to an agent.

15. Kripke, "A Puzzle about Belief," 134–135.

6

Intentional Identity and True Negative Existential Statements

It is essential to our understanding of everyday and scientific discourse that we know when different people (or the same person on different occasions) intend to refer to one and the same object, even though we may not be able to identify that object or even to know whether the intended reference succeeds. We may, for example, understand two astronomers who speak of the planet Vulcan's being near the sun, without ourselves agreeing that Vulcan exists. The same is true in historical, anthropological, and archeological discourse. We may want to know whether two cultures worship the same god or whether various intentions to refer to a historical person are intentions to refer to the same person, without being committed to the existence of the god or of the alleged historical person. Thus far, we have primarily been discussing cases in which we may attribute the same belief, the expression of which contains a vacuous name within the belief context, to two agents on the basis of their both satisfying the same instance of the BCS, without discussing in much detail the conditions under which two agents express the same belief when they satisfy different instances of the BCS. But as we have previously stated, sometimes an attributer may be enabled to attribute the same belief to two agents even if the agents fail to satisfy the same instance of the BCS. This occurs when, for example, the agents use different names that putatively denote the same object, even if nonexistent, and the putative proposition that is attributed to both agents as accepting, is purportedly about "this object." It may also occur when the two agents speak different languages, but are putatively expressing the same proposition that they both, respectively, accept. The problem of when we may attribute to two people an intention to refer to the same object (or proposition), without ourselves being able either to identify the object or to know that their intentions to refer to the object succeed, and the problem of the logical form of such attributions are at the heart of the problem of intentional identity.

In this chapter, I apply various notions and analyses of chapters 4 and 5 and introduce other notions in order to help to solve the problems of intentional identity and true negative singular existential statements. In section 6.1, I seek to clarify the problem of intentional identity. In order to make sense of intentional identity statements, we must make sense of the notion of two agents purporting to be talking about the same thing from a given agent's perspective. I then present conditions under which we may apply that notion. By applying these conditions to intentional identity statements, we are providing the conditions under which we deem these statements appropriate without requiring that the mentioned non-existent entity exist. I end the chapter by applying some of these notions to the problem of true negative singular existential statements, the problem of explaining how we can meaningfully assert that an object, α, does not exist.

6.1   The Problem of Intentional Identities

P. T. Geach has pointed out that one can "refer" to the same entity across *intentional* contexts.[1] Consider, for example, his sentence:

(1)   Hob thinks a witch has blighted Bob's mare, and Nob wonders whether she (the same witch) killed Cob's sow.

In this sentence the pronoun "she" seems to refer back to the same witch that is referred to by the phrase "a witch has blighted Bob's mare," which lies within the intentional context "Hob thinks."

Now the problem of *intentional identity,* as set out by Geach, is how to construe the pronoun 'she' in sentence (1) and similar uses of pronouns in sentences like (1), where the person reporting the sentence need not be committed to the *existence* of the entity to which the pronoun seemingly refers. In fact, the reporter may believe that no such entity actually exists.

It might appear that we can construe the occurrence of the pronoun "she" in (1) as an occurrence of a variable bound by "a witch." The problem with such a reading is that if the expression "a witch" is construed as lying inside the scope of the intentional context (Hob thinks), then since

1. P. T. Geach, "Intentional Identity," *The Journal Of Philosophy* 64 (1967): 627–632.

the term "she" lies outside the scope of this context, the sentence is syntactically not well formed. But if we construe the phrase "a witch" as lying outside the scope of "Hob thinks," then we obtain an incorrect reading of the sentence. For although we then have the well-formed sentence

(2)   Some witch is such that Hob thinks she has blighted Bob's mare, and Nob wonders whether she killed Cob's sow,

(2) implies that there are witches. Now this is false even though (1) may be true. (Even if there *are* witches, the reporter of (1) may very well consistently deny that there are witches.) Hence (2) is not an adequate paraphrase of (1).

Moreover, as Geach points out,

(3)   Someone is such that Hob thinks she is a witch and has blighted Bob's mare, and Nob wonders whether she killed Cob's sow

also fails to be an acceptable reading of (1) because it implies that Hob and Nob have some one person in mind. But there may not be any actual person focused on, even though both are allegedly referring to the same object.

Geach also notes that a tempting paraphrase of sentences such as (1) would treat the problematic pronoun as what Evans calls an E-type term, serving as proxy for a definite description that is recoverable from the clauses governed by the pronoun's antecedent. Thus the pronoun "she" in (1) would go proxy for the definite description "the witch who has blighted Bob's mare." We then obtain

(4)   Hob thinks a witch has blighted Bob's mare, and Nob wonders whether the witch who has blighted Bob's mare killed Cob's sow.

This sentence consists in a conjunction each conjunct of which is an unproblematic sentence beginning with an opaque context, and yet the sentence attributes to Hob and Nob a common (purported) reference to "the same witch."

One problem with this sentence, Geach argues, is that it requires that Nob have thoughts about Bob's mare, yet he may not. Without knowing whether Nob has any thoughts about Bob's mare, the reporter may know that when they both used the words "the witch," they were "referring" to the same entity. For example, knowing that they both believe that there is exactly one witch in town, a reporter may overhear Hob say, "The witch blighted Bob's mare" on one occasion and Nob say, "I wonder whether the witch killed Cob's sow" on another. Nob may have no thoughts about Bob's mare, yet a reporter in such circumstances would be justified in using (1) to report the situation, but not (4).

Geach goes on to raise a second objection to (4) as an analysis of (1).[2] Geach agrees with Russell that

(5)   The witch who blighted Bob's mare killed Cob's sow

is analyzable as

(6)   Just one witch blighted Bob's mare and she killed Cob's sow.

But Geach maintains that it is unlikely that (6) may always be substituted for (5) *salva veritate* in the context of "Nob wonders whether." When we append this prefix to (5), we obtain

(7)   Nob wonders whether the witch who blighted Bob's mare killed Cob's sow,

which is the second conjunct of (4). But this conjunct, Geach contends, should be analyzed *not* as

(8)   Nob wonders whether (the following is the case) just one witch blighted Bob's mare and she killed Cob's sow

but rather as

(9)   Nob assumes that just one witch blighted Bob's mare, and Nob wonders whether she (that same witch) killed Cob's sow.

According to Geach, we cannot use Russell's analysis of definite descriptions within the context of "wonders whether." Thus Geach's second objection to (4) as an analysis of (1) is that the second conjunct of (4) merely introduces the same problem of intentional identity over again. For if (9) is a correct analysis of the second conjunct of (4), then the occurrence of "she" in (9) is problematic in just the way it was in Geach's original sentence (1).[3] Thus Geach leaves us with the problem of intentional identity unsolved.

Now on my view, the problem of intentional identity itself requires further clarification before progress can be had in offering a solution. More

2. For a detailed discussion and a proposed partial solution to Geach's problem of intentional identity, see Michael McKinsey, "Mental Anaphora," *Synthese* 66 (1985): 159–175. The following discussion of Geach's second objection to (4) is based on this article.

3. Geach, "Intentional Identity," 631.

specifically, it is necessary to distinguish between two questions that have to be answered regarding propositional attitudes in general, and intentional identity statements in particular. First, whatever the precise logical form of a propositional attitude is, there remains the problem of what is the object of a belief or propositional attitude. In the ordinary case, it is generally taken that a belief (or other propositional attitude) is a relation to a proposition.[4] But when the surface structure of the belief has the form 'α is F', where 'α' stands in for a nondenoting proper name or a pronoun failing to refer to anything (and 'F' stands in for a predicate), what, if anything, can this proposition be? Since the problematic anaphoric pronoun in the second conjunct of intentional identity statements fails to refer to anything, it is not clear which proposition, if any, is the object of the agent's belief. This is one of the problems of chapter 5.

Second, there is the problem of under what conditions do we attribute beliefs, and in particular, under what conditions is it correct to make intentional identity statements, such as (1)? As we stated in chapter 4, Kripke has introduced customarily accepted principles of belief attribution adequate to many ordinary attributions of belief. Once again, the principle that concerns us is, Kripke's principle 2':

Principle 2': A normal English speaker who is not reticent will be disposed to sincere reflective assent to 'P' if he believes that P.

Here, as in chapter 4, we discover a class of cases that this principle fails to capture. In particular, this principle runs into difficulties with intentional identity statements. For notice that in (1) above, Nob may not have any thoughts about, or even heard of, Hob, Bob, or Bob's mare. Thus in such circumstances, from Nob's own resources alone, he cannot sincerely assent to the sentence P that expresses the belief that we attribute to him. Nevertheless, there are conditions under which our practice deems it correct for us to make the attribution expressed in the second conjunct, even though Nob is not in a position to do so. That is, there are conditions under which it is correct to attribute a belief to an agent even though that

4. I am aware of the difficulties about the nature of a proposition, whether they are objects of belief and how to individuate them. For present purposes, whatever one considers a proposition to be, how to individuate them, and even whether such entities can serve as an object of belief, I consider the cases discussed in what follows problematic for expressing a proposition.

agent may not sincerely upon reflection assent to the sentence that expresses the object of the belief attributed to him or her.

Moreover, when making such an attribution by means of an intentional identity statement, we are claiming that two people are mentioning the same nonexistent entity from the given agent's perspective in a manner that does not require the existence of "nonexistent" entities. Thus the second problem of specifying the conditions under which we make true intentional identity statements requires (a) that we specify the conditions under which two people are mentioning the same non-existent entity from a given agent's perspective and (b) that in attributing a belief (or propositional attitude) to an agent, we do not require the agent to assent, sincerely and upon reflection, to the sentence that expresses the object of belief attributed to him or her, that is, we do not require Kripke's principle 2' to hold.

The first problem of what, if anything, is the object of a belief (or propositional attitude) when the sentence expressing the belief contains a non-denoting proper name or a pronoun failing to refer to anything and the second problem of under what conditions we correctly attribute such beliefs are the questions that we dealt with in chapter 5. In section 6.2, we thus look at a few examples of intentional identity statements and apply to them the notions and conditions formulated in chapter 5.[5]

6.2   Idealized Rational Agents, Epistemically Complete World Views, and a Given Agent's Perspective

We want to present the conditions under which we can make intentional identity statements that we deem correct. But, first, what are we to understand here by an agent's perspective? As mentioned in chapter 4, we are not concerned with an agent's beliefs that are mere "hunches" or "feelings in one's bones." Moreover, since in such cases the agent fails to assent to the sentence that expresses the attributed belief, the notion of agent's per-

---

5. In section 6.2, where we specify these conditions that do not require the agent sincerely to assent upon reflection to the sentence that expresses the object of belief attributed to him or her, we are not claiming that we are presenting principles other than Kripke's that avoid the paradox or puzzle about belief in such cases that lead to such paradox or puzzle. Rather, we are simply claiming that these principles or conditions that we present apply to various nonpuzzling cases of belief attribution made in intentional identity statements without requiring Kripke's otherwise customarily accepted principle stated earlier.

spective cannot be constituted merely by either the agent's occurrent be-liefs or by the agent's dispositions to assent or dissent under query, even upon reflection. Rather, it involves what the agent should assent to were the agent presented with a certain class of facts (discussed in chapter 4). Since this "should" is based upon our belief about the agent's beliefs and what the agent is committed to, given these beliefs, I try to explicate what tacit information about the agent we are assuming and committed to, and the sense in which it captures the agent's point of view or perspective.

I assume we are dealing with idealized rational agents whose epistemic and doxastic life have at least the following four dimensions:

1. The agent has a "worldview" which in some cases may be "epistemi-cally complete."
2. The agent has the generalized intention to apply this worldview and reason and judge in accord with it.
3. Obviously, the agent has a language, and we attribute a semantics to it. The semantics of the agent's language places certain constraints on the agent's beliefs. I call such constraints *semantic commitments* that the lan-guage imposes on the agent.
4. The agent can reflect and reorganize his or her beliefs when he or she realizes or is told what follows from them or what he or she is committed to, given these beliefs. This realization of what follows from an agent's be-liefs places certain constraints on these beliefs. I call such constraints *ra-tional commitments* of the agent. (The notions of semantic and rational commitments were introduced in chapter 5.)

We explain each of these dimensions in turn.

Regarding the first dimension, an agent has a worldview if, first, he or she believes in certain kinds of entities and that certain kinds of predicates can or cannot apply to these entities. For example, it may be part of some-one's worldview that there are only physical entities, or that there are mathematical entities as well, but not supernatural entities. Certain predi-cates, such as 'is married' or 'is not married', cannot apply to, say, mathe-matical entities.

Second, the agent believes that these entities enter into causal relations or special interactions with one another. Depending upon one's world-view, one might regard physical events as caused exclusively by other phys-ical events, or alternatively sometimes by divine intervention. One might believe in objective moral values that require one to engage in or refrain from certain actions, and so forth.

Third, the agent also believes, or is committed to the view, that explanation (and prediction) of phenomena requires appealing to the causal relations or special interactions that these entities have with one another. (A subgroup of the agent's community may try to develop theories that make use of only such explanation and prediction for a given domain of kinds of entities.) The agent may also believe that there are special kinds of entities that defy these normal patterns of explanation by appeal to such causal or special interactions. People who believe in witches, for example, may believe that, though they are physical entities, they may fly on a broomstick and thus defy physical laws.

Fourth, a worldview contains claims about how the agent might get knowledge, which could lead to *second-order epistemic beliefs*. That is, the agent not only has beliefs, including beliefs about a particular belief. Such an agent also has beliefs about classes of beliefs, for example, beliefs that one's beliefs should be relatively consistent, a posteriori beliefs should be based on certain kinds of evidence, and so on. Such second-order epistemic beliefs also include beliefs about how we get evidence and what the agent's relationship is vis-à-vis this evidence. Evidence may, for example, be inductive or be based on divine revelation. It may be evidence that anyone can seek, or it may be evidence revealed to only a special member of the community. It may be beliefs that in science we never accept hypotheses (e.g., Popper). (Second-order beliefs, as we will see in what follows, give rise to norms or constraints on the agent's acceptance and change of beliefs.) A worldview that satisfies this fourth condition, as well as the other three conditions above, is an *epistemically complete worldview.*

These beliefs that form such a worldview are obtained neither by random guesses nor by rote procedure. Most people have only a rough picture, or parts, of a worldview that they inherit whether they are aware of it or not. They are relatively coherent. In various domains or "mini-worlds," a certain subgroup within the community is recognized, usually as "the experts," as having special competence in that domain or mini-world. These experts are expected to develop and have a more refined picture of their worldview for that domain. We say that such agents have *institutional competence* for that domain or mini-world. Most people generally rely on these experts to help them form their rough picture and fill in the gaps of their worldview. (As we will see later, the greater the agent's expertise in a given domain, the stronger we feel about attributing to that agent beliefs in that domain that the agent is committed to, given the agent's worldview.) I believe that this is all in the spirit of Hilary Putnam's sociolinguistic hypothesis about the division of linguistic labor and the role he assigns to experts in this hypothesis.[6]

A worldview is roughly an agent's picture of what can or cannot be, what property a given kind of object can or cannot have, what and how we can or cannot know, and what we can (or must) or cannot (or must not) do. The relevant sense of "can" in the above formulation usually is not what is logically possible. Rather, it is what is possible given the constraints imposed by the agent's worldview. Thus the agent's beliefs must be compatible with the agent's worldview, which is part of the agent's point of view, or perspective.

In the example in chapter 4 involving Kripke and my student Mary, we assume that in Kripke's worldview, he believes that an agent wrote the paper rather than, say, the paper just came into existence, it was produced by a god, or it was typed randomly. He also believes that only a brilliant person can produce such a product. If we consider the domain in which Kripke is an expert as a mini-world, we take it that his mini-worldview is sophisticated and developed enough to have certain beliefs about certain abilities, such as brilliance, of agents who produce products in this mini-world. When Kripke examines an agent's product in this domain, we thus have no problem attributing to him beliefs regarding what that agent can or cannot produce. That is, given Kripke's expertise and his examination of an agent's product in this domain, we may attribute to him beliefs regarding certain abilities, such as brilliance (i.e., a very high intellectual ability), of that agent.

We can make sense of a given community's worldview even though it differs from our own. There may be no theoretical agreement between them and us, and hence they do not share our institutional competence. In fact, they may even have very different community-wide beliefs and may even countenance radically different kinds of entities than we do. What is crucial, however, is that their worldview must be intelligible to us. Otherwise, it is not clear how we could be interpreting them. Thus disagreement presupposes intelligibility. And intelligibility rules out the coherence of attributing to them an alternative logic (in the sense of accepting simple

6. See Hilary Putnam, "The Meaning of 'Meaning.'"

contradictions). Hence a constraint on any worldview is that it must not require an alternative logic in order to accept it. It is also crucial that though a given community may countenance different entities than we do, we can still make sense of how they individuate, which is crucial for understanding their mechanisms of reference. In making sense of an agent's worldview, we are thus attributing a *cognitive competence* to the agent. This is essential in order to attribute to an agent any propositional attitude directed toward an actual or merely purported object, even though from our perspective we may doubt that there is such an entity. It is of special interest to us in discussing the problem of intentional identity.

Regarding the second dimension, a rational agent has general intentions. General intentions often do not invoke those specific intentions that we "say to ourselves." They are not like having the intention to buy the newspaper today or to go to the movies this weekend. They are more like having a policy that we may not be aware of, but with which we act in accordance. We may have general intentions to eat breakfast before leaving for work, to be careful while driving, and to speak the language of our current community even if we are bilingual. General intentions are often intentions without which we would find daily aspects of life too difficult. Like any intentions, they cannot be accounted for by habit. Having a general intention to be careful while driving a car, for example, does not tell us, let alone condition us, to turn the steering wheel five degrees to the right or to the left in a given situation. Rather, these general intentions are carried out by the operation of our various skills and abilities in specific situations.

Now (our idealization of) a rational agent is someone who has the general intention to make sense of the world and to apply his or her worldview to specific cases in accordance with the agent's epistemically complete world view. The agent's general intention to apply his or her second-order epistemic beliefs give rise to various norms; that is, the agent's general intention to apply his or her second-order epistemic beliefs place two kinds of constraints on beliefs. These constraints are the third and fourth dimensions that our idealization of a rational agent must have. We call these constraints the agent's *commitments*.

The first kind of constraint (the third dimension), is due to the agent's language. We have discussed this constraint in chapter 5 and have called it the agent's *semantic commitment*. Agents express beliefs in a language. If the agent uses language in a normal way, then certain things follow from the agent's discourse. For example, proper names are taken to be designating expressions and to designate whatever they normally designate. The agent has a general intention to use language in the normal way, and thus the agent is committed to certain beliefs based upon these semantic constraints whether the agent realizes it or not. For example, the agent is committed to referring to the object designated by the proper name he or she uses whether the agent realizes that that is, indeed, the object to which he or she is referring. Proper names may, of course, fail to designate. Indeed, an agent may use a name in a language without believing or even being committed to the name designating. Someone may assent to the sentence "Santa Claus has a beard" without believing or even being committed to the existence of Santa Claus. But as a user of the language, when an agent uses the name "Santa Claus," the name is taken as if it designates, regardless of the agent's beliefs, and *the agent is semantically committed to taking the name as if it designates*. (We say more about this in section 6.3.) Accordingly, we may say that *an agent is semantically committed to a proper name's (or directly referential term's[7]) having a genuine naming (or genuine designating) condition*. If this condition is satisfied, the agent is semantically committed to the name's (or directly referential term's) designating the unique satisfier of its A-B condition even if the agent is unaware of this condition or its unique satisfier.

Also, as we said in chapter 5, an agent may have a belief about a particular person or object but not be in a position to express this belief with the name of the person or object due to ignorance of this name. Nevertheless, the agent is semantically committed to accepting the belief, even when it is expressed by means of using the correct name of the person or thing that the agent's belief is about. Accordingly, we are justified in attributing such a belief to the agent expressed by means of this name (or directly referential term), even though the agent may not realize that his or her belief is about

7. What I mean by a directly referential term's having a genuine designating condition is, say, that demonstratives are used in a context, regardless of whether they designate anything in that context, and pronouns are given an anaphoric background that determines an assignment that assigns a value to the variable that represents the pronoun, regardless of whether the A-B condition determines any such assignment. See my remarks in chapter 4 and in this chapter for detail.

this name's (or term's) referent. A rational agent also has a second-order epistemic commitment to take these semantic commitments seriously.

In addition to semantic commitments, an agent has various "semantic" beliefs regarding his or her language and how the world can or must relate to it. For example, an agent may not only believe that when we use proper names we purport to refer, but also that (barring rare exceptions) every person has a name, but particular tables and chairs normally do not. (Also, as will prove to be important, the agent may believe that if an expression is meaningful in the agent's language, then it expresses a thought or is about something.) The agent's semantic beliefs regarding how the agent's language functions place further constraints on the agent's beliefs.

Now Hilary Putnam has developed a sociolinguistic hypothesis regarding how semantic competence may vary within a linguistic community. He calls his hypothesis "The Universality of the Division of Linguistic Labor,"[8] which basically states the following: "Every linguistic community 'possesses at least some terms whose associated "criteria" are known only to a subset of the speakers who acquire the terms, and whose use by other speakers depends upon a structured cooperation between them and the speakers in the relevant subsets.'"[9]

I want to develop further Putnam's key insight that in various communities semantic competence may vary by extending this view to other semantic competencies that may vary within a community. Further, I want to add that reliance on community experts in these various competencies and to recognize and accept the role of people having certain "rights" in virtue of their semantic competence is part of what we are assuming it is to be a rational agent. For example, in our culture we recognize certain *rights of entitlement* that various members of the community have for introducing a name. One such right is given to certain agents to name certain entities that have a special relation to them. Names introduced into the community this way often carry a special legal status. For example, in the United States, the parents of a baby have an entitlement right to name their baby, and that name is the legal name of their baby. The presupposition is that they are indeed naming (or intending to name) *their* baby. Another such right is based on certain agents having *institutional compe-*

8. Hilary Putnam, "Meaning and Reference."
9. Hilary Putnam, "Meaning and Reference," 126.

tence. A certain subgroup within the community is recognized, usually as "the experts," as having special competence in a given domain, and they may purport to name something within that domain. For example, the science community may purport to name a planet. But someone without such institutional competence trying to introduce a name into our community by merely guessing that there is a tenth planet, and then calling it "Glub," is not likely to succeed, even if a tenth planet is discovered. For in the absence of good theoretical reasons that have the status of *institutional competence* backing up this guess, it is not likely that we would use this name to "refer" to the tenth planet. As we will see, these semantic competencies and beliefs place further constraints on belief attribution.

The second kind of constraint (the fourth dimension) on the agent's beliefs resulting from the agent's general intention to apply his or her second-order epistemic beliefs we have also discussed in chapter 5 and have called the agent's *rational commitments.* These are due to the agent's theory or discourse. As an example, if the agent realizes that Q follows from P, and the agent believes P, then he or she *should* either accept Q or reject or suspend judgment P. These constraints on an agent's beliefs due to these norms determine what the agent is *rationally committed to.* When attributing a belief to an agent, we are justified in taking into account the rational commitments of the agent. A rational agent has a second-order epistemic commitment to take these rational commitments seriously.

The strength of an agent's rational commitments generally depends upon those beliefs that play a central role in the agent's worldview or that deductively follow from the agent's "entrenched" beliefs, that is, those strongly held beliefs that the agent in practice cannot easily reject. These include beliefs such as that the Atlantic Ocean exists, that the agent has a mother, and so on. They also include statements and theories that an agent accepts on the basis of being both lawlike (i.e., containing semantically well-defined projectible predicates) and lawful (i.e., they are well-confirmed now, even if later they are disconfirmed, and hence not laws). For example, in the nineteenth century, Newtonian mechanics was both lawlike and lawful, even if for us now, Newtonian mechanics merely contains limiting cases of laws. (The strength of the agent's commitments depends also upon other considerations to be discussed later.)

The normative notions of semantic commitments and an agent's rational commitments require that we have an analysis of the content of a belief on which the content (captured by the consequences that follow from the proposition that is the object of a given belief, rather than patterns of assent or dissent under query) individuates the belief.

But as we stated in chapter 5, when we attribute a belief to an agent, we do not attribute to the agent every belief that is in the deductive closure of an agent's beliefs. For that would be too strong a requirement. Often an agent has contradictory beliefs, and we do not want to attribute to the agent any arbitrary belief on the grounds that any belief is a consequence of a contradiction. Moreover, we could not always make sense of the activity or enterprise of an agent if we were to attribute to the agent the deductive closure of his or her beliefs. Mathematicians strive to prove theorems in part because they may not already believe all the consequences of their axioms. Also, many mathematicians tried to trisect an angle with compass and straightedge alone, even though it is a consequence of their axioms that it is impossible.

In practice, various factors, such as the agent's verbal dispositions and dispositions to act in certain ways, together with what we would regard as "reasonable" for the agent in a given activity or enterprise to realize is a deductive consequence of his or her beliefs, restrict what we attribute to an agent. Tension among these factors and an agent's semantic and rational commitments give rise to puzzles about belief.

As in the case of a de dicto belief attribution, in attributions of intentional identity we must make sense of a given agent's perspective. Now the notion of a given agent's perspective is simply the agent's epistemically complete worldview applied to specific cases in accordance with the agent's rational *and* semantic commitments.

In our example involving Kripke and my student, we believe that Kripke has institutional competence in the domain of Mary's dissertation, that is, he is a member of a certain group of experts having special competence with a sophisticated mini-worldview and strong rational commitments in this domain; as a result of his institutional competence, he has strong cognitive contact with her dissertation; he has the belief that only a brilliant person could have produced such a dissertation and he has the semantic competence to know that people in our culture have names. These facts enable him to have a belief about Mary *from his own perspective,* even though he cannot express this belief, since he does not know of any directly referential expression that refers to the author of the dissertation he just read. Accordingly, these facts, which constitute Kripke's applying his worldview to the case of evaluating the author of the dissertation in accordance with his rational and semantic commitments, are the justification we have for attributing to Kripke the belief that Mary is brilliant. In doing so, we have captured Kripke's own perspective even though he can not assent to the sentence "Mary is brilliant" since he does not know her name.

Such belief attribution thus embodies the attributer's view of what the agent would (or should) acknowledge as one of the agent's own beliefs if, over time, the agent learns certain "semantically relevant facts" about the agent's own semantic commitments that are compatible with the agent's worldview and rational commitments.

The notion of an agent's perspective, and with it the notion of what an agent is rationally and semantically committed to, are central to our interest in the intentionality of belief (and in the notion of intentional identity). They are also central to the notion of a belief individuated by content. Any completely adequate theory of belief must pay attention to the intentionality of belief, and thus to the notions mentioned above.

6.3 Mentioning an Object

In order to state the conditions for making intentional identity statements that we deem appropriate, we now introduce some additional notions and terminology. We define the term "designating expressions" broadly so as to include more than terms that literally designate. In addition to names and pronouns, we include definite and indefinite descriptions. A definite description will be taken to designate the object that uniquely satisfies the description. An indefinite description, when uniquely satisfied or intended to have a unique satisfier, will be taken to designate the object that uniquely satisfies the description.

Designating expressions constitute a linguistic category, where the category is determined by a linguistic function in the language. A designating expression (in virtue of, say, its syntax or its position in a sentence) is to be interpreted under normal use *as if* there is an object, α, that the expression denotes or that satisfies the expression. Whenever we use a designating expression, our language commits us to the existence of an object that is designated by the expression or that satisfies it. Indeed, it is a presupposition that the designating expression denote an object or be satisfied by it in order for any sentence containing the expression to have a truth value. We say that such an expression *mentions an object,* α, regardless of whether or not α exists. When such a denoted object or satisfier does exist, the expression is said to "succeed in designating."

A designating expression mentions an object in virtue of its having an A-B condition in the language or occurring in a context of use. If the expression is a name, its A-B condition may not be a genuine naming condition, as, say, in the case of a name introduced in fiction. Thus such a name could never have its A-B condition satisfied. Nevertheless, this name from fiction mentions an object.

Accordingly, all designating expressions mention objects. The name 'John', for example, mentions John according to how names are used in natural language. That is, when we use the name 'John', our language commits us to the existence of an object, John, that the name denotes. But mentioning, unlike designating or referring, is not a success term, and thus does not entail the existence of an object that the expression mentions. Analogous remarks apply to other designating expressions.

Now often a speaker may use a designating expression without even *purporting* or *intending* to refer with the expression. The speaker need not believe that the expression designates—or even that it is possible for the expression to designate. The speaker may mention various angels, witches, or even fictional characters, and not believe that the designating expressions he or she uses could possibly designate, even though these expressions, in virtue of being designating expressions, mention things. We thus say that a speaker is *mentioning the object* (which his designating expression mentions), even though the speaker need not believe that the expression used in mentioning designates or has a satisfier. In using a name, a speaker is semantically committed to there being a naming condition that is satisfied even though the speaker may not believe that the condition is satisfied, or perhaps even deny that there is such a condition. In such a case, the speaker's semantic commitment thus requires that the speaker have a pretense (as discussed in chapter 5) that there is a naming condition that is satisfied, and accordingly that the name designates.

When I say "Santa Claus has a beard," the name 'Santa Claus' mentions someone, namely, Santa Claus; I mention the person, namely, Santa Claus, when I use this expression, even though I do not purport to refer when using this expression, since I do not believe that Santa Claus exists. Thus when I utter the sentence "Santa Claus has a beard," it is a pretense on my part that there is a person, Santa Claus, and that he has a beard.

Viewed intuitively, mentioning is what speakers are committed to in virtue of their language on the surface level without the benefit of paraphrase or logical construction, that is, in virtue of the designating expressions they use, rather than in virtue of their beliefs. Indeed, a speaker need not be committed to believing that his or her designating expression that mentions something is about (or designates) anything. Although the designating expression as such might seem to be about something, the *speaker,* in using the designating expression, need not *purport* to be referring to anything. Thus one speaker may be mentioning the same thing as another speaker, regardless of either speaker's beliefs concerning whether his or her own designating expression designates, and if so, which object it designates. Mentioning an object is the minimal semantic commitment of a designating expression. It merely commits the speaker to enough of an understanding of the expression so that he or she can use it as a designating expression, regardless of whether the expression designates.

Last, we consider the notion of mentioning the same thing. Clearly, two expressions mention the same thing when they designate the same thing. But what could it mean to say that two expressions mention the same thing when neither expression designates and the two expressions describe the mentioned object in different ways? For such cases in general, the notion of mentioning the same thing, where the mentioned object fails to exist, only makes sense relative to a given agent's perspective (as discussed in the previous section). In section 6.4, we present conditions for two agents to be mentioning the same non-existent object from a given agent's perspective and apply these conditions to intentional identity statements.

6.4 Mentioning the Same Thing from a Given Agent's Perspective and Intentional Identity Statements

We consider next the notion of *mentioning the same thing from a given agent's perspective.* In section 6.2 we said that the notion of a given agent's perspective is simply the agent's epistemically complete worldview applied to specific cases in accordance with the agent's rational and semantic commitments. The notion of *mentioning the same thing from a given agent's perspective* involves the agent's conception of a given mentioned entity based in part upon this worldview of the agent. Intuitively, two agents ("agent$_1$" and "agent$_2$," respectively, hereafter) are mentioning the same thing from a given agent's perspective if and only if, assuming that their theories were true and their terms were to denote, then it would deductively follow that they would be denoting the same entity. This is the picture, although, as we will see, it requires further refinements. We nevertheless try to work out some details of a theory while we acknowledge counterexamples. For convenience, I state the conditions for this notion to hold as necessary and sufficient conditions, even though, for reasons to be stated later, they are strictly neither. In fact, the conditions are deliberately stated with imprecise criteria, which is appropriate because they are often applied as a matter of degree.

Now an agent may be rationally committed to the view, perhaps because it deductively follows from the agent's theory, that a given designating expression mentions an entity that satisfies certain conditions uniquely. Thus the agent is committed to the view that any designating expression that mentions the satisfier of one of these conditions mentions the same thing as the given designating expression in question. Accordingly, we call these special conditions *u-conditions* ("u" for uniqueness), even though there may be cases in which these conditions by themselves do not imply that they be uniquely satisfied. Thus other people may disagree with the agent that there is any such thing as "the unique satisfier" of such a condition. For example, if Barbara believes that her apartment was burglarized yesterday and also believes that there is a unique person satisfying the condition of being a burglar that committed a burglary in her town yesterday, then this condition is one of Barbara's u-conditions for her designating expression 'the burglar of my apartment'. Thus Barbara is rationally committed to the view that anyone who has a designating expression that mentions a satisfier of 'x is a burglar that committed a burglary in her town yesterday' mentions the satisfier of Barbara's designating expression's satisfaction condition, namely, 'x is the burglar of Barbara's apartment'.

Accordingly, we say that *two agents* (with respect to their respective designating expressions in question) *mention the same thing from a given agent's perspective,* if in fact, their respective designating expressions fail to refer,[10] and if either of the following two conditions obtains:

Condition 1: $Agent_1$ is rationally committed or semantically committed to his or her designating expression's mentioning a satisfier of one of $agent_2$'s u-condition ("u-condition$_2$," hereafter) or the A-B condition for $agent_2$'s designating expression.

If condition 1 is satisfied, then $agent_1$ and $agent_2$ are mentioning the same thing from $agent_2$'s perspective. We may thus substitute a pronoun anaphoric upon $agent_1$'s designating expression in question within the intentional context of the belief attributed to $agent_2$.

The most obvious example of $agent_1$'s semantic commitment to his or her designating expression's mentioning a satisfier of the A-B condition for $agent_2$'s designating expression is when both agents are using the same designating expression that is on the same anaphoric chain. Surely in that case they are mentioning the same thing from $agent_2$'s perspective. This may arise without either agent's being aware of his or her designating expression's mentioning the satisfier of the given A-B condition for this designating expression. This may also arise without either agent's being rationally committed to his or her designating expression's mentioning the satisfier of the given A-B condition for this expression.

As an example of $agent_1$'s being rationally committed to his or her designating expression's mentioning a satisfier of u-condition$_2$, consider the following. In our example above, where Barbara's designating expression is "the burglar of my apartment," Barbara believes that anyone who committed a burglary in her town, say, Crawfordsville, yesterday, say, January 17, 1979, is the burglar who burglarized her apartment. It follows from this belief that anyone having a designating expression that mentions someone who committed a burglary in Barbara's town on that same day mentions, by Barbara's lights, the same burglar that her designating expression mentions. Suppose Frank ($agent_1$) knows that he lives in Crawfordsville and believes he was burglarized on January 17, 1979. Then from Barbara's perspective ($agent_2$), they are mentioning the same burglar. (We will discuss this example in more detail in what follows.)

---

10. When their respective referring expressions do, in fact, refer, two agents are mentioning the same thing if and only if their respective referring expressions are indeed referring to the same thing, regardless of whether from a given agent's perspective they are or are not mentioning the same thing.

If the following condition is satisfied, we may substitute a proper name or pronoun anaphoric upon a proper name for the agent's designating expression within the intentional context of the belief attributed to the given agent. Thus if this condition is satisfied, the attributer and the agent are mentioning the same thing from the agent's perspective.

Condition 2: A given agent is rationally committed or semantically committed to his or her designating expression's mentioning the satisfier of the A-B condition for a given name.

If condition 2 is satisfied, we may substitute this name (or a pronoun anaphoric upon it) or a name form[11] that is on the same anaphoric (historic) chain as the given name (and is thus its translation in a given language or community) for the agent's designating expression within the intentional context of the belief attributed to the given agent.

In our contrary-to-fact example in chapter 5 regarding how the name 'Vulcan' is introduced, we supposed that this name was introduced only to designate the one and only one intra-Mercurial planet. Hence the A-B condition for this name is being the one and only one intra-Mercurial planet. We further supposed that Leverrier is rationally committed to his designating expression "the planet that produces the perturbing effect on Mercury" mentioning the satisfier of this A-B condition since he later came to believe, based on his scientific calculations, that the planet that produces the perturbing effect on Mercury is also the one and only one intra-Mercurial planet. It is for this reason that Leverrier's designating expression mentions Vulcan, and we may substitute that name within the intentional context to form the belief attribution

(10)   Leverrier believes that Vulcan is small.

We consider next one important special case of condition 2 that is based upon both agents' semantic commitments and not their rational commitments, which is worthy of mention as a corollary of this condition.

---

11. Here, using the terminology of chapter 2, we say that a term is not merely a syntactic item. Rather, it is individuated by an anaphoric (historical) chain of intentions to corefer, going all the way back to and including the initial baptismal step. Alternatively, we may say that syntactic items that are names with different syntactic and phonetic structure constitute different names without any loss of significance to the above condition or corollary and relevant example of this corollary to follow. See the relevant example of the corollary that follows for details.

Corollary: Suppose two agents' respective designating expressions are on the same anaphoric (historic) chain that determines what these expressions mention by terminating in some A-B condition, or set of conditions, for a proper name. Then we may substitute that name or a name form that is on the same anaphoric (historic) chain as the given name (and that name or name form is thus its translation in a given language or community) for the agents' designating expressions, respectively, within the intentional contexts of the belief attributions for these agents.

An example of the above corollary is where two children who do not know the name 'Santa Claus' but know the basic story regarding Santa Claus have the designating expressions, "the big man who has a beard and comes down every child's chimney on the eve of December 24" and "the reindeer driver in the sky," respectively. Since these designating expressions are on the same anaphoric (historic) chain that terminates in a story, that is, a set of A-B conditions for the name 'Santa Claus', they mention the same person, namely, Santa Claus. (We discuss this example in more detail in what follows.)

As another example, we consider a case that involves two agents using different syntactic and phonetic forms of the same name.[12] Suppose Johannes uses the name 'Wotan' and Peer the name 'Odin'. Since 'Wotan' is the German name for 'Odin', these expressions are on the same anaphoric (historic) chain originating in the language of Old Norse. (The southern, i.e., German, form of his name was 'Woden'; the 'd' is pronounced like a 't'. The Norse and German mythology regarding Odin and Wotan are very similar. For example, Odin was the All-Father, supreme among gods and men, with a daughter named 'Brynhild'; in German mythology, Wotan occupies a similar position, with a daughter named 'Brunnhilde'.) The A-B condition for these expressions, according to Norse mythology, is being-the-sky-father-god-that-is-supreme-among-gods-and-men. Now neither Johannes nor Peer may be aware of this fact. Indeed, they may both be confused and think their respective designating expressions are names of Greek gods. Nevertheless, they are both semantically committed to their respective designating expressions mentioning the satisfier of the A-B condition stated above. If Johannes believes that the All-Father, supreme among gods and men, went down to the Well of Wisdom, Peer can appropriately report

12. Again, terms are not individuated merely syntactically; see footnote 11.

to his community, "Johannes believes that Odin went down to the Well of Wisdom."

There are many constraints that apply to the two conditions under which it is true that *two agents* (with respect to their respective referring expressions in question) *mention the same thing from a given agent's perspective,* when in fact, their respective referring expressions fail to refer. Two such constraints are:

a.   If there are (entrenched) theories of both agents required in order to deduce agent$_2$'s A-B conditions, these theories must not conflict.

(We allow the exception of one theory being a limiting case of another.)

b.   If there are such theories, the traits used in the theories from which they countenance the mentioned entity must not conflict.

We consider next a few examples of intentional identity statements and subject them to the conditions under which we may attribute to an agent's mentioning the same thing from the agent's own perspective. In these statements, the attributer is attributing a propositional attitude to two agents. In the case of agent$_1$, the attributer is attributing a de dicto belief (or other propositional attitude) to agent$_1$, where the sentence within the belief context contains a designating expression, mentioning an object O, used or accepted by agent$_1$ in expressing agent$_1$'s belief. In the case of agent$_2$, the attributer, in attributing a belief to agent$_2$, is stating that agent$_2$ has a belief that from agent$_2$'s perspective also mentions O. Further, *from agent$_2$'s perspective,* it is the same object as that mentioned by the attributer in making the attribution. The attributer mentions O within the intentional context of the attribution by substituting a name or pronoun for agent$_2$'s designating expression that occurs in a sentence that expresses agent$_2$'s belief; agent$_2$ mentions O by entertaining this belief expressed with a designating expression that mentions O. Thus the intentional identity attribution uses an expression that, from agent$_2$'s point of view, mentions the same object as that mentioned with a designating expression that appears in a sentence that expresses one of agent$_2$'s beliefs. Moreover, the attribution and agent$_2$'s belief in question predicate the same thing of the mentioned object.

Consider Geach's example of an intentional identity statement.

(1)   Hob thinks a witch has blighted Bob's mare, and Nob wonders whether she (i.e., the same witch) killed Cob's sow.

Notice that the first conjunct of (1) states a certain de dicto thought (propositional attitude) of Hob's (agent$_1$). The sentence within the intentional context expressing this thought contains the designating expression 'a witch' that mentions an object, O, that satisfies this expression from Hob's perspective (i.e., the satisfier that blighted Bob's mare). The second conjunct of (1) contains the pronoun 'she'. This pronoun is anaphoric upon the designating expression 'a witch' occurring in the first conjunct of this sentence, and thus the pronoun mentions the same object as the designating expression 'a witch'. Since the pronoun 'she' occurs within the sentence that expresses a propositional attitude to Nob (agent$_2$), the attributer is claiming that Nob is mentioning the same thing as Hob from Nob's perspective. Last, we note that this attribution is correct if from agent$_2$'s perspective, the attributer is mentioning the same object as is agent$_2$ in the expression of one of agent$_2$'s beliefs.

To illustrate the fact that the sentence within the intentional context of the second conjunct—*from Nob's perspective*—mentions the same witch that the thought attributed to Hob mentions, consider a typical situation in which we would assert (1). Suppose that both Hob and Nob share the belief that there is exactly one witch in town and that being the one and only one witch in town is their shared *A-B condition* for their respective use of the referring expression 'the witch'. Suppose further that we may correctly assert the following:

(11)   Nob wonders whether the witch killed Cob's sow.

In this situation, the sentences expressing the objects of Hob's and Nob's propositional attitudes (thinking that and wondering whether, respectively) mention the same witch, that is, the one and only one witch in town, from Nob's (or even Hob's) perspective. For their designating expressions are on the same anaphoric chain that terminates with the same A-B condition. We may thus say that Hob is semantically committed to his use of the term 'a witch' mentioning the same thing as Nob is mentioning with his designating expression ('a witch'). That is, given Hob's use of the term 'a witch' in this situation, and given Hob's and Nob's shared A-B condition for their respective designating expressions, it follows that they are mentioning the same thing from both their perspectives. We thus feel justified in asserting (1), even if Hob and Nob do not know each other and even if Nob has no thoughts concerning Bob's mare. That is, we feel justified in attributing to Nob the expression of an intentional identity.

Our general condition for agent$_1$ and agent$_2$ to mention the same thing from agent$_2$'s perspective is satisfied. Agent$_1$'s (Hob's) A-B condition for his term 'the witch' is being the one and only one witch in town. But this condition is identical with agent$_2$'s (Nob's) A-B condition. It follows that agent$_1$ is semantically committed to his designating expression's mentioning the satisfier of the A-B condition for agent$_2$'s designating expression. Hence our general condition of mentioning the same thing from a given agent's perspective is satisfied by satisfying condition 1 of this notion. If Nob were to know the anaphoric background condition for Hob's expression (i.e., that it is the same condition as his own), he would obviously agree that they are mentioning the same witch.

It seems natural to suppose that the anaphorically used pronoun within the intentional context of the second conjunct of a sentence expressing an intentional identity has as its A-B condition part of what is expressed by the sentence within the intentional context of the first conjunct of such a sentence. As such, the pronoun should be treated as what Gareth Evans calls an E-type term, a term that goes proxy for a definite description that is recoverable from the clauses governed by the pronoun's antecedent. (See chapter 7 for details.) But as we have seen in section 6.1, this is plainly false. The following attribution illustrates the problem with such an interpretation of the anaphorically used pronoun:

(12)   Hob believes a witch has blighted Bob's mare, and Nob thinks she has not blighted Bob's mare.

The second conjunct may at first seem strange to us because, we, who are reading this sentence, have no A-B condition to determine, what, if anything, is the referent of the pronoun 'she' other than being the witch that has blighted Bob's mare. Accordingly, we mistakenly interpret the second conjunct as expressing a certain de dicto belief attribution, where the pronoun 'she' is an E-type term that goes proxy for "the witch that has blighted Bob's mare." But on that reading, we would be attributing the following self-contradictory belief to Nob:

(13)   Nob thinks that the witch that has blighted Bob's mare has not blighted Bob's mare.

There is, however, a natural way of interpreting (12) as true and that does not attribute an absurdity to Nob. Let us suppose, as previously, that Hob and Nob have as their A-B condition for their respective designating expressions being the one and only one witch in town. Let us further suppose that while Hob thinks that that particular witch has blighted Bob's mare, Nob has the contrary belief that mentions the same witch, namely, that the one and only one witch in town has not blighted Bob's mare. In this case, it is natural and correct to assert (12). But in so doing, we are not attributing a contradictory belief to Nob. Rather, we are attributing beliefs that are in conflict to Hob and Nob about the same mentioned object from both their perspectives.

From the previous example, it may appear that the agents must know what their respective designating expression's A-B condition is in order for us to make a correct intentional identity statement about them. But this is not correct, as the following example illustrates.

Suppose non-Western anthropologists visit the West during Christmas time and hear Johnny and Sue talking. When they return to their own environment, they report the following:

(14)   Johnny believes that a big man with a white beard comes down his chimney on the eve of December 24, and Sue believes that he drives a sleigh pulled by reindeer.

Now neither Johnny nor Sue may agree on the A-B background condition that this man must satisfy if he is to be the referent of their respective referring expressions. Nevertheless, what enables us to use these expressions to mention the same object is that both designating expressions are on the same anaphoric (historical) chain that terminates in a shared background story, that is, a set of community A-B conditions for the name 'Santa Claus'. Although it is not necessary to know which condition is the A-B condition for the agents', Johnny's and Sue's, respective designating expressions, their expressions are linked to the same set of A-B conditions that determine what these designating expressions mention. It is not necessary for anyone in the community to *know* exactly what this set of A-B conditions is in order for the designating expressions in question to mention the same thing from a given agent's perspective. All that is required in this example is that these designating expressions are on the same anaphoric chain that terminates in the same (set of) A-B condition(s).

Let us say that Johnny's designating expression is 'the big bearded man who comes down chimneys once a year'. Johnny believes that his designating expression mentions someone satisfying the condition of being the big man who has a beard and comes down every child's chimney on the eve of December 25. This condition need not be the A-B condition for the name of the person mentioned by this designating expression. This condition may simply be some part of Johnny's background story of what happens on Christmas Eve. Nevertheless, Johnny's designating expression is on the anaphoric (historic) chain terminating in the A-B condition or set of A-B conditions a unique satisfier of which would be the reference for the name of the mentioned person of his designating expression. That is to say, although for the agent and for the community it may not be clear what exactly is the A-B condition for the name of the mentioned person of a given designating expression, nevertheless an agent may be semantically committed to the given designating expression's mentioning the satisfier of this A-B condition.

Now let us say that Sue's designating expression is 'the reindeer driver in the sky'. Let us further suppose that for her, too, there is a background story (about what happens on Christmas Eve) from which this condition originates for her. Although the details of the story told to her may differ from the story told to Johnny, loosely speaking, their stories are linked to a common anaphoric background. Moreover, Sue's (agent$_2$'s) designating expression is on the same anaphoric (historic) chain that terminates in the same set of A-B conditions for the name of the mentioned person of both their respective designating expressions. Hence, condition 1 of two agents' mentioning the same thing from agent$_2$'s perspective is satisfied. It seems clear that if Sue were to know that Johnny's referring expression is on the same anaphoric (historic) chain that terminates in the same set of A-B conditions for the name of the reindeer driver in the sky, she would agree that she and Johnny are mentioning the same person. Hence, from Sue's perspective, she and Johnny are mentioning the same person. Thus once again, the general condition for making correct intentional identity statements is satisfied. We are thus justified in substituting the anaphoric pronoun 'he' for Sue's designating expression 'the reindeer driver in the sky' in the sentence that expresses one of Sue's beliefs to form the second conjunct of (14).

The next example shows not only that in order to make a correct intentional identity statement the respective designating expressions of the two agents that mention the same thing from a given agent's perspective need not be members of the same anaphoric chain that goes back to a common anaphoric background condition. It also shows that the two agents need not even share a belief, theory or even a u-condition such that each believes that his or her respective designating expression mentions the satisfier of this condition.

Suppose that Frank and Barbara live in the same town of Crawfordsville and do not know each other, and that each mistakenly believes that his or her apartment has been burglarized. Suppose further that Frank notices that after the alleged burglary, blue paint is on his floor, and he believes that the burglar deliberately did this as some sort of trademark. In fact, Frank believes that whoever is burglarized in his town and then has blue paint on the floor was burglarized by the same person. On the same day (say, January 17, 1979), Barbara mistakenly believes her apartment is burglarized, and she notices that there is, in fact, blue paint on her floor after the supposed burglary. Barbara reads in the paper that a lot of apartments were burglarized that day in her otherwise safe and low-crime town. As a result, Barbara believes that all the apartments burglarized in her town that day were burglarized by the same person. Barbara forms no belief regarding the alleged burglar of her apartment and the blue paint on her floor. Frank forms no belief regarding the alleged burglar of his apartment and the other burglaries in his town on that day (except for those involving blue paint).

It seems to me that it is correct to attribute the following beliefs to Frank and Barbara:

(15)   Frank believes that a burglar broke into his apartment in Crawfordsville on January 17, 1979, and Barbara believes that he (i.e., the same person) broke into her apartment.

Our general condition for two agents to mention the same thing from agent$_2$'s perspective applies to this case as well. The A-B condition for Frank's designating expression 'the burglar' is being the burglar who broke into Frank's apartment in Crawfordsville on January 17, 1979. Similarly, on the basis of his belief regarding being burglarized in his town and then having blue paint on the floor, with respect to his designating expression Frank is rationally committed to the following u-condition: being a burglar in Crawfordsville on January 17, 1979, and leaving blue paint on the floor.

The A-B condition for Barbara's designating expression is being the burglar who broke into Barbara's apartment in Crawfordsville on January 17, 1979. Now Barbara believes that on January 17, 1979 (on which day she believes her apartment was burglarized), all apartments broken into in her town were burglarized by the same person, that is, by the person who she believes burglarized her apartment. In other words, Barbara has the following belief:

Anyone who burglarized an apartment in Crawfordsville on January 17, 1979, is the burglar who broke into her apartment.

Based on this belief, Barbara is rationally committed to her referring expression as having the u-condition being a burglar who burglarized an apartment in Crawfordsville on January 17, 1979.

It follows from the A-B condition that Frank is semantically committed to and the u-condition that Barbara is rationally committed to that Frank's designating expression mentions something that satisfies Barbara's u-condition. Hence, our general condition for agent$_1$ and agent$_2$ to mention the same thing from agent$_2$'s perspective applies to this example since condition 1 of this notion is satisfied. Barbara and Frank are, from Barbara's own perspective, mentioning the same burglar. If Barbara were to know Frank's belief and the fact that whatever mentions the satisfier of the A-B condition for his designating expression mentions the satisfier of her u-condition, she would agree that she and Frank are mentioning the same burglar. Thus, from Barbara's own perspective, she and Frank are mentioning the same burglar.

Analogous considerations apply to Frank's u-condition regarding the blue paint on the floor. If Frank were to know that Barbara lives in his town and he were to believe that she found blue paint on her floor after she was burglarized, from Frank's own perspective, he would agree that he and Barbara are mentioning the same burglar.

We can correctly make an intentional identity statement regarding Frank and Barbara even though (i) they do not know each other, (ii) their respective designating expressions are not members of the same anaphoric chain and do not share the same anaphoric background condition, and (iii) Frank and Barbara do not even share a belief, theory, or even a (simple)[13] u-condition such that each believes that his or her respective designating expression ('the burglar') mentions the satisfier of this condition.

---

13. That is, we exclude the following sort of condition: if condition P is a u-condition for a given referring expression and is entailed by condition Q, we exclude condition Q from the class of simple u-conditions for a given referring expression.

This example, slightly modified, also serves to illustrate the fact that intentional identity statements need not be symmetrical. That is, there are situations when we are enabled to attribute to agent$_1$ mentioning the same (nonexistent) object as that which agent$_2$ mentions from agent$_2$'s perspective, but not from agent$_1$'s perspective. For suppose that there is no blue paint on Barbara's floor after she believes it is burglarized or that Frank has no beliefs concerning the burglar painting the floor blue. Still, it would be correct to say that, from Barbara's perspective, she is mentioning the same object that Frank is mentioning for the reason stated earlier, even though we could no longer claim that, from Frank's perspective, Barbara is mentioning the same object that he is mentioning. Given his own perspective, there would be no basis for Frank to agree that he and Barbara are mentioning the same burglar.

That there will be further refinement and modification of my formulations of mentioning the same thing from a given agent's perspective are inevitable. Nevertheless, this is the general picture.

6.5   Conditions under which Intentional Identity Statements Are Appropriate

Under what conditions are intentional identity statements deemed appropriate? To answer this question, we draw on certain notions introduced in chapter 5 and on the notion of mentioning the same thing from a given agent's perspective. In chapter 5, I argue that when a proper name n is introduced into the language with the intention of its succeeding in designating, the A-B condition for n must be *authentic*. When a name's A-B condition is authentic, we know exactly what would have to be the case in order for the name to designate. I further state that an agent in expressing a belief with the use of the name n is semantically committed to the existence of an object o into which the A-B function for n maps the given context of introduction and that n designates.

In order to generalize, when an agent uses a designating expression that may or may not be a name, we say that the designating expression's designating condition is the condition that must be met for the expression to designate. The designating condition is authentic if we know exactly what would have to be the case in order for the expression to designate. We call a function that represents the designating condition (authentic or not) for an expression d the *designating function* f_d. Without any specific commitment as to how the semantic machinery works, we say that f_d maps a relevant context into the denotation (or satisfier), if any, of the designating expression with respect to that context. An agent in expressing a belief with the use of a designating expression d is semantically committed to the existence of an object o into which the designating function f_d for 'd' maps a given relevant context and that 'd' designates in that context.

In discussing the enabling conditions of a belief attribution that contains a vacuous name within the belief context, we appealed to the Belief Commitment Schema (BCS):

(BCS) $\exists f_{A\text{-}B}\exists c_i\exists C_s\exists c_u$(A is committed to believing that $\exists o((f_{A\text{-}B}(c_i) = o) \wedge C_s(c_u) = \text{that-S} \wedge S)$,

where 'S' stands in for a sentence containing the name n, o is an object, C_s is the character of 'S', c_i is the context of introduction, c_u is a context of use, A is the agent of c_i and c_u, and $f_{A\text{-}B}$ is the anaphoric background function for the name 'n' that A is committed to denoting o.

Now in the case of designating expressions in general, we may introduce the following generalized belief commitment schema (GBCS) as follows:

(GBCS) $\exists f_d\exists C_s$(A is committed to the belief that $\exists o((f_d(c_p) = o) \wedge C_s(c_u) = \text{that-S} \wedge S)$,

where 'S' stands in for a sentence containing the designating expression d, o is an object, C_s is the character of 'S', 'c_p' is the relevant context (be it a context of introduction or context of use), A is the agent of a relevant context, and f_d is the designating function for 'd'.

As in the case for names, each instance of this schema corresponds to a singular term ⌜that-S⌝ allegedly denoting a definite proposition. Each instance also corresponds to the belief attribution ⌜A believes that-S⌝ and to the designating condition for 'd' contained in the sentence S.

We are now in a position to apply this schema to intentional identity statements. Consider again,

(1)   Hob thinks a witch has blighted Bob's mare, and Nob wonders whether she (the same witch) killed Cob's sow.

The first conjunct (partially) formalized in quantification theory in the standard way is the following:

Hob thinks that $\exists x(Wx \ \& \ Bxm)$,

where 'Wx' is 'x is a witch' and 'Bxm' is 'x blighted Bob's mare'. In order for Hob to think that there is a witch, Hob must be committed to there being a witch, in particular, one who has blighted Bob's mare. We may formalize this as an instance of the (GBCS) as follows:

$\exists f_{d_1} \exists C_{s_1}$ (Hob is committed to the belief that $\exists o_1 (f_{d_1}(c_{w_1}) = o_1) \wedge C_{s_1}(c_{u_1}) =$ that-$S_1) \wedge$ (Hob thinks that-$S_1)^{14}$

where 'S_1' stands in for the sentence "a witch blighted Bob's mare," 'o_1' is an object (the witch who Hob thinks blighted Bob's mare), 'C_{s_1}' is the character of 'S_1', 'c_{u_1}' is the relevant context of use, for agent$_1$'s (Hob's) designating expression 'a witch', and f_{d_1} is the designating function for 'd' ('a witch', as used by Hob) that Hob is committed to use to designate o_1. This condition is what entitles Hob to think that a witch has blighted Bob's mare and is a necessary condition for enabling an attributer to make this attribution to Hob.

Now the second conjunct of (1) commits Nob first to there being a witch of whom he wonders whether she killed Cob's sow, and second to "this witch" being the same witch who Hob thinks blighted Bob's mare. Again, we make use of the (GBCS) to formalize Nob's first commitment as follows:

$\exists f_{d_2} \exists C_{s_2}$ (Nob is committed to the belief that $\exists o_2 (f_{d_2}(c_{u_2}) = o_2) \wedge C_{s_2}(c_{u_2}) =$ that-$S_2) \wedge$ (Nob wonders whether that-S_2),

where 'S_2' is the sentence "a witch killed Cob's sow," 'o_1' is an object (the witch of whom Nob wonders whether she killed Cob's sow), C_{s_2} is the character of 'S_2', c_{u_2} is the relevant context of use, for agent$_2$'s (Nob's) designating expression, 'd_2', and f_{d_2} is the designating function for 'd_2' that Nob is committed to designating o_2. This condition is what entitles Nob to wonder whether a witch killed Cob's sow and is a necessary condition for enabling an attributer to make this attribution to Nob.

But as things stand, it does not follow that Nob's second commitment is satisfied, namely, that "this witch" is the "same witch" as the one Nob thinks blighted Bob's mare. It follows, however, if Nob's designating expression mentions the same thing as Hob's designating expression from Nob's perspective. On the assumption that this is true, then it follows that

---

14. We change the last clause of the GBCS in accord with the relevant propositional attitude that the agent has toward that-S.

Nob is committed to $\exists o_2((f_{d_2}(c_{u_2}) = o_2) \wedge (o_2 = o_1))$. Putting this all together gives us

$\exists f_{d_1} \exists C_{s_1}$ (Hob is committed to the belief that $\exists o_1(f_{d_1}(c_{u_1}) = o_1) \wedge C_{s1}(c_{u_1}) =$ that-S_1) $\wedge$ (Hob thinks that-S_1) and $\exists f_{d_2} \exists C_{s_2}$ (Nob is committed to the belief that $\exists o_2((f_{d_2}(c_{u_2}) = o_2) \wedge (o_2 = o_1)) \wedge C_{s_2}(c_{u_2}) =$ that-S_2) $\wedge$ (Nob wonders whether that-S_2).

The analysis in section 6.4 presents the conditions under which we may attribute what comes after the word "and" above. The condition after the word "and" is what entitles Nob to wonder whether the same witch killed Cob's sow and is a necessary condition for enabling an attributer to make this attribution to Nob.

We deem it appropriate to make an intentional identity statement (1) only if these conditions obtain. These conditions generalize by substituting the names of agent$_1$ and agent$_2$, for 'Hob' and 'Nob', respectively, and for substituting the relevant sentences for S_1 and S_2. Accordingly, analogous to the case of belief attributions that contain vacuous names within the belief context, with the aid of the (GBCS) we have stated conditions that entitle agent$_1$ and agent$_2$ to have a propositional attitude toward that-P, even when 'that-P' contains a nondesignating expression. These conditions must be met if an attributer is enabled to make an intentional identity statement that we deem appropriate.

6.6   True Negative Existential Statements

In this chapter and in chapter 5, we have been arguing that although a belief attribution or even an intentional identity statement may contain a vacuous name or pronoun that fails to refer, we can still make sense of such statements. We have shown that we can even state conditions under which an attributer is enabled to make such attributions. But the problem still arises regarding whether we can coherently express true singular negative existential statements.

The problem with such statements is that it appears that in order to make such a statement, we have to assert the very existence of something that we claim does not exist. Thus in the sentence "Sherlock Holmes does not exist," it appears that we are asserting of this definite person, Sherlock Holmes, that he does not exist. If the sentence is true, then how can the sentence express something about Sherlock Holmes, who, according to this sentence, does not exist?

In his John Locke lectures, Kripke develops two views regarding a name occurring in fictional discourse. First, as mentioned in chapter 5, such a name in its primary sense, in the sense of primordial, is merely a pretended name and that sentences containing such a name "pretend to express a proposition rather than really doing so."[15] Second, if there is enough of a story involved in the pretense, an ontology of fictional characters is set up. The pretense thus creates a fictional character, as there is a fictional character, Hamlet, but not a fictional character Bigozo (a name I just made up).

Now a thoroughgoing Millian will be very attracted to Kripke's second view regarding names from fiction. For according to it we can truly say that Hamlet exists, and even that Vulcan exists, where the name 'Vulcan' is viewed as naming a mythological planet that is (mistakenly taken as) the cause of the perturbations of Mercury. On this view, it is simply false to say that Vulcan does not exist or that Sherlock Holmes does not exist. Of course, it remains true on this view that Sherlock Holmes is not a real person or that Vulcan is not a real planet. But since these names refer, there is no problem in making such statements.[16]

In this chapter, as in chapter 5, I have not taken a thoroughgoing Millian view. Rather, I have been talking about enabling conditions that license belief attributions containing vacuous names and about mentioning conditions. It seems to me that these notions and the machinery developed in these two chapters apply to the problem of "true" negative existential statements as well.

When we assertively utter the sentence 'n does not exist', where 'n' is a proper name, we are mentioning n. Mentioning n semantically commits the speaker to the existence of n. The user of 'n' is semantically committed to the claim that the A-B condition for 'n' is satisfied. But mentioning n

---

15. Saul Kripke, "Reference and Existence" (The John Locke Lectures, presented at Oxford University, 1973).

16. See Nathan Salmon, "Nonexistence," *Noûs* 32, 3 (1998): 277–319, for a defense of this position. Another influential view regarding true negative existential statements is to go metalinguistic, that is, to claim that such statements are really about the names and whether they denote. I consider Kripke's objections to this view in his "Reference and Existence" essay (The John Locke Lectures) quite conclusive. Thus I do not intend to discuss this view here.

does not entail that n exists, and sometimes we may explicitly want to deny the existence of n, which can only be done by mentioning n. This is the problem of "true" negative existential statements that make use of proper names.

In using a name in assertively uttering the sentence 'n does not exist' we are not treating the name *as if* it denotes. Rather, we are treating it as if we are saying, "the purported object, n, does not exist." But this use of the name in the negative existential sentence is problematic for two reasons. First, this is not the normal use of a name when we assertively utter a sentence that contains the name. For instance, in order for the sentence 'n is ϕ' to express a true proposition, the name 'n' used in the sentence must denote an object that has property ϕ. For we are not asserting that the *purported object* has property ϕ. Perhaps someone questioning the existence of n may utter the sentence 'n is ϕ'. The person may only want to be committed to mentioning n rather designating it. But in such cases, can we really say that the person is *assertively* uttering 'n is ϕ', that is, making a claim that the sentence expresses a true proposition? I think not. But then what is the basis for the exception in the use of the name merely to mention n, rather than to presuppose the existence of n, when asserting that n does not exist?

Second, what does it mean to say the purported object, n, does not exist? One is tempted to ask, "And which object is that?" It seems that this just leads us back to the original problem about true negative existential statements. For if there is no particular thing that is "the purported object," then to what are we ascribing nonexistence? But if "the purported object" is a particular thing, then it appears that we are ascribing of this definite thing that it does not exist.

Still, there is some sense in which whoever asserts that n does not exist is merely mentioning n and asserting that there is no object n. But to say even this is paradoxical. For the speaker who says this is mentioning n and thus is semantically committed to n's existence, which the assertion that n does not exist seems to deny.

There are, nevertheless, cases in which agents may override their commitment. An analogy with the speech act of promising may be useful here. Suppose someone promises to do act X. Then this promise commits the agent to performing X. Still, while an agent may well be aware of this commitment, the agent may consistently say, "Although I promised to do X, I won't for such-and-such reasons." That is, the agent may override this commitment by presenting some justification for not performing X. In an analogous way, a speaker may override his or her semantic commitments to the existence of n when using the name 'n'. Now my claim is that this is precisely what happens when a speaker adds after the name the expression 'does not exist'.

A discussion of Moore's paradox may be useful to explain how this works. When Jones asserts a statement of the form 'P but I don't believe that-P', semantically speaking, there is no paradox or contradiction in what Jones says. For someone saying 'P and Jones does not believe that-P' has said the same thing as Jones. The propositions that they both express are the same. But clearly there is no paradox or contradiction in these propositions being conjointly true. Moore's paradox is on the level of *speech acts*. For when Jones asserts that-P, this very speech act seems to commit him to the belief that-P, which the second part of his speech act commits him to denying.

The paradox arises apparently because when speech act and semantic commitments conflict, speech act commitments seem to override semantic commitments. Now it is my contention that although assertively uttering a sentence containing the name 'n' semantically commits the speaker to the existence of n, there are certain speech acts that override the speaker's semantic commitments to the existence of n. This is not an analysis of true negative existential statements. Rather, it is an explanation of the nature of this speech act.

How then should we analyze true negative existential statements? For even if we have resolved how someone may not be committed to a contradiction or a paradox at the speech act level, an analysis of true negative existential statements involving proper names requires that at the semantic level these statements are literally true and coherent. But this is what I deny is the case. Instead, as in our analysis of belief attributions containing vacuous names within the belief context and our analysis of intentional identity statements, we present the conditions that entitle an agent to assert a negative existential statement and that enable a reporter to attribute such a statement to an agent. As in our discussion of 'that-ϕ_α', within a belief context or in intentional identity statements, where 'α' is a vacuous name or a pronoun that fails to refer, we do not present an analysis of what, if anything, such a proposition as 'that n does not exist' could be.

First, what are necessary and sufficient conditions that entitle us correctly to assert that n exists? Clearly if we use a name 'n' in making the true assertion that n exists, then the name 'n' designates and thus has a genuine naming condition that is satisfied by n. In fact, *necessarily* if we use a name 'n' in making the true assertion that n exists, then the name 'n' has a genuine naming condition that is satisfied by n in the context of introduction for that name. For whenever there is a possible world in which 'n' is used to make the true assertion that n exists, then the name 'n' has a genuine naming condition that is satisfied by n in its context of introduction. To be sure, the genuine naming condition may not be satisfied by n, if satisfied at all, in a given possible world in which it is true that n exists. Nevertheless, in order to use the name 'n' to make a true assertion that n exists in a given possible world w, n must be the satisfier of the genuine naming condition for 'n' in the context in which the name is introduced into the community. (Recall from chapter 5 that we called this context in which a name is introduced at the initial baptismal step, by means of its A-B conditions, the "context of introduction" for that name.)

For example, let us assume that the name 'Neptune' was introduced into the language as the name for the planet that caused such-and-such perturbations in the orbital path of certain other planets. If so, then the authentic naming condition for the name 'Neptune' is being the planet that caused such-and-such in the orbital path of certain planets, and the context of introduction for the name is the actual world in which Neptune does indeed satisfy this condition. But it could have been the case, as Kripke rightly states in *Naming and Necessity,* that Neptune, while still existing, had been knocked off its course one million years earlier and thus would have caused no such perturbations and even that some other object might have caused the perturbations in its place. What we are describing is a situation in which either some other object satisfies the A-B condition for the name 'Neptune' or nothing at all in a given possible world. But in order to use the name 'Neptune' to make the true assertion that Neptune exists in this given counterfactual situation, that is, in the given possible world so described, Neptune must be the satisfier of the genuine naming condition for 'Neptune' in the real world, under the actual conditions. This is the context of introduction for the name 'Neptune'.

So far, we have established of necessity that a necessary condition for making the true assertion that n exists with the use of the name 'n' is that its authentic naming condition be satisfied by n in the name's context of introduction. But can n satisfy the authentic naming condition for 'n' in the name's context of introduction without its being the case that we are necessarily making a true assertion that n exists when using the name 'n'? Surely this is possible, as the following hypothetical case illustrates. Suppose that Neptune had been not merely knocked off its course one million years earlier, as in the previous example, but had been obliterated from existence one million years ago. Or, better still, suppose that there had been something in the makeup of the early solar system that prevented Neptune from ever coming into existence. Clearly, although the satisfier, Neptune, of the authentic naming condition for the name 'Neptune' with respect to the context of introduction for that name, actually exists, it does not exist in the possible world described. We thus cannot make a true assertion with respect to the possible world just described that Neptune exists, by using the name 'Neptune' (or any other name denoting Neptune). Yet Neptune satisfies the authentic naming condition for the name 'Neptune' in the context of introduction for that name.

Nevertheless, the previous illustration suggests a condition that necessarily is sufficient for making the true assertion that n exists with the use of the name 'n'. The sufficient condition suggested is that with respect to the possible world in which we may make this true assertion, there exists the satisfier of the authentic naming condition for 'n', with respect to the context of introduction. Since 'n' is a rigid designator, in any possible world w, 'n' denotes n in any possible world, that is, 'n' denotes the satisfier of its authentic naming condition with respect to the context of introduction in any possible world, if it denotes at all. So if the satisfier of this condition with respect to the context of introduction exists in world w, then n exists in w.

Considering the inverse, if in any possible world we cannot make a true assertion that n exists by using the name 'n' with respect to a possible world w, then it is not the case that in w there exists the satisfier of the authentic naming condition for 'n' with respect to the context of introduction. There are three cases in which such a satisfier can be absent. First, as in the illustration above, there is such a satisfier of the authentic naming condition with respect to the context of introduction, but the satisfier doesn't exist in the possible world w. Here we are literally expressing a proposition when we say 'N does not exist with respect to world w'.

Second, there is no satisfier of the authentic naming condition with respect to the context of introduction. This is illustrated by the name 'Vulcan', as in chapter 5. Last, there may not be any authentic naming conditions for a given name. Hence there cannot be a satisfier of such a condition. This, again as observed in chapter 5, is illustrated in the case of a name from fiction, where there is only a pretense that there is an authentic naming condition for the name.

We have thus established that the following condition is necessarily equivalent to the assertion that n exists when using 'n' to make this assertion:

$$\exists x A(\text{Sat}(x, C_{A\text{-}B}, c_i)) \wedge x \, \varepsilon \, w,$$

where 'A' is the actuality operator (we are assuming that the context of introduction contains the actual world) and '$\text{Sat}(x, C_{A\text{-}B}, c_i)$' is true if and only if x satisfies the A-B condition (we are assuming that the A-B condition is an authentic naming condition) with respect to the context of introduction and '$x \, \varepsilon \, w$' is true if and only if x is in world w. In the more familiar terminology of chapter 5, we state that the assertion that n exists, when using 'n' to make this assertion, is necessarily equivalent to the following:

$$\exists x(x = f_{A\text{-}B}(c_i)) \wedge x \text{ is in } w$$

where $f_{A\text{-}B}$ is the A-B function for the name n, and c_i is the context of introduction.

We should not confuse this necessarily equivalent condition for asserting that n exists when using the name 'n' to make this assertion with necessarily equivalent conditions for the existence of n or, equivalently for the proposition that n exists. Clearly, in general an object n can exist without the existence of human language, let alone a particular name that denotes n if n exists.

Thus, as in the case of belief attributions that contain vacuous names within the belief context and the case of intentional identity statements, in establishing this necessarily equivalent condition to the assertion that n exists when using 'n' to make that assertion, we are establishing the entitlement condition for making this assertion. When this condition is not met, we deem it appropriate to make the assertion that n does not exist even when there literally is no proposition that n does not exist that we are expressing.

III

Pronouns and Anaphora

7

Anaphoric Pronouns: Some Proposed Analyses

In this chapter, I discuss and evaluate various proposed logical analyses of pronouns anaphoric upon indefinite noun phrases. We say that an expression is used anaphorically when its reference in that use is dependent upon certain semantical information given in sentences (most often in prior sentences, sometimes in the same or even in later ones) of a given discourse. The sentences upon which the reference of the anaphoric expression depends we call the *anaphoric background sentences* (hereafter, A-B sentences) of that expression for that discourse. The expressions themselves, the references of which are dependent upon certain semantic information derived from their A-B sentences, we call *S-type* expressions ('S' for 'satisfying-some-given-condition(s)'). In the final chapter of the book, I present a formal semantics for sentences containing anaphoric expressions, that is, a semantics that provides truth conditions for these sentences.

The reader should note that my project differs from those that I discuss in this chapter. The latter projects are attempts to present *the logical analysis* of sentences containing anaphoric expressions. My interest is primarily to present a formal language with the aid of which we may provide truth conditions for such sentences. Nevertheless, these various proposed analyses each present problems or reveal limitations that we find useful to consider. For example, some analyses do not provide an account of a large class of anaphoric pronouns, say, plurals; others fail to give a satisfactory treatment of the notion of *scope,* especially in connection with intensional operators.

7.1   Some Problems in the Analysis of Anaphoric Uses of Pronouns

It is widely held that anaphoric pronouns and sentences containing these pronouns strongly resist satisfactory logical analysis. An example often cited is the case, due to Peter Geach,[1] of the so-called donkey sentences. Consider the following two sentences:

(1)   Pedro owns a donkey and he beats it.

(2)   If Pedro owns a donkey, then he beats it.

The truth conditions for (1) and (2) may be written simply enough as (1′) and (2′), respectively.

(1′) $\exists x((Donkey(x)\ \&\ Owns(p,x))\ \&\ Beats(p,x))$.

(2′) $\forall x((Donkey(x)\ \&\ Owns(p,x)) \rightarrow Beats(p,x))$.

   Many linguists and philosophers of language seek to represent the relation between the pronoun 'it' and its anaphoric antecedent by means of *restricted* or *binary* quantifiers. Restricted quantifiers have the following form:

$(Qx: \Phi(x))$,

where 'Q' is a quantifier that may stand not only for the quantity expressions 'some' and 'all', but also for expressions like 'most', 'many', 'the', 'a', 'few', 'no', 'one', 'two' (hereafter such expressions are to be called *quantifiers*) and where 'Φ' stands for any common noun. Following Evans, we call an expression consisting of a quantifier plus a common noun (such as 'a boy', 'each girl', 'many children', etc.) a *quantifier expression*.[2] Thus the restricted existential quantifier, '$(\exists x: \Phi(x))$' is to be read as 'for some x such that x is a Φ . . .' or, more simply, as 'some Φ, x, is such that . . .'.

   When a sentence contains pronouns as well as a quantifier expression serving as their anaphoric antecedent, we may then represent the form of the sentence with the aid of these restricted quantifiers. We proceed as follows: We assign the restricted quantifier expression a scope wide enough to bind those pronouns that have this expression as their anaphoric an-

---

1. Peter Geach, *Reference and Generality* (Ithaca: Cornell University Press, 1962).

2. Gareth Evans, "Pronouns, Quantifiers, and Relative Clauses (1)," in *Collected Papers* (Oxford: Clarendon Press, 1985), 90.

tecedent. Then we replace each pronoun that is bound by this quantifier expression with an occurrence of the same variable contained in the quantifier expression. The result will be a quantified sentence in which these pronouns have been replaced with variables bound by their (quantified) anaphoric antecedent. Thus, according to this analysis, (1) and (2) are represented, respectively, as

(1″)   ($\exists$x: Donkey(x))(Owns(p,x) & Beats(p,x)).

(2″)   ($\forall$x: Donkey(x))(Owns(p,x) $\rightarrow$ Beats(p,x)).

The problem with either (2′) or (2″) as a logical analysis of (2), however, is that the indefinite noun phrase 'a donkey' apparently means the same in (2) as it does in (1). Yet in providing the logical analysis of (1) as either (1′) or (1″), we represent the noun phrase as an existential quantifier (restricted or not), whereas in providing the logical analysis of (2) as either (2′) or (2″) we represent this phrase as a universal quantifier (restricted or not).

It might appear that we can account for the universal quantifier in (2) by appeal to a prenex rule that gives the logical equivalent of

(3) $\exists$x(Px) $\rightarrow$ Q

as

(4) $\forall$x(Px $\rightarrow$ Q).

Thus it would appear that a sentence, which according to its surface grammar seems to contain an existential quantifier, would contain instead a universal quantifier derived from that existential quantifier simply by means of this prenex rule.

But appeal to the above prenex rule must fail in the analysis of (2). For the prenex rule changes the wide scope of the universal quantifier in the deep structure of the sentence to the narrow scope of the existential quantifier at the surface level, and this change leaves the variable 'x' in the consequent of (2′) and (2″) unbound. Moreover, this rule gives narrow scope to 'a donkey' in (2), whereas our analysis of (1) gives 'a donkey' wide scope. Thus it would appear that pronouns that are anaphorically dependent upon indefinite noun phrases cannot be analyzed as variables bound by their anaphoric antecedents. For such an attempt must either represent the same noun phrase at times as a universal quantifier and at other times as an existential quantifier or else give an incorrect scope to the quantifier.

There are, of course, some occurrences of pronouns (the anaphoric antecedents of which are quantifier expressions) that are correctly analyzed
as bound variables, at least in the sense of providing the correct truth conditions. Examples are 'he' and 'himself' in (5) and (6), respectively.

(5)   Every man works hard for the thing he loves.

(6)   Every misanthrope hates himself.

The problem, then, of giving a logical analysis of anaphorically used
pronouns as well as their indefinite noun phrase antecedents is to find
a uniform treatment for them that provides the correct truth conditions
for sentences such as the "donkey sentences." Usually, linguists and philosophers require that this analysis provide also the logical form of such
sentences, or of the propositions such sentences express, or both. This
requirement places further constraints upon the analysis.

7.2   The Analysis of Anaphoric Pronouns as Descriptive
Referring Expressions

One proposed analysis of the anaphoric use of pronouns treats such pronouns in certain cases as proxies for their antecedent phrases. Peter Geach,
who holds this view, calls such pronouns "pronouns of laziness."[3] They are
surrogative, merely, for avoiding repetition of the antecedent phrases, for
which they go proxy. For example, the analysis of the pronoun 'one' in

(7)   A pronoun in this sentence is one of laziness

is a referring expression that goes proxy for 'a pronoun'.[4] In providing this
analysis, Geach does not intend to deny that some uses of pronouns the
anaphoric antecedents of which are indefinite noun phrases are correctly analyzed as bound variables. Quite the contrary, his main contention is that,
with the minor exception of pronouns of laziness, pronouns (generally with
a singular term or a quantifier expression as its anaphoric antecedent) are to
be analyzed as variables bound by their anaphoric antecedents.

3. See Peter Geach, *Reference and Generality.*

4. Geach modifies his notion of pronouns of laziness to include definite descriptions formed by nominalizing their antecedent noun phrases. See Geach, "Referring Expressions Again," in *Logic Matters* (Berkeley and Los Angeles: University
of California Press), 97–98.

Gareth Evans[5] maintains that although some occurrences of pronouns with quantifier expressions as their anaphoric antecedents are correctly analyzed as variables bound by their anaphoric antecedents and other occurrences are correctly analyzed as pronouns of laziness, there is a use of pronouns that cannot be correctly analyzed as either of these. He contends that such occurrences of pronouns are "assigned a reference and their immediate sentential contexts can be evaluated independently for truth and falsehood."[6] For example, according to Evans, the logical form of (1) and of

(8)   Socrates owns a dog and it bit him

is that of a conjunction of two propositions, and the pronoun 'it' in the second conjunct is a referring (singular) term. Such a pronoun, he asserts, is a singular term whose reference is rigidly fixed, in Kripke's sense, by a definite description derived in part from the anaphoric antecedent of the pronoun. Evans calls these pronouns "E-type." The indefinite noun phrase antecedent is analyzed in accordance with its surface structure as an (restricted) existential quantifier with a narrower scope than that of the connective in the sentence in which the noun phrase appears, and thus it does not bind the E-type pronoun.

Using this analysis, Evans purports to solve the problem posed by the donkey sentence

(2)   If Pedro owns a donkey, then he beats it

by treating it as composed of two sentences joined by a conditional connective, and by treating the pronoun 'it' as a referring term the reference of which is fixed by the definite description 'the donkey owned by Pedro'. In this way, Evans does not need to represent the indefinite noun phrase 'a donkey' as a restricted quantifier having a scope wider than the connective in the sentence. He can represent the noun phrase 'a donkey' in both (1) and (2) as a restricted existential quantifier with a scope narrower than that of the connective, leaving (2) as expressing two independent propositions, since the pronoun is not bound by the quantifier.

I find that Evans is not clear about the semantics he proposes for E-type pronouns. He does not provide a rigorously presented formal semantics

5. See Evans, "Pronouns, Quantifiers, and Relative Clauses (1)."
6. Evans, "Pronouns, Quantifiers, and Relative Clauses (1)," 104.

that includes a modal model theory. Hence it is difficult to determine whether he is offering a clear semantic proposal, especially in view of the fact that what he describes as his semantics and what he actually presents as his "formal" semantics may be inconsistent with each other. Scott Soames,[7] for example, maintains that in his "formal" semantics, Evans, despite his claim throughout the rest of the article, does *not* analyze E-type pronouns as terms the reference of which is rigidly fixed by their nominalized anaphoric antecedents. Rather, a pronoun used as an E-type pronoun is analyzed as a definite description the scope of which is the largest clause containing the pronoun but not including the clause containing its anaphoric antecedent. Evans mistakenly believes that by attributing the large scope to the definite description he is assuring that the E-type pronoun rigidly refers to its referent. This second analysis, which is in conflict with his first, treats E-type pronouns as proxies for definite descriptions formed from their anaphoric antecedents.[8]

According to the second analysis, the definite description, 'the donkey owned by Pedro', is to be used explicitly in the paraphrase of (2). But this description "must be understood as having a scope narrower than the connective."[9] Thus this analysis also allows us to represent the noun phrase 'a donkey' in both (1) and (2) as a restricted existential quantifier with a scope narrower than that of the connective. Since in this analysis, as in the first, the pronoun is not bound by the quantifier, (2) again expresses two independent propositions.

7.2.1   Evans's Objections to the Bound Variable Analysis and an Evaluation of His Objections

Evans has two main criticisms of the analysis of certain uses of pronouns as variables bound by their anaphoric antecedents. "The first is purely semantic: interpreting the pronouns as being bound by the quantifiers does not enable us to capture the most natural interpretation which these sen-

7. Scott Soames, review of *Collected Papers* by Gareth Evans, *The Journal of Philosophy* 86, 3 (March 1989): 141–156.

8. I am less convinced than is Soames that Evans's "formal semantics" commits him to this second analysis. Again, the problem is the lack of a rigorous formulation of his semantics. At any rate, I certainly doubt that the second analysis is his intended analysis.

9. Evans, "Pronouns, Quantifiers, and Relative Clauses (1)," 113.

tences have. The second . . . is the ill-formedness of [certain] sentences"[10] that such an analysis must countenance as meaningful.

In regard to the first criticism, consider the following sentences. According to the bound variable analysis, the pronoun 'it' in

(8)   Socrates owns a dog and it bit him

is correctly analyzed as a variable bound by its anaphoric antecedent, 'a dog', and thus (8) is equivalent to

(9)   A dog is such that Socrates owns it and it bit Socrates.

But then, according to this analysis, the pronoun 'them' in

(10)   John owns some sheep and Harry vaccinates them

is correctly analyzed as a variable bound by its anaphoric antecedent, 'some sheep', and thus (10) is equivalent to

(11)   Some sheep are such that John owns them and Harry vaccinates them.

Although there may be a possible construal of (10) as (11), surely this is not the most natural interpretation of (10). Under the most natural interpretation, for (10) to be true, Harry would have to vaccinate *all* the sheep that John owns. On that reading, a correct paraphrase of (10) would be

(12)   John owns some sheep and Harry vaccinates the sheep that John owns.

The same point is illustrated by the following sentence:

(13)   Few MPs came to the party, but they had a marvelous time.

This sentence is not equivalent to the paraphrase based on its bound variable analysis:

(14)   Few MPs are such that they both went to the party and had a marvelous time.

Similarly,

(15)   Mary danced with many boys and they found her interesting

is not equivalent to the paraphrase based on its bound variable analysis:

(16)   Mary danced with many boys who found her interesting.

10. Evans, "Pronouns, Quantifiers, and Relative Clauses (1)," 111.

In both pairs of sentences, the supposed paraphrase fails to capture what the first sentence of the pair entails. Thus (13) entails, while its supposed paraphrase, (14), does not, that few MPs went to the party and also that *all* the MPs that came to the party had a marvelous time. And (15) entails, while its alleged paraphrase, (16), does not, that Mary danced with many boys and also that *all* the boys who danced with Mary found her interesting. What these sentences strongly suggest, Evans argues, is that the correct analysis of (10), (13), and (15) reveals them to be conjunctions of two sentences the quantifier scope of which goes only to the end of the first conjunct and the pronoun of which is a singular term that has its reference fixed, in part at least, by nominalizing its anaphoric antecedent.

The first criticism does indeed show that in these cases the immediate anaphoric antecedent does not bind the variable occurrence representing the anaphoric pronoun. That analysis of the binding of the anaphoric pronoun applied to (10), (13), and (15) does not yield the most natural interpretation of the sentences. Usually in linguistic literature when it is argued that an anaphoric pronoun should not be analyzed as a bound variable, what is argued is simply that the immediate anaphoric antecedent does not bind the variable occurrence representing the pronoun as in the case above. But it does not follow that the pronoun is not to be analyzed as a bound variable. For it is possible to analyze the pronoun as a bound variable without regarding it as bound by the immediate anaphoric antecedent. (We return to this point in section 7.3.)

Evans's second objection to the bound variable analysis of certain uses of pronouns is that such an analysis admits as meaningful certain sentences that are, in fact, ill-formed.

For if the bound variable analysis is correct, then substituting a different quantifier in a meaningful sentence should result in a sentence that preserves well-formedness. But the results of replacing the quantifiers 'some', 'few' and 'many' with 'no' in (10), (13), and (15) are, respectively:

(17)   John owns no sheep and Harry vaccinates them

(18)   No MPs came to the party but they had a marvelous time

and

(19)   Mary danced with no boys and they found her interesting,

which according to Evans are ill-formed. But if (17), (18), and (19) are ill-formed, then this fact, Evans maintains, is inexplicable if we accept the view that their pronouns are bound by their anaphoric antecedents. For, according to such a view, (17), (18), and (19) are true if and only if the complex predicate formed by removing the quantifier 'no' from each of these sentences is satisfied by no sheep, no MPs, and no boys, respectively. Thus on the bound variable analysis of the pronouns in (17), (18), and (19), the alleged ungrammatical sentence, say (19), is rendered as

(20)   Mary danced with no boys such that they found her interesting,

which according to the bound variable analysis must count as well-formed.

But according to the Evans analysis, pronouns in (10), (13), and (15) are analyzed as denoting expressions the reference of which is fixed, respectively, by the descriptions 'the sheep that John owns', 'the MPs that came to the party', and 'the boys who danced with Mary'. On this analysis, we can reject (17), (18), and (19) as ill-formed, and "then we can explain why E-type pronouns cannot follow sentences whose quantifier is 'No' + common noun."[11]

Now this second objection advanced by Evans against the bound variable analysis is based, in my opinion, on both a mistaken linguistic intuition and a confusion. Let us first discuss the mistaken linguistic intuition.

I do not believe that sentences (17), (18), and (19), which Evans cites as ungrammatical, are in fact ungrammatical. To see that these sentences are well-formed, consider, first, the sentence

(19)   Mary danced with no boys and they found her interesting.

It is not hard to imagine a context in which this sentence would have a clear semantic interpretation and would be true. Imagine two girls at a party having the following conversation:

A: Boys are interested in you only if you dance with them.
B: Nonsense! Mary danced with no boys and they found her interesting.

If we switch the conjunction 'and' to 'but' in (19), or if we add the word 'anyway' to the end of sentence (19), it should be even more obvious that (19) makes sense and has a clear interpretation. The pronoun 'they' refers to boys or, in the situation under discussion, to the boys at the party.

Consider, next, the sentence

(18)   No MPs came to the party but they had a marvelous time.

11. Evans, "Pronouns, Quantifiers, and Relative Clauses (1)," 111–112.

Once we realize that the pronoun 'they' refers to MPs or to the MPs under discussion, I think that it is obvious that this sentence makes sense and is clearly not ill-formed.

Finally, consider the sentence

(17)   John owns no sheep and Harry vaccinates them.

Now imagine the following conversation:

A: Who owns and takes care of the sheep on the farm we went to yesterday?
B: I don't know for sure, but I know this much. John owns no sheep and [but] Harry vaccinates them.

The pronoun 'them' in this dialogue refers to sheep or to the sheep under discussion, that is, the sheep on the farm.

I suspect that Evans has fallen victim to a faulty linguistic intuition regarding these sentences for two reasons. First, he may well believe that changing the quantifier in a sentence containing a pronoun and its quantifier anaphoric antecedent does not change the reference of the pronoun. But this is clearly wrong. The pronoun 'they' in a sentence of the form 'Some A's are B's and they are C's' (in which the anaphoric antecedent has existential force) refers to A-B things. But the same pronoun in a sentence of the form 'All A's are B's and they are C's' or of the form 'No A's are B's and they are C's' (in both of which the anaphoric antecedent has universal force) refers not to A-B things, but to A's (not, that is, to A's that are B's, but to A's that might or might not be B's). We will have more to say about rules governing the reference of anaphoric pronouns in chapter 8.

Second, Evans may falsely assume that when a pronoun is anaphoric upon a quantifier expression within a given sentence, if we change the quantifier expression within that sentence, the pronoun is now anaphoric upon the new quantifier expression. But this is simply false. The pronoun may no longer be bound to the quantifier expression within the sentence. It may be anaphoric upon some antecedent sentence or some assumed (even if not stated) anaphoric background and anaphoric background statement. This is what we have seen in the examples above.

It is also worth noting that Evans is mistaken in claiming that—on both of his own analyses—sentences (17), (18), and (19) are ill-formed.

Recall that according to his first analysis of E-type pronouns, an E-type pronoun is a rigidly referring expression the reference of which is fixed by the definite description formed from its anaphoric antecedent. It is not clear what is meant for a term to refer rigidly to what is fixed by a plural noun phrase. Does the term rigidly refer to all the members of the class of things denoted by the plural noun phrase in the actual world or, like a natural kind term, to the class of things denoted by the noun phrase in a given possible world? Let us assume that Evans means the former. Thus the anaphoric pronouns in (10), (13), and (15)—that is, 'them', 'they' and 'they'—rigidly denote, respectively, the sheep that John owns, the MPs who came to the party, and the boys who danced with Mary. Let us use these descriptions, respectively, to fix rigidly the references of three names, say, 'Baba', 'Bill', and 'Ben'. These names, then, rigidly denote the empty set, and should play the same semantic role as the corresponding E-type pronouns that occur in (17), (18), and (19). If we substitute these names in these three sentences, respectively, we get

(21)   John owns no sheep and Harry vaccinates Baba

(22)   No MPs came to the party but Bill had a marvelous time

and

(23)   Mary danced with no boys and Ben found her interesting.

And these three sentences, according to Evans's claim about his own analysis, would have to be meaningless.

But on this analysis these sentences are not meaningless. To see this, let us assume that the first conjuncts of (17), (18), and (19) are true. Then the first conjunct of (21) is true by assumption. The second conjunct is true if and only if Harry vaccinates Baba, where the term 'Baba' is an S-type term referring rigidly to all the sheep that John owns. Thus the second conjunct is true if and only if Harry vaccinates all the members of the class of sheep that John owns, namely, all the members of the empty class, which is trivially true, since anything you like is true of all the members of the empty class. Analogous remarks apply to (22) and (23). Hence Evans's claim that, according to his own (first) analysis, sentences (21), (22), and (23) do not have clear truth conditions and are rendered meaningless is false.

To be sure, this first analysis of E-type pronouns does assign incorrect truth conditions to (17), (18), and (19). (I have more to say about Evans's analyses assigning the wrong truth conditions in 7.2.2.) At any rate, it does not assign to these sentences the more natural interpretation we gave them when we showed above that they are meaningful. If this analysis is what

Evans intends, then, he is open to the same objection that he raised against Geach's version of the bound variable analysis: the Evans analysis fails to give the most natural interpretation of certain sentences.

Now let us consider Evans' second analysis of an E-type pronoun, that is, as a definite description the scope of which is the largest clause containing the pronoun but not including the clause containing its anaphoric antecedent. Then sentences (17), (18), and (19) once again turn out to be meaningful. Indeed, all three sentences would necessarily be false. For example, (17) would have the following truth conditions.

(24)   "John owns no sheep and Harry vaccinates them" is true iff John owns no sheep and the sheep that John owns is vaccinated by Harry.

On a Russellian analysis, the truth of the first conjunct entails the falsity of the second conjunct, since the existential quantifier used in the definite description 'the sheep that John owns' includes the entire second conjunct. But to say that the sentence is false is not to say that it is meaningless. Even if one takes a Strawsonian line on the truth value of sentences the presupposition of which fails, the second conjunct of (17), though failing to have a truth value, is nevertheless meaningful. Similar remarks apply to sentences (18) and (19). Once again, we have an analysis of E-type pronouns assigning truth conditions to sentences (17), (18), and (19) that are not in accord with their natural interpretation.

Thus the same examples that Evans uses in objecting to Geach's version of the bound variable analysis turn out to have an unnatural interpretation on Evans's own analyses. For as we have just seen, the truth conditions assigned to (17), (18), and (19) on his analysis, under the two most plausible interpretations of his semantics for E-type pronouns, are not the proper truth conditions for (17), (18), and (19).

7.2.2 An Evaluation of the Proposed Semantic Analyses of E-Type Pronouns

We consider next various additional objections to Evans's view concerning what he calls "E-type pronouns." These objections center around two main issues: (i) Are such E-type pronouns really rigid designators? and (ii) Does Evans's analyses of these pronouns always provide the correct truth conditions? We discuss each in turn.

Are E-type pronouns rigid?

Michael McKinsey and later Scott Soames and Stephen Neale have challenged Evans's view that E-type pronouns rigidly refer to their referents.[12] McKinsey's position is that E-type pronouns are simply proxies for the relevant descriptions. He argues that if the reference of the pronoun 'them' in (10) is supposed to be fixed rigidly by the description "the sheep that John owns" "then [(10)] is true only in those possible worlds in which Harry vaccinates the sheep that John owns in the actual world. But in that case we cannot explain how the following sentence can express a truth:

[(25)]   John in fact owns no sheep, but it might have been the case that John owns some sheep and Harry vaccinates them."[13]

Another example that McKinsey offers in support of his own view is

(26)   A woman will be nominated but it is doubtful that she will win the election.

McKinsey argues that the speaker who utters (26) "would not be expressing a doubt concerning any particular woman's winning the election, but would be expressing a doubt as to whether the woman who will be nominated, whoever she may be, will win. But it seems that in order for [(26)] to have this interpretation, 'she' must be construed as short for the description 'the woman who will be nominated'".[14]

Scott Soames, in his review of Gareth Evans's *Collected Papers*, objects in a similar way to the view that E-type pronouns are rigid designators. In considering

(27)   Boston has *a Mayor* and *he* used to be a Democrat,

(where 'used to be' is to be formalized with a tense operator) Soames says,

Nevertheless, it is clear that E-type pronouns are not, in fact, rigid designators. The leading idea is that an occurrence of such a pronoun is supposed to refer to the verifiers of the clause containing its antecedent. Since this clause will typically have different verifiers at different circumstances of evaluation, an occurrence of an E-type pronoun associated with it will refer to different things in different circumstances. If this were not so, and if 'he' in [(27)] rigidly referred to the actual present mayor of Boston (call him 'Kevin'), then [(27)] would be true at an arbitrary

12. See Michael McKinsey, "Mental Anaphora," *Synthese* 66 (1986): 159–175; Soames, review of *Collected Papers* by Gareth Evans; and Stephen Neale, *Descriptions* (Cambridge, MA: MIT Press, 1990), 186.

13. Michael McKinsey, "Mental Anaphora," 161.

14. Michael McKinsey, "Mental Anaphora," 161.

circumstance of evaluation E in which a lifelong Republican was Mayor of Boston at E, provided that Kevin used to be a Democrat in E. Since this is incorrect, E-type pronouns are typically not rigid designators.[15]

The McKinsey-Soames-Neale objection to the Evans analysis is that if an E-type pronoun is taken to be a rigid designator, then the wrong truth conditions result for the most natural interpretation of sentences containing such pronouns. That is, Evans's first analysis of E-type pronouns provides the wrong truth conditions.

Before evaluating the McKinsey-Soames-Neale objection to Evans's first analysis of E-type pronouns, notice that when we consider Evans's second analysis of E-type pronouns, we find that he is mistaken in believing that the large scope of the definite description makes the E-type pronoun a rigid designator. For example, the truth condition that this second analysis provides for (27) is

(28) $\exists x(Mx)$ & $\lambda y P(Dy)(\iota x)(Mx)$,

where 'Mx' is 'x is a mayor of Boston', 'P' is a past tense operator to be read "it used to be the case that," and 'Dx' is 'x is a Democrat'. (The lambda operator is an operator that forms complex predicates, and the expression '$\lambda y P(Dy)$' is to be read as "is an object y such that in the past y is a Democrat." The iota operator that forms singular terms, and the expression '$(\iota x)(Mx)$' is to be read as "the mayor of Boston.")[16]

But (28) does not treat the pronoun 'he' as a rigid designator. When we evaluate (28) in a possible circumstance w, the satisfier of the definite description is a mayor of Boston *in w*. In general, such a satisfier varies from possible world to possible world, and the variable in (28) bound by the iota operator (after removing this operator) will be given different assignments of satisfiers in different possible worlds.

The McKinsey-Soames-Neale objection that *certain occurrences* of pronouns do not refer rigidly is incorrect. In my view, with the exception of pronouns of laziness, all pronouns, such as "he," "she," "it," "they," "them," and so forth, are rigid designators wherever used, even in the examples of McKinsey and Soames. To see this, notice that we do not have

---

15. Soames, review of *Collected Papers* by Gareth Evans, 145.

16. Using the lambda operator, a large-scope reading of the definite description corresponds to the lambda operator having the large scope, as opposed to the past tense operator. Alternatively $\exists x(Mx$ & $(y)(My \rightarrow y = x$ & $P(Dx))$.

the same intuitions regarding pronouns being assigned different objects in different possible worlds as we have regarding definite descriptions.

Compare, for example,

(29)   Boston has a (Republican) mayor and he used to be a Democrat

with

(30)   Boston has a (Republican) mayor and the mayor of Boston used to be a Democrat.

In (29), the assignment to the pronoun 'he' is determined by the satisfier of its anaphoric background condition, that is, whoever is the mayor of Boston at the time of evaluation of the first conjunct. It remains so even within the intensional context of a temporal operator. But in (30), the occurrence of the definite description within the intensional context, unlike the occurrence of the pronoun 'he' in (29), refers to the (unique) satisfier of the description at some time prior to the evaluation of the first conjunct. We may no longer be referring to whoever is the mayor of Boston at the time of evaluation. At best, one might argue that (30) is ambiguous between these two readings. But even then, one would have to formulate (30) as (29) if one intended the first reading to be unambiguously stated.

The mistake in the McKinsey-Soames-Neale position appears to be based on two implicit assumptions, one of which I reject, the other I consider false. First, they appear to assume a Fregean-, rather than a Russellian- or Tarskian-, style semantics. In Fregean semantics, an occurrence of a term may have, in a particular context, say that of a nonextensional context, a reference other than its standard one. Second, they appear to assume that all kinds of rigid designator terms, or at least all pronouns, determine their extension in the same way. They thus assume that the same formal semantics is required to represent the way in which we are to determine these terms' extension and then evaluate whether they are rigid designators. In particular, McKinsey, Soames, and Neale appear to presuppose the double indexing formal semantics due to Hans Kamp as developed by David Kaplan for the semantics of demonstratives, in which he employs the notions of contexts of use and circumstances of evaluation.

Regarding the first assumption, in standard Russellian or Tarskian formal semantics, a variable may stand in place of a pronoun in the formalization of the sentence containing the pronoun. A quantifier will then bind this variable in order for the formalization to represent the sentence containing that pronoun. Of course, an occurrence of a bound variable does not refer, let alone rigidly. Nevertheless, in order to determine the truth of this formalized sentence, we employ standard inductive clauses that determine its truth by means of first determining the semantic value of its parts. According to these clauses, we determine the truth of a quantified sentence by first removing the quantifier and determining the truth of the resulting expression relative to an assignment of a value to the resulting free occurrences of that variable that represents the pronoun. Now, in Russellian or Tarskian semantics, *each such occurrence* of the variable, *under a given assignment* of objects to variables, is assigned the same object, even when the variable occurs within a nonextensional context.

Regarding the second assumption of McKinsey, Soames, and Neale, I contend that there are different kinds of rigid designators, the extensions of which are determined in different ways. First, there are proper names. Once a proper name has been introduced into a language, it rigidly refers to its referent in all possible worlds or circumstances of evaluation, regardless of the name's context of use. Thus a name is not context-sensitive.

In order for the name to succeed in referring, its A-B condition must be satisfied. (See chapter 5 for details.) These conditions are either that the object named is named by ostension or that the reference of the name is fixed by description. The former condition is satisfied if the right causal connection between the name and an object obtains. The latter condition is satisfied if all the conceptual apparatus for uniquely specifying the name's reference is in place and the world cooperates—that is, all descriptions used in fixing the reference when introducing the name are true and are conjointly satisfied uniquely. The A-B condition for proper names is what we have called the baptismal step, and the context in which the name is introduced is what we have called the context of introduction. The A-B condition for proper names may be represented by a function that maps contexts of introduction into the name's referent. Given this context of introduction, the name rigidly refers to its referent in all possible worlds relative to the possible world of the context of introduction. Thus for proper names, there is no distinction between a context of use and a possible circumstance of evaluation, and hence there is no need for double indexing that employs both these notions.

But not all rigid designators have their extension determined in the same way as proper names. To represent the second kind of rigid designators, demonstratives, we must make use of Kaplan's innovative development of double indexing. According to this formal semantics, a demonstrative accompanied by a demonstration (i.e., a completed demonstrative) and an indexical expression are rigid designators relative to a context of use. A variable representing such a demonstrative or indexical will have its reference covary rigidly with what it is assigned in a given context of use. But given a context of use, as Kaplan has shown, completed demonstratives and indexicals rigidly refer to their referent in all possible worlds, or circumstances of evaluation. For completed demonstratives and indexicals, there is no distinction between a context of introduction and a context of use and hence no need for double indexing that employs both these notions.

Now my claim is that there is a third kind of rigid designator that requires still another formal semantics to represent how we determine its extension, namely, anaphorically used pronouns. Consider the formalization of a sentence containing a pronoun. As we stated above, in Russellian and Tarskian semantics, after removing the quantifier that binds the variable representing the pronoun in the formalization, the same object is assigned to each resulting free occurrence of the variable, even if the occurrence is within a nonextensional context. The (free) variable given this assignment may thus be used to represent a pronoun that refers rigidly. An anaphorically used pronoun is rigid relative to an assignment of an object to the variable that represents the pronoun. It rigidly refers to the assigned object in any possible world accessible from the possible world in which the variable is assigned that object.

This then is the central problem that I find with the McKinsey-Soames-Neale argument that E-type pronouns are not rigid designators: Its proponents fail to realize that anaphorically used pronouns, including E-type pronouns, are represented by a (free) variable relative to a given assignment of the pronoun's referent and thus rigidly refer to this assigned object in any possible world accessible from the possible world in which the variable is assigned this object. Their failure to realize this, I believe, is due to their failure to distinguish among three kinds of rigid designators and the relevant class of possible worlds in which these terms rigidly designate the same object.

First we have a rigid designator *simpliciter,* or relative to a *context of introduction,* such as a proper name; such a rigid designator rigidly designates the same object in all possible worlds accessible from the possible world of the context of introduction. Second we have a rigid designator relative to a *context of use,* such as a completed demonstrative or indexical; such a term rigidly designates the same object in all possible worlds accessible from the possible world of the context of use. Third we have a rigid designator relative *to an assignment of a value to a variable,* such as an anaphoric pronoun; such a term rigidly designates the same object in all possible worlds accessible from the possible world in which the variable is assigned that object, that is, the possible world from which the A-B statement for the term makes a claim.

Now in the case of anaphorically used pronouns, the A-B condition determines the pronoun's referent. The referent is this condition's satisfier from the possible world in which the condition must obtain in order for the pronoun to refer. It is with respect to this possible world that the variable represents an anaphorically used pronoun as a rigid designator. For our third kind of rigid designator, anaphoric pronouns, reference thus covaries rigidly with what we assign to this variable, where the assignment is from the possible world in which the anaphoric background condition must obtain. This possible world may be the possible world of the context of introduction, the context of use, or a possible circumstance of evaluation. Thus in the formal semantics for the third kind of rigid designators, there is no need to distinguish these three notions. These rigid designators are simply rigid relative to an assignment of values to the variables representing them.

Let us consider

(31)   Boston has a mayor and it might have been the case that he used to be a Democrat.

Unlike a rigid designator simpliciter, the pronoun 'he' is represented by a variable. Thus its reference (when we remove the quantifier binding the variable) is determined relative to a possible world, or circumstance of evaluation, in which its A-B condition (Boston's having a mayor) is supposed to obtain. This, in turn, will determine the relevant assignment of a referent to the variable that represents the pronoun. In particular, the proposition expressed by sentence (31) is true in any possible world w if and only if at the time of evaluation there is a mayor of Boston *in w* and there is a possible world w' (accessible to w) such that *that person* (i.e., the mayor of Boston in w) at a time prior to the evaluation in w is a Democrat in w'.

More explicitly, the truth condition for (31) is the following:[17]

(32) ($\forall$w) (31) is true with respect to w iff the first conjunct is true in w and the second conjunct is true with respect to two parameters—w *and* an assignment of a referent to the pronoun, 'he', namely, the assignment to the pronoun of the mayor of Boston in w.

We observe first that the pronoun 'he' is treated like a bound variable, in a fashion analogous to the way the variable 'x' in the closed formula '$\exists$x(Fx)' is treated in connection with the open sentence 'Fx', that is, '$\exists$x(Fx)' is true if and only if

(33) Fx is true under some assignment of a value for x.

We next observe that for every assignment, a, of referents to pronouns, and for every possible world w, the pronoun 'he', under a given assignment a refers with respect to w to a('he'), that is, in any possible world, the referent of 'he' in that world is whatever a assigns to 'he'. In our previous example, for any two worlds w and w', the pronoun 'he' refers—with respect to w' and under the assignment a that assigns the mayor of Boston in w to the pronoun 'he'—to the mayor of Boston in w. Accordingly, the second conjunct is true if and only if there is a possible world w' such that a(he) = the mayor of Boston in w and at a time prior to the evaluation in w, the mayor of Boston in w is a Democrat in w'. Since the result of applying the assignment a to 'he' is not dependent upon any other possible world w', 'he' is a rigid designator under a given assignment with respect to the possible world w.

The same analysis applies to McKinsey's example:

(25) John in fact owns no sheep, but it might have been the case that John owns some sheep and Harry vaccinates them.

The proposition expressed by sentence (25) is to be evaluated in the actual world. But the relevant domain with respect to which the anaphoric background condition determines the referent of the pronoun 'them' is not the actual world. Although the first conjunct is supposed to hold in the actual world, the second conjunct is a statement about what obtains in some possible world w, namely, that John owns some sheep and Harry vaccinates them. And it is the first half of the second conjunct ("it might have been

17. Nathan Salmon in numerous conversations has helped me in formulating these views, which he also shares.

the case that John owns some sheep") that is the A-B statement for the pronoun 'them'. Thus the pronoun 'them' refers to members of sheep from the domain of a world w in which John owns some sheep. In particular, it refers to the sheep that John owns in w. For it is after the modal operator that the quantifier binding the variable that represents 'them' occurs.

To appreciate that 'them' in (25) is a rigid designator, suppose that, after asserting (25), we go on to say

(34)   Harry wouldn't vaccinate them if they were owned by Bob.

In (34), the pronoun 'them' refers only to the sheep that John might have owned, that is, the sheep John owns in w. Let us assume that Bob owns these sheep in w'. Then in order for the proposition expressed in sentence (34) to be true, in w', Harry doesn't vaccinate the sheep assigned to the pronoun 'them' in w', that is, the sheep owned by John in w.

We thus conclude that a so-called E-type pronoun is a rigid designator. It refers rigidly to the object that satisfies the A-B condition in the domain of the relevant world in which this condition is supposed to obtain. This object is assigned to the variable representing the pronoun, and thus relative to this assignment, the pronoun refers rigidly to this object in all possible worlds accessible to this relevant world.

Do the analyses of E-type pronouns always provide the correct truth conditions?

First, Evans's analyses fail to provide the correct truth conditions for sentences containing plural E-type pronouns. In (10), (13), and (15), the pronouns 'them' and 'they' are used as plural E-type pronouns. But we cannot treat these pronouns as having their reference fixed by a definite description or literally going proxy for the description, if such a description is analyzed in the standard Russellian way, that is, as an expression that is to be interpreted as having a *unique* satisfier, if satisfied at all. (For as plural pronouns, they refer to more than one thing.)

Second, the problem is exacerbated if the E-type pronoun is singular, but the sentence containing it does not warrant a uniqueness claim. Thus in (1), the first donkey sentence, the pronoun 'it' may refer to more than one donkey owned by Pedro. This example illustrates that if we analyze the pronoun as having its reference fixed by a definite description or as going proxy for that description, we no longer have a uniform treatment of an E-type pronoun with a quantifier expression as its anaphoric antecedent.

Yet this is a central goal of an analysis of these pronouns. Instead, Evans's analyses require further rules to distinguish when a singular E-type pronoun is to be treated as a definite description from when it is to be treated as something that permits more than one satisfier. Moreover, we need to distinguish the analysis of singular pronouns having more than one satisfier from the analysis of plural pronouns, which have more than one satisfier. It is not clear that this or any variant substitute proposal can achieve this in a manner that satisfies the motivations of Evans's analyses.

In an attempt to meet the objection that sometimes E-type singular pronouns may not refer to a unique satisfier of a definite description, Evans suggests that the speaker be *"prepared to answer upon demand,* the question 'He? Who?' or 'It? Which?' In order to effect this liberalization we should allow the reference of the E-type pronoun to be fixed not only by predicative material explicitly in the antecedent clause, but also by material which the speaker supplies on demand."[18] It is as if the pronoun in (2) has its reference fixed by the definite description "the donkey owned by Pedro that the speaker has in mind" or goes proxy for it. Thus, for Evans, the pronoun succeeds in referring if the speaker, upon request, can provide a description that uniquely identifies the referent of the E-type pronoun.

Moreover, Evans states that fixing the reference with the aid of additional predicative material supplied by the speaker can involve cancellation of explicit predicative material in the antecedent. He illustrates this point with the following Strawsonian example:

A: A man jumped out of the crowd and fell in front of the horse.
B: He didn't jump, he was pushed.[19]

Here the reference of 'he' is apparently determined either by a focusing or by the speaker's "having some referent in mind." The description obtained from the anaphoric antecedent is used ascriptively, as a speaker's reference, rather than a semantic reference, that is, rather than attributively. In Evans's example, the pronoun refers to the object that the speaker mistakenly *took* to satisfy the predicative material in the anaphoric antecedent. Hence the use of this term is F-type and not S-type.

One problem in Evans's semantic analysis of E-type pronouns is his failure to distinguish between F-type and S-type uses of terms, and his failure

18. See Evans, "Pronouns, Quantifiers, Relative Clauses (1)."
19. See Evans, "Pronouns, Quantifiers, Relative Clauses (1)."

to appreciate the fact that these two kinds of uses differ in their semantics. By failing to distinguish between F-type and S-type terms, his semantics for E-type pronouns betrays confusion.

Now it is my contention that although Evans's E-type pronouns can on occasion be used as F-type expressions, they are more usually S-type. Consider again the sentence

(8)   Socrates owns a dog and it bit him.

According to Evans, the pronoun 'it' in (8) is E-type. There is, of course, a clear reading of this sentence in which the pronoun 'it' is used as an F-type term, for example, when the speaker has in mind either a particular dog owned by Socrates or the dog that is the historic source of the belief now being relayed. There is, however, a clear reading of (8) in which the pronoun 'it' is used as an S-type term, namely, the case in which the speaker, having no particular dog in mind, believes that there is at least one dog owned by Socrates and at least one such dog, whichever it may be, bit him.

On my view, when a pronoun is used as an F-type term, its reference is ultimately determined by means of focusing. Hence the predicative material (in the anaphoric antecedent) that forms a description is not part of the content of such terms any more than descriptions used in introducing F-type terms are part of the content of these terms.[20] In both cases the description is used ascriptively, to aid in determining the speaker's reference, and it may be denied that the referents of these terms satisfy these descriptions. In (8) above, when the pronoun 'it' is used as an F-type term, someone can interject, "The dog wasn't owned by Socrates."

On the other hand, when a pronoun is used as an S-type term, the predicative material (in the anaphoric antecedent) that forms a description is relevant to the determination of the term's reference. Here the description is used attributively and thus contributes to the truth conditions of sentences containing the S-type term. In that case, however, it does not make sense in (8) above, for example, to interject, "The dog wasn't owned by Socrates."

In any event, we cannot analyze an E-type pronoun as having its reference fixed by a definite description derived from its anaphoric antecedent or as going proxy for the description regardless of whether the E-type pronoun is F-type or S-type. For example, we cannot analyze the pronoun 'it' in sentence

20. This is not to say that the predicative material (in the anaphoric antecedent) that forms a description is part of the content of S-type terms.

(35)   If John owns a sock, he owns another one that matches *it*

as a definite description derived from its anaphoric antecedent. The pronoun cannot be analyzed as a definite description (with wide scope in appropriate clauses) because then we would get

(36)   If John owns a sock, he owns another one that matches the sock that John owns.

The definite description 'the sock that John owns' cannot be satisfied if taken attributively. Even if we allow for material not explicitly in the antecedent clause, and accept material that the speaker supplies on demand (whether taken descriptively or ascriptively), there still may not be any object that satisfies this additional predicative material. The speaker may have no particular sock of John's in mind or any further description that, together with the predicative material, applies to one and only one of these socks. The main problem, however, is that 'the sock that John owns' implies that there is one and only one sock that John owns. Thus he cannot also own another sock that matches the one and only one sock that he owns. Thus for all these reasons, the sentence serves as a counterexample to the analysis that E-type pronouns are definite descriptions (with wide scope) or are singular terms the reference of which is fixed by the definite descriptions derived from their anaphoric antecedents; and this is so even when there is supplementary material that the speaker can supply upon request.

Stephen Neale has offered a proposal (in the spirit of Evans's analysis) designed to meet the two problems raised in this section: to provide correct truth conditions for (i) sentences containing plural E-type pronouns and (ii) sentences containing singular E-type pronouns where the sentence does not warrant a uniqueness claim.[21] Neale's project is to defend the Russellian analysis of indefinite descriptions as existential quantifiers in any sentential context. He proposes to analyze these anaphoric pronouns themselves, rather than indefinite descriptions in certain contexts, as introducing universal quantification. According to his analysis, these anaphoric pronouns, even when singular (e.g., 'he', 'she', and 'it'), are abbreviations for universal descriptive phrases, and thus, according to Neale, go proxy for universal restricted quantifiers.

---

21. Stephen Neale, "Descriptive Pronouns and Donkey Anaphora," *The Journal of Philosophy* 87, 3 (March 1990), and *Descriptions*. In what follows, I will often talk about E-type pronouns even though I do not believe that there are such pronouns. More accurately, I should say "what Evans calls 'E-type pronouns.'"

Specifically, Neale analyzes singular anaphoric pronouns as variables bound by an existential quantifier in some sentential contexts, while they go proxy for a restricted universal quantifier in still other contexts. In order to distinguish the two sentential contexts that distinguish his two readings of singular anaphoric pronouns (i.e., as bound variables and as restricted universal quantifiers), Neale represents the syntactic structure of the sentence containing the pronoun by a syntax tree. He then makes use of the linguistic rule known as the c-command rule:

A phrase α *c-commands* a phrase β iff the first branching node dominating α also dominates β and neither α nor β dominates the other.

A node is said to *dominate* an expression α iff there is a downward path through the tree from this node to the expression α.

Using these notions, Neale provides the following criterion (which was implicit in Evans) for an anaphoric pronoun to be interpreted as a variable bound by its anaphoric quantifier antecedent:

A pronoun P that is anaphoric on a quantifier Q is interpreted as a variable bound by Q iff Q c-commands P.

For example, in the sentence "Some boy in the class thinks he is smart," the quantifier expression 'some boy in the class' c-commands the pronoun 'he' and thus the pronoun is interpreted as bound by this restricted quantifier expression. In sentence (2), "If Pedro buys a donkey, then he vaccinates it," however, the quantifier expression 'a donkey (bought by Pedro)' does not c-command the pronoun 'it'. Thus the pronoun is to be interpreted as an E-type pronoun for Evans and as a restricted universal quantifier expression for Neale.

Before examining Neale's analysis, it is important to recall that providing an analysis is not merely providing the correct truth conditions. It is also exhibiting the correct logical form and, at least according to the way the notion of analysis was originally used by early-twentieth-century analytic philosophers, providing the correct meaning of the analysands.

It is unclear what constitutes the "logical form" of an expression, at least, independently of the embedding language. Linguists in the Chomskyan tradition regard logical form as a level of syntactic structure below the surface structure and as the level where quantifier binding occurs. From this level of syntactic structure there are algorithmic rules that allow us to derive, or "generate," the surface structure. Many linguists often ignore questions of meaning in an analysis and replace it with those rules from which one can derive the surface structure from the syntactic level of logical form.

Although linguists may describe their project this way, surely this is misleading. For, no one would postulate a logical form of '$(x)(\sim\!F \rightarrow \sim\!A)$' for any sentence that has the same surface structure as, say, "All apples are fruit" simply because we can have a rule to derive such a surface structure from its logical equivalent at the level of logical form. Thus there are more constraints on logical form and rules mapping logical form into surface structure than simply deriving the correct surface structure. Accordingly, in evaluating Neale's analyses of anaphoric pronouns that are E-type, we will be concerned with more than whether these analyses provide us with the correct truth conditions. Of course, since truth conditions are a necessary condition for a correct analysis, if Neale's analysis fails to provide the correct truth conditions, as I intend to show, he thereby fails to provide a correct analysis.

We should first note the unnaturalness of Neale's analysis of a singular anaphoric pronoun as going proxy for a restricted universal quantifier in some sentential contexts. An anaphoric singular pronoun ('he', 'she', or 'it') would seem to have a more natural analysis as simply an existentially bound variable in all contexts. Further, Neale's analysis requires giving up a univocal, and hence a uniform, treatment of singular anaphoric pronouns. This is ironic since the lack of a uniform treatment is Neale's central objection to analyzing an indefinite description as having existential force in some contexts while having universal force in others. Indeed, it seems more plausible to argue that there is a universal quantifier reading of indefinite descriptions, as in the generic reading of "A whale is a mammal," than to claim that there is any such reading of a singular anaphoric pronoun. In fact, Neale cannot account for the universal reading of "A whale is a mammal" since there is no pronoun in the sentence that he can claim goes proxy for a restricted universal quantifier and, hence, nothing for him to account for the sentence's universal character.

Second, we should note that not only is the analysis of a singular anaphoric pronoun as going proxy for a restricted universal quantifier in certain sentences unintuitive. The resulting analysis and logical form of these sentences is also highly unnatural and unintuitive. Neale analyzes singular E-type pronouns occurring in sentences that do not warrant a uniqueness claim as a restricted universal quantifier, the form of which he expresses as '[whe x:Fx]', that is, "whoever/whatever is F." This latter expression he calls a "numberless description." An example of such a pronoun is 'it' in the second donkey sentence (2). He then proposes the following truth conditions for such sentences containing singular E-type pronouns that do not warrant a uniqueness condition:

(37)   '[whe x: Fx](Gx)' is true iff $|F-G|= 0$ and $|F| \geq 1$.

(The vertical bars are to be read as "the cardinality of.")

The resulting analysis and logical form of sentences that contain such singular anaphoric pronouns may appear somewhat natural only when we use Neale's restricted quantifier notation to express the form of these sentences. But the difficulty is that his restricted quantifier notations actually serve only to abbreviate the standard quantification expression with the same truth conditions proposed by Neale in introducing these notations. For we do not have an understanding of these notations prior to or independent of his introduction of the truth conditions expressed in (37).

That Neale is well aware of this is clear from his discussion of a singular definite description 'the F' as a restricted quantifier. He introduces the following truth conditions for his restricted quantifier '[the x: Fx]', where 'F' is singular:

(38)   '[the x: Fx](Gx)' is true iff $|F-G| = 0$ and $|F| = 1$.

He then states, "To treat a singular definite description 'the F' as a restricted quantifier '[the x: Fx]' is not to propose an alternative to Russell's theory; it is just to find a more congenial way of stating it. In effect, [(38)] stipulates that '[the x: Fx](Gx)' is equivalent to '$(\exists x)(Fx \,\&\, (\forall y)(Fy \supset y = x) \,\&\, Gx)$'."[22]

But we cannot solve a problem of analysis merely by introducing an abbreviation. What Neale offers is the exact opposite of Russell's classic analysis of the definite article 'the' in 'the F is G'. There Russell showed how we can define contextually and thus eliminate as merely an abbreviation the definite article 'the' (or, in quantification theory, the iota operator). Now, Neale's restricted quantifier expressions are introduced *only* by stating truth conditions for sentences containing these expressions. Thus

---

22. Neale, "Descriptive Pronouns and Donkey Anaphora," 122n.23. Also in *Descriptions*, 45, with the phrase 'stipulates that' replaced with *'definitionally equivalent to'*.

these truth conditions constitute all we know regarding what these expressions mean or abbreviate. But when we substitute sentences expressed in accordance with both Neale's truth conditions and logical form for sentences containing the anaphoric pronouns in question, what results is something far from natural and intuitive.

To see the unnaturalness of this analysis, notice the truth conditions in (37) for a sentence that contains a singular E-type pronoun and does not warrant a uniqueness claim. These truth conditions are nothing more, in familiar terminology, than 'all F's are G's and there is at least one F'. For example, the standard analysis and logical form of

(2)   If Pedro owns a donkey, then he beats it

is

(2′) $\forall x((\text{Donkey}(x)\ \&\ \text{Owns}(p,x)) \rightarrow \text{Beats}(p,x))$.

But applying Neale's analysis, we have

(2″) $\exists x(\text{Donkey}(x)\ \&\ \text{Owns}(p,x)) \rightarrow [\forall x((\text{Donkey}(x)\ \&\ \text{Owns}(p,x)) \rightarrow \text{Beats}(p,x))\ \&\ \exists x(\text{Donkey}(x)\ \&\ \text{Owns}(p,x))]$.

Now this analysis and logical form attributed to (2) is counterintuitive. It requires, beyond what is given in a standard analysis, an extra conditional the antecedent of which requires an existential sentence—$\exists x(\text{Donkey}(x)\ \&\ \text{Owns}(p,x))$—and an extra sentence in the consequent, namely, the same existential sentence.

A more central problem with Neale's analysis is that in many cases his truth conditions for sentences containing anaphoric pronouns that he analyzes as going proxy for a universal quantifier are simply wrong. Neale provides two analyses for singular E-type pronouns, one in which the pronoun warrants a uniqueness claim, the other in which the pronoun is analyzed as a numberless description. But he fails to offer any (syntactic) criterion to determine which of these two analyses apply to a singular pronoun in a given sentence. In any event, both analyses fail to provide the correct truth conditions for certain sentences containing singular E-type pronouns.

Consider the sentence

(39)   John bought a donkey and Harry vaccinated it.

Neale analyzes the pronoun in (39) as warranting a uniqueness claim, and analyzes it as

(39′)   John bought a donkey and Harry vaccinated *the donkey John bought.*

He states that we may, therefore, represent the logical form of (39) as follows:

(39″)   [an x: donkey x](John bought x) & [the x: donkey x & John bought x](Harry vaccinated x),

where the determiner 'an x' is interpreted as a restricted existential quantifier.

Neale, like Evans, apparently accepts sentences like (39) as expressing a uniqueness claim, that is, that John bought exactly one donkey and Harry vaccinated it. But no such uniqueness claim is implied by (39). For someone can consistently assert after (39), "In fact, he owns another donkey and Harry vaccinated that one, too. But Harry doesn't vaccinate all of John's donkeys because John owns still another donkey and Bill vaccinates it." The consistency of this added assertion indicates that no such uniqueness claim for the pronoun in (39) is warranted. Any such uniqueness claim is at best only a conversational implicature. Furthermore, it shows that the pronoun in (39) analyzed as a numberless description also fails since Harry does not vaccinate *all* the donkeys John owns.

Even if (39) were to be analyzed as a conjunction of two sentences, the second conjunct of which expresses a uniqueness claim, Neale's analysis would still fail to provide correct truth conditions for other sentences. For as a Russellian, he should accept the following rules of English regarding the scope of the negation operator:

Rule I: When we have a binary truth functional connective followed by "it is not the case that," then the negation is to be treated as a sentential operator applying to the second sentence of the (binary) truth functional connective.

For example, a sentence in English of the form 'A and it is not the case that B' or 'If A then it is not the case that B' should be expressed as 'A & ~B' and 'A → ~B', respectively.

Rule II: In a sentence that contains the expression 'not' before the predicate of the sentence, place the negation sign in front of the predicate of the sentence.

Applying these rules enables Neale to assign to sentences (40) and (41):

(40) If a man buys a donkey, then the present king of France does not vaccinate it

(41) If a man buys a donkey, then it is not the case that the present king of France vaccinates it

the correct truth conditions:

(40′) [an x: man x]([a y: donkey y](Bxy)) → [whe x: man x & [a y: donkey y](Bxy)]([whe y: donkey y & Bxy]([the z: Kz](~Vzy)))

(41′) [an x: man x]([a y: donkey y](Bxy)) → ~[whe x: man x & [a y: donkey y](Bxy)]([whe y: donkey y & Bxy]([the z: Kz](Vzy)))

respectively, where 'Kx' is to be interpreted as 'x is a present king of France'.

Now, although applying rule I to

(42) Pedro owns a donkey and it is not the case that Pedro beats it

correctly yields on Neale's analysis the following truth conditions:

(42′) [an x: donkey x](Owns(p,x)) & ~([the x: donkey x & Opx](Bp))

(i.e., (1) with the negation of the second conjunct), when we apply this rule to

(43) If a man is sick, then it is not the case that he is happy.

Neale's analysis is

(43′) [an x: man x](Sick x) → ~([the x: man x & Sick x](Hx)),

that is, a conditional with the negation operator applied to the consequent. But (43′) clearly does not have the same truth conditions as (43). For, (43′) in familiar quantification terminology is

(43″) $\exists x(\text{Man }(x) \ \& \ \text{Sick }(x)) \to \sim(\forall x((\text{Man }(x) \ \& \ \text{Sick }(x)) \to \text{Happy}(x)) \ \& \ \exists x(\text{Man}(x) \ \& \ \text{Sick}(x)),$

which, unlike (43), is true in the case where there is a sick man who is happy and a sick man who is not.[23]

In fact, Neale's analyses fail in general to provide correct truth conditions or consistent rules for sentences containing the phrase "it is not the case that" within the consequent of a conditional. They also fail to provide correct truth conditions or consistent rules for such sentences when a

---

23. Moreover, the situation cannot be rectified by treating the determiner 'the' as a plural or by changing the determiner to 'whe', that is, as expressing a number-less description. These, too, fail to provide the correct truth conditions for (43).

pronoun is anaphoric on an indefinite noun phrase embedded within the scope of a universal quantifier or within the antecedent of a conditional.

For example, suppose we apply rule II to

(44)   Every man who buys a donkey is not happy

and

(45)   If a man is sick, then he is not happy

to obtain on Neale's analysis

(44′)   [every x: man x & [a y: donkey y](Bxy)](~Hx)

and

(45′)   [an x: man x](sick x) → [whe x: man x & sick x](~Hx),

which yield correct truth conditions for (44) and (45), respectively.

But sentences equivalent in English do not turn out to be equivalent on Neale's analyses. Consider

(46)   If a man is sick, then it is not the case that he is happy,

which on Neale's analysis yields

(46′)   [an x: man x](Sx) →~[whe x: man x & Sx](Hx).

Now, although (45) and (46) are equivalent, their respective analyses are not. (46′) can be true if all but one sick man is happy, whereas (45′) provides the correct truth conditions, which require that all sick men be unhappy.

Consider also:

(47)   Every man who buys a donkey does not vaccinate it

(48)   If a man buys a donkey, then he does not vaccinate it

(49)   If a man buys a donkey, then it is not the case that he vaccinates it

Although these sentences are equivalent on the natural reading of all three, they fail to be so on Neale's analyses. Applying rule (2) to (47) correctly yields

(47′)   [every x: man x & [a y: donkey y](Bxy)]([whe y: donkey y & Bxy](~Vxy)).

Similarly, applying rule (2) to (48) correctly yields

(48′)   [an x: man x]([a y: donkey y](Bxy)) → [whe x: man x & [a y: donkey](Bxy)]([whe y: donkey y & Bxy](~Vxy)),

which is equivalent to (47′).

But in order for Neale to formalize (49), he must apply rule I; we then have

(49′) [an x: man x]([a y: donkey y](Bxy)) → ~[whe x: man x & [a y: donkey](Bxy)]([whe y: donkey y & Bxy](Vxy)) ,

which is allegedly equivalent to (47′) and (48′) expressed with external negation. But the truth condition for the consequent of (49′) is that it is not the case that for any man (who buys a donkey) and for any donkey that he buys, the man vaccinates that donkey. Unlike (47′) and (48′), (49′) is true if a man buys several donkeys and vaccinates all but one of them.

What these examples show is that Neale needs to make a distinction between external negation that is and external negation that is not equivalent to internal negation. For, in the vacuous description case, such as 'the present king of France', external negation is not equivalent to internal negation, while in the case of nonvacuous descriptions it is. But Neale cannot provide nonarbitrary and non–ad hoc syntactic (or even semantic) rules to make this distinction. For, it is a matter of fact, and not one of syntax, whether a given description is or is not vacuous.

7.3   Discourse Semantics, Dynamic Predicate Logic, and a Semantics for Monadic Second-Order Logic

We consider next the systems of Heim and Kamp,[24] which may be thought of as another defense of pronouns as bound variables. On their view, when we have an anaphoric expression within a discourse, nothing short of the entire discourse expresses a proposition, and only the entire discourse is to be assigned a truth value.[25]

24. For Discourse Representation Theory, see Hans Kamp, "A Theory of Truth and Semantic Representation," in J. Groenendijk, T. Janssen, and M. Stokhof, eds., *Formal Methods in the Study of Language* (Amsterdam: Mathematisch Centrum, 1981); Hans Kamp and Uwe Reyle, *From Discourse to Logic* (Dordrecht: Kluwer, 1993); Irene Heim, *The Semantics of Definite and Indefinite Noun Phrases*, Ph.D. diss., University of Massachusetts at Amherst, 1982. For Dynamic Predicate logic, see Jeroen Groenendijk and Martin Stokhof, "Dynamic Predicate Logic," *Linguistics and Philosophy* 14 (1991): 39–100.

25. In addition to the references in footnote 22, see also Irene Heim, "File Change Semantics and the Familiarity Theory of Definiteness," in R. Bauerle, C. Schwarze, and A. von Stechow, eds., *Meaning, Use and Interpretation of Language* (Berlin: de Gruyter, 1983), 164–189; Irene Heim, "On the Projection Problem For Presuppositions," in D. Flickinjer et al., eds., *Proceedings of the Second West Coast Conference on Formal Linguistics* (Stanford: Stanford University Press, 1983). Irene

Heim's formal semantics is based on Stalnaker's (1978) context change analysis of assertion with Karttunen's (1976) discourse referent analysis of indefinite noun phrases. Following Stalnaker, Heim (1982 and 1983, "File Change Semantics") makes fundamental use of a possible-world account of propositions, which is built into her semantics for a discourse containing an anaphoric expression. The meaning of a sentence is given by an algorithmic rule that determines the sentence's contribution to the proposition expressed by a given discourse containing that sentence. The basic idea of her semantics for a discourse is to start with the class of all possible worlds, which can be thought of as the initial context, or common ground. We are to consider in turn each sentence of the sequence of sentences constituting a discourse, and then eliminate those possible worlds incompatible with the sentence under consideration. Each such sentence with the context of possible worlds compatible with all prior sentences of the discourse form a new context consisting of those possible worlds in the above mentioned context *and* compatible with the given sentence under consideration. We are to form new contexts in this systematic manner, the end result of which is the class of possible worlds compatible with all the sentences in the discourse. This class of possible worlds is the proposition that, according to this semantics, the entire discourse expresses.

Kamp's semantical system, which he calls Discourse Representation Theory (DRT, hereafter), and Heim's are essentially the same in that they both assign truth conditions for an entire discourse by proceeding in effect with the same rules. Following Kamp, we are to proceed by means of what he calls *construction rules* for embedding natural language into formal structures that he calls *discourse representation structures*. Of special interest is his treatment of indefinite noun phrases and pronouns occurring in later sentences of the discourse, anaphoric upon these indefinite noun phrases. According to Kamp's construction rules, we first replace the article in the indefinite noun phrase with a variable to form an open sentence (e.g., from 'a boy' we obtain 'Boy x'). Next, the variable, which Kamp calls a "reference marker," is set aside to be used with other open sentences

---

Heim, "E-Type Pronouns and Donkey Anaphora," *Linguistics and Philosophy* 13 (1990): 137–177, seems to retract this claim and much of her former work, arguing instead for a modified version of Evans's E-type pronouns. Several of my objections to Kamp and Heim's earlier works are in this 1990 article.

formed from various sentences of the discourse containing pronouns anaphoric upon this indefinite noun phrase (e.g., from 'He is happy' we obtain 'Happy x'). These open sentences, or "conditions" as Kamp calls them, are all conjoined to form a conjunction of open sentences that places satisfaction conditions on the referent of an anaphorically used pronoun in a given discourse. These conditions are also part of the truth conditions for the whole discourse. The set-aside variables, or reference markers, together with these conditions, are the discourse representation structures (DRS, hereafter) for this discourse. Finally, since we have formed a conjunction of open sentences from all the sentences of the discourse, we may now bind the open sentence with an unrestricted quantifier determined by the construction rules governing the clause in which the noun phrase that introduced the variable occurs. Specifically, we bind the open sentence with an existential quantifier unless the noun phrase (or phrases) that introduces the variable (or variables) used in forming the open sentence is (or are) in the antecedent of a conditional clause or in a universal clause. In the case of the conditional sentence, we connect the antecedent to the consequent with the conditional connective and bind the result with a universal quantifier. A universal sentence, is, in effect, treated the same way. The result of this process is that only an entire discourse can have a truth condition, have a truth value, and express a proposition.

For example, the truth conditions for a discourse consisting of two sentences of the form 'Some P is Q' and 'He/she/it is R' is obtained by forming the open sentences, conjoining them to form '(Px & Qx & Rx)' and then binding the result with an existential quantifier to obtain a sentence of the form '$\exists x(Px \,\&\, Qx \,\&\, Rx)$'. The truth conditions for a discourse consisting of a sentence of the form 'If an A is a B, then it is a C' or of the form 'Each A that is a B is a C' is obtained by first forming the two open sentences 'Ax' and 'Bx', next conjoining them with a conjunction to form '(Ax & Bx)' and then connecting the result to the open sentence 'Cx' with a conditional to form '$((Ax \,\&\, Bx) \rightarrow Cx)$'. Last, we bind the result with a universal quantifier to obtain a sentence of the form '$\forall x((Ax \,\&\, Bx) \rightarrow Cx)$'.

The semantics for DRT is defined in terms of the notion of a *verifying embedding* of a DRS into a model M. Such an embedding is a function that assigns elements of the domain of M to the reference markers of the DRS such that *all conditions* of the DRS come out true in M. Further, *truth of a DRS in a model* M is defined in terms of the notion of a verifying embedding, in particular, as the existence of at least one verifying embedding for that *entire* DRS in M. In other words, truth in DRT requires the existence of a verifier (or verifiers) or a satisfier (or satisfiers) from this domain such that all the conditions contributed by each sentence of the discourse are satisfied.

One central problem with this approach is that there is no way to assign a truth value to individual sentences of a discourse. For example, consider, again, the following sentence:

Some woman will land on Mars in the year 2051.

Now let it again be the A-B sentence for the S-type term 'she' in

She will be an American.

Further suppose that someone disagrees and interjects:

She won't be an American; she will be a Russian.

It should be clear that in this discourse, one speaker is uttering a true sentence and the other speaker a false sentence regarding whether this person will be an American. But within the Kamp-Heim formal semantics, it is only this entire discourse that is assigned a truth value, and it must be assigned false. For the discourse contains contradictory sentences that, in effect, get treated as contradictory conjuncts and thus fails to hold in any possible world. Equivalently, the discourse is treated as containing contradictory, or impossible, conditions which cannot be conjointly satisfied. Thus the DRS representing the entire discourse fails to have at least one verifying embedding.

The problem is that only some sentences of the discourse restrict the truth conditions of sentences uttered in later conversation—in effect, by restricting the domain of possible satisfiers of an S-type term—while others do not. For example, in the discourse above, the sentence "she will be an American" does not restrict the truth conditions of the sentence "she will be a Russian." That is, any assignment to the S-type term 'she' in this sentence, though restricted to a member of the class of women who land on Mars in the year 2051, is not further restricted to the class of women who are American. But there is no way within the Kamp-Heim semantics to prevent some sentences from restricting the truth conditions of the discourse, or in effect, from restricting the domain of possible satisfiers of an occurrence of an S-type term that appears later in the discourse.

It may appear that in Dynamic Predicate Logic (DPL, hereafter), developed by Jeroen Groenendijk and Martin Stokhof, this problem is alleviated. But their semantics fares no better. This semantics is basically a modification or alternative formulation of Kamp's, designed to handle the principle of compositionality, which is lacking in the original formulation (1981) of Kamp's formal semantics.[26] Both the semantics of DRT and DPL assign the same truth conditions to a given discourse. Furthermore, DPL is still committed to assigning a truth value only to an entire discourse and to regarding only the entire discourse as expressing a proposition.

The difference between DRT and DPL is that the latter adds semantic interpretations to conjunctive and existentially quantified formulas. These interpretations are defined so that an existential quantifier, in effect, binds an occurrence of the same variable that appends to this quantifier even when the occurrence extends into a conjunct that lies outside the quantifier's syntactic scope (e.g., '$\exists x(Px \ \& \ Qx)$' in DPL has the same truth conditions as and is equivalent to '$\exists x(Px) \ \& \ Qx$').

To understand these interpretations, recall that in standard semantics of predicate logic, the interpretation of a formula may be thought of as a set of assignments, namely, those assignments that satisfy the formula in a given model M. In analogy with a "semantics" for programming languages, the interpretation of a formula Φ in DPL is thought of as a class of ordered pairs of assignments, "possible input–output pairs." Intuitively, we are to think of a given ordered pair, <g, h>, as "in the interpretation of a formula Φ" or as "satisfying Φ in a given model, M" if and only if when Φ is evaluated with respect to assignment g, h is a possible outcome of the evaluation procedure, that is, the output assignment h is to be construed as a possible assignment that satisfies Φ, with respect to input assignment g, in a given model M.

Accordingly, in evaluating a conjunct of a formula in conjunctive form, the input assignment is to be construed as a possible assignment that satisfies all conjuncts of the conjunction already evaluated in this procedure. The output is to be construed as a possible assignment that satisfies

---

26. Since then, Kamp and others have formulated DRT so that it can handle the principle of compositionality. See, for example, Jan van Eijck and Hans Kamp, "Representing Discourse in Context," in J. van Bentham and A. ter Meulen, eds., *Handbook of Logic and Language* (Cambridge, MA: MIT Press, 1997); R. Muskens, "Anaphora and the Logic of Change," in J. van Eijk, ed., *European Workshop on Logics in AI*, Springer Lecture Notes (Berlin: Springer-Verlag, 1991), 414–430, and R. Muskens, "Combining Montague Semantics and Discourse Representation," *Linguistics and Philosophy* 19: 143–186.

the conjunct under evaluation in this procedure, with respect to the given input assignment. This output assignment, in turn, becomes the input assignment in the evaluation of the next conjunct of the conjunction. (Similarly, if Ψ is a subformula of an existential formula Φ, the output assignment of Ψ becomes the input assignment of the next subformula in the evaluation procedure of Φ.) All assignments that satisfy the conjunction Φ are taken to be possible outputs with respect to input g. Truth for a formula Φ with respect to g is, in turn, defined as the existence of an output h that is in the interpretation of Φ, that is, the existence of a satisfier (from the domain of M) of the formula Φ.

DPL, like DRT, represents simple sentence sequencing in a discourse as conjunction, with each sentence of the discourse represented by an open sentence and the entire discourse represented as a conjunction of these open sentences all bound by the same quantifier. Each sentence of the sequence thus restricts the satisfier class of the discourse (or the formula Φ that represents the entire discourse).

So for both DRT and DPL, despite their differing terminology, truth is of an entire discourse, or of a formula Φ representing the entire discourse, and requires the existence of a satisfier assignment h from the domain of M such that each open sentence, or subformula, representing a sentence in the discourse is satisfied by h.

But that is precisely our problem for these systems: There is no way within the semantics of DRT or of DPL to prevent some sentences from restricting the class of possible assignments that satisfy later sentences in the discourse. A sentence Ψ within the context of a discourse does not have its own class of assignments in the interpretation of Ψ, and thus the sentence cannot be viewed as having a truth value. Rather, the class of possible assignments of a sentence Ψ in a given discourse is restricted to the class of assignments that satisfies every prior sentence in the discourse. That is, both DRT and DPL assign truth to only the entire discourse and require all sentences of a given discourse to be satisfied in order for the discourse to be assigned the truth value true. There is no way within these systems to assign a truth value to individual sentences of a discourse.

Further, we note that DPL, as formulated by Groenendijk and Stokhof, offer no construction rules for embedding simple plural pronouns, such as occur in (50), into a standard first-order language.

(50)   All apples on the table are red; *they* are tasty.

A more serious objection is that plural quantification as expressed in the Geach-Kaplan "critics" sentence ("Some critics admire only one another") cannot be formalized into DRT or DPL since the embedding language of these systems is a standard first-order language, and such sentences have been proven to be non-first-order formalizable.[27]

Irene Heim and Angelika Kratzer argue against the traditional linguistic distinction between "deictic" and "anaphoric" uses of a pronoun on the grounds that it has no semantical role to play in linguistic theory.[28] A pronoun is used *deictically* when it receives its reference from the extralinguistic context of utterance, such as an associated demonstration in the case of a demonstrative (as we have seen in discussing Kaplan in chapter 3). A term is used *anaphorically* if its referent is determined (at least in part) from another phrase or phrases in the surrounding text. According to Heim and Kratzer (and recent trends among certain generative syntacticians and many philosophers discussed earlier), there are some anaphorically used pronouns that do not differ in any theoretically relevant way regarding their semantics from deictic uses. These anaphoric uses of pronouns, according to Heim and Kratzer, are referential (or coreferential) and accordingly, like deictically used pronouns, are to be analyzed as free variables under an assignment.

According to Heim and Kratzer, intersentential anaphora must always involve coreference rather than variable binding. Their argument is based on certain syntactic constraints on movement; in particular, it would require the determiner phrase (DP, hereafter) to be "raised high enough to c-command the entire two-sentence text."[29] One consequence and advantage of this view over DRT and DPL (though Heim and Kratzer do not state this) is that, unlike those two systems, it can now assign truth values to individual sentences in a discourse. For if such anaphorically used pronouns always involve coreference, they are free variables under an assignment in the sentences in which they occur. There is no quantifier from

27. Simple plural pronominalization, such as (6), can be represented in later formulations of DRT. See, for example, Kamp and Reyle, *From Discourse to Logic*. Their formulations cannot, however, represent complex plural quantification, such as the Geach-Kaplan "critics" sentence.

28. Irene Heim and Angelika Kratzer, *Semantics in Generative Grammar* (Oxford: Basil Blackwell, 1998).

29. Heim and Kratzer, *Semantics in Generative Grammar*, 241.

another sentence that binds the variable and thus forces us to treat both sentences as one.

Nevertheless, Heim and Kratzer's argument that certain syntactic constraints on movement require that intersentential anaphora must always involve coreference rather than variable binding is not convincing. When certain syntactic constraints conflict with intuitive semantic principles regarding the binding of a variable, linguists should give up the view that there is always a match between syntactic structure and semantic representation, and furthermore the view that the former must always constrain and dictate the form of the latter. Semantic intuitions must not be flouted for the sake of syntactic rules. Rather, the conclusion that should be drawn from the above conflict is that binding theory does not belong entirely to syntax.[30]

Moreover, Heim and Kratzer's claim regarding intersentential anaphora and coreference conflicts with another claim of theirs, namely, that whenever an anaphoric pronoun has a quantifier as its antecedent, it cannot be referential. "Anaphoric pronouns with quantifier antecedents are the paradigm cases of bound variable pronouns."[31] Now these two claims are incompatible.

Consider, for example, the following:

(51)   Some students in the class are intelligent. They will do well in graduate school.

The anaphoric pronoun 'they' has a quantifier expression as its anaphoric antecedent. Thus according to Heim and Kratzer, it should be analyzed as a bound variable. But since this is a case of intersentential anaphora, they are also committed to the claim that this must involve coreference rather than variable binding.

According to Heim and Kratzer, there are also pronouns that are neither bound variables nor referential. An example they offer is the following:

(52)   Every host bought just one bottle of wine and served it with the dessert.

---

30. Linguists who present views similar to my own in this respect are Peter W. Culicover and Ray Jackendoff. See their "*Something Else* for the Binding Theory," *Linguistic Inquiry* 26, 2 (Spring 1995): 249–275, and "Semantic Subordination despite Syntactic Coordination," *Linguistic Inquiry* 28, 2 (Spring 1997).

31. Heim and Kratzer, *Semantics in Generative Grammar*, 245.

According to them, the pronoun 'it' in (52) cannot have a bound variable analysis since (52) does not have the truth conditions of "for every host, there is just one bottle that he bought and served with dessert."[32] But 'it' in (52) is not referential either. For, they argue, "What could its referent possibly be? The bottle of wine that host John bought? If that were its reference, [(52)] should mean that every host bought just one bottle of wine and then served the one that John bought for dessert."[33]

Now, of course, it is correct that (52) does not have the truth conditions stated in quotation marks. But it is incorrect to conclude from this, as do Heim and Kratzer, that the pronoun 'it' in (52) should not be analyzed as a bound variable. This conclusion, as we have seen earlier in discussing Evans, is a mistake. All one can conclude from the fact that (52) does not have the truth conditions stated in quotation marks is that the pronoun 'it' in (52) is not bound by its antecedent quantifier Determiner Phrase, 'every host'. When linguists speak of a pronoun's occurring not as a bound variable, they usually mean that its antecedent quantifier Determiner Phrase does not bind the variable occurrence representing the pronoun. But to conclude from this that an occurrence of such a pronoun as, say, in (52) is not to be represented by an occurrence of a bound variable is a mistake.

Sentence (52) is similar in structure to the kind of sentences that have led McKinsey, Soames, and Neale to argue that E-type pronouns are not rigid designators. What all these sentences structurally have in common is that they are all sentences containing a conjunction sign and a pronoun occurring after the conjunction sign. The pronoun is anaphoric upon a nonrigid expression that occurs before the conjunction sign. In a way similar to the McKinsey-Soames-Neale view, Heim and Kratzer's view is that E-type pronouns can always be paraphrased by certain definite descriptions. In particular, Heim and Kratzer analyze the pronoun 'it' in (52) as having the same semantics as the Determiner Phrase '*the bottle* of wine y (that) host x bought'. Accordingly, they paraphrase (52) as

(53) Every host bought just one bottle of wine and served *the bottle of wine he had bought* with the dessert.[34]

32. Heim and Kratzer, *Semantics in Generative Grammar*, 288.
33. Heim and Kratzer, *Semantics in Generative Grammar*, 288.
34. Heim and Kratzer, *Semantics in Generative Grammar*, 288.

But as we have already seen, this analysis does not even preserve the same truth conditions. (Since the pronoun 'it' is rigid but the above definite description in (53) is not, simply place a modal operator just after the word 'and' in (52) and (53), respectively, to reveal the different truth conditions.)

Be that as it may, Heim and Kratzer adopt an analysis due to Robin Cooper[35] that the pronoun in (52) is an E-type pronoun that is to be analyzed as a definite description together with a two-place predicate containing a bound variable as well as a free variable. By means of a standard technique of reducing n-place predicates to one-place predicates known as Currying (or the Schonfinkelization of) n-place predicates, the two-place predicate can be thought of as a function mapping individuals into a one-place predicate. The intuitive idea applied to the pronoun in (52) is that the two-place predicate is 'x bought *just one* bottle y', where the "free variable" is y and the bound variable is x, in this case bound by the universal quantifier, 'every host x'. In this way, the values of the "free" variable covaries with the values assigned to the bound variable after removing the quantifier that binds this variable. Alternatively, we may treat the two-place predicate as a characteristic function for a relation R, mapping ordered pairs of arguments into 1 or 0, respectively, depending upon whether the ordered pair bears the relation R, that is, whether the ordered pair is in the extension of the predicate representing R. We are to consider the member of the ordered pair assigned to the "free variable" as dependent upon the other member of the ordered pair assigned to the bound variable after removing the quantifier binding the bound variable.

But both variables, x, a host, and y, the bottle bought by x, are not free in an analysis of (52). We have already seen this in discussing the McKinsey-Soames-Neale position on E-type pronouns. As Bertrand Russell taught us, definite descriptions and uniqueness conditions are analyzed as having their variables bound by existential quantifiers. Russell had envisioned such cases as that above and developed his theory of descriptions precisely to deal with such or analogous cases. Consider, for example, the following:

(54)   Just one person authored *Waverley* and he is Scottish.

35. See R. Cooper, "The Interpretation of Pronouns," in F. Heny and H. Schnelle, eds., *Syntax and Semantics, Vol. 10: Selections from the Third Groningen Round Table* (New York Academic Press, 1979), 61–92.

Analogous to example (52), (54) cannot be analyzed as (55)

(55)   Just one person authored *Waverley* and is Scottish.

Unlike (54), (55) is compatible with more than one person authoring *Waverley*, but only one of them being Scottish. But this is not an argument showing that, therefore, the pronoun in (54) is not bound to the Determiner Phrase 'just one person'. As Russell taught us, the pronoun 'he' is a variable bound to the existential quantifier in the formalization of 'just one person authored *Waverley*'.

Analogous remarks apply to the pronoun in (52). After removing the universal and existential quantifiers of x and y, respectively, the value of y, the bottle bought by x, will covary with the host that we assign to x. But the pronoun 'it' in (52) is represented by a bound occurrence of the variable y.

Finally, we consider the proposal of Heim and Kratzer for the semantics of a variable under an assignment. Given a context utterance c and a variable assignment g_c, determined by c (if at all), they formulate the following appropriateness condition for logical forms, LFs, with free pronouns.

(56)   *Appropriateness Condition:* A context c is *appropriate* for an LF ϕ only if c determines a variable assignment g_c whose domain includes every index which has a free occurrence in ϕ.[36]

This condition is trivially true as long as we are dealing with pronouns used like demonstratives, that is, deictic uses of pronouns. But as we mentioned above, a central semantic thesis of Heim and Kratzer regarding pronouns is that the traditional linguistic distinction between "deictic" and "anaphoric" uses of pronouns has no semantical role to play in linguistic theory. Thus there are many anaphoric uses of pronouns that they analyze as free variables under an assignment in a given context. But as we have seen, their examples that certain anaphoric uses of pronouns are to be treated this way is not convincing. Accordingly, the semantic distinction between "deictic" and "anaphoric" uses of pronouns appears intact. Nevertheless, if they wish to incorporate anaphoric uses of pronouns as free variables under an assignment, a lot more has to be said about contexts of utterance. But they mention nothing further. There is no mention, for example, of which parameters constitute a context of utterance. Hence it

36. Heim and Kratzer, *Semantics in Generative Grammar*, 243.

is not at all clear what in the context determines the assignment to the variable when the pronoun is used anaphorically and analyzed as a free variable under an assignment.

Heim and Kratzer claim that as semanticists it is not their concern to formulate what determines such an assignment. This attitude may be reasonable with regard to a deictic use of a pronoun. But assignments to anaphoric uses of pronouns are dependent upon semantic features of the term's anaphoric background. Consequently, it clearly is part of the semanticist's task to discover rules that determine the binding or assignment to the pronoun. Indeed, to present an algorithm that determines this is a central task attempted in DRT and DPL.

What is missing from Heim and Kratzer's semantic account of any kind of anaphoric use of pronouns, as with Kaplan's account (discussed in chapter 3), is the role of A-B sentences and anaphoric chains in determining what value we assign to the variable that represents the anaphoric pronoun (after removing the quantifier that binds it). In particular, it is the A-B sentence of an anaphoric term and the anaphoric chain in which that term occurs that is essential in determining its referent by determining its Pronominal Satisfier Class. (Remember that the PSC is the class from which we may choose a referent for the S-type term the A-B condition of which helped to determine this class.) An assignment of a value to a free variable that represents such a pronoun must come from this class. In the next chapter, I present a formal semantics that makes precise the notion of an anaphoric chain and present some rules that determine the PSC for a term, given the anaphoric chain in which the term occurs.

I end this chapter with a few brief comments on George Boolos's semantics for plural quantification. It is well known that certain kinds of plural quantification cannot be formalized in standard first-order logic, that is, by a formal language containing variables x, y, z, . . . , ranging over individuals, the quantifiers $\forall$ and $\exists$, the truth-functional connectives and the equal sign. The most famous example is perhaps the Geach-Kaplan sentence

(57)   Some critics admire only one another.

Although this sentence can be formalized in second-order monadic logic as

(58) $\exists X(\exists x Xx \,\&\, \forall y \forall z[Xy \,\&\, Admires(y,z)) \rightarrow (y \neq z \,\&\, Xz)])$,

the standard interpretation of the second-order variable is to have it range over classes. Yet many people's ordinary intuitions regarding sentence (57) is that it need only be about individual critics. In order to remedy this problem, George Boolos presents a new interpretation of second-order monadic logic variables without requiring quantifying over classes.[37] His new interpretation of the second-order quantifier '∃V' is 'there are some Vs such that', and his new interpretation of the wff 'Vv' is 'v is one of the Vs'. He achieves this by adding to the language of second-order set theory a new predicate containing two first-order variables 's' and 'F', and one second-order variable, R (where R and the sequence s satisfy the formula F) that is assigned some (or perhaps no) ordered pairs of second-order variables and first-order objects. One may then define 'x is a value of the second-order variable V with respect to R' as 'R<V,x>'. The second-order formula, *Vv*, consisting of a second-order and first-order variable, respectively, is satisfied by R and a sequence, s, of first-order objects iff R<V,s(v)>. The intuitive interpretation of 'R<V,x>' is that R<V,x> holds iff x is one of the plurality of objects assigned to the second-order variable V.

Although the truth conditions that our respective semantics assign to the Geach-Kaplan sentence are the same, both our syntax and model theory differ. In my system, such sentences of plural quantification are analyzed as complex plural pronominalization (a view to which Boolos was sympathetic). Since all variables range over first-order objects, I do not make use of a second-order language as such. Instead, I employ devices that make it more perspicuous as to what we are pronominalizing on. Hence the anaphoric relations are more perspicuous as well. Further, my semantics can also formalize intersentential binding. Anaphoric relations, intersentential binding, and plural quantification all are treated as one problem and receive a uniform treatment within my semantics.[38]

37. For an excellent discussion and defense of this view, as well as a presentation of how the Geach-Kaplan sentence may be treated semantically in second-order logic, see George Boolos, "To Be Is To Be a Value of a Variable (Or To Be Some Values of Some Variables)," *The Journal of Philosophy* 84 (1984): 430–449. Also see his "Nominalist Platonism," *The Philosophical Review* 94 (1985): 327–344. I wish to thank the late George Boolos for carefully going through my model-theoretic semantics and for our discussions on the relation of my semantics of plural quantification with his.

38. Unlike Boolos, I have no interest in taking up other questions, such as whether plural quantification is "really" logic—for example, is ontologically neutral, general, and has a natural extension to n-adic second-order logic. I also do not have nominalist scruples.

8

A Formal Semantics for Plural Quantification, Intersentential Binding, and Anaphoric Pronouns as Rigid Designators

As chapter 7 made clear, there are two main challenges to the formalization of parts of natural language by the devices of standard first-order logic: plural quantification as represented in the Geach–Kaplan critics sentence, and sentences containing anaphoric pronouns bound to quantifier antecedents in prior sentences of a discourse.

In this chapter, I present a formal language and a model-theoretic semantics (hereafter, "a formal model structure") for such plural quantification and for anaphoric expressions requiring intersentential binding.

In section 8.1, I offer some examples of formalization in our language. In section 8.2, I present a formal language and also introduce an operator that will enable us to formalize the notions of *one of them, some of them,* and *all of them*. In order to construct our model-theoretic semantics, I then introduce and make precise the notions of *anaphoric chain* and *pronominal satisfier class*. Our model-theoretic semantics will interpret this language as an extension of first-order quantification theory.

It is my view that both plural quantification of the Geach-Kaplan variety and intersentential cross-reference make essential use of anaphora. Our model theory thus presents a uniform representation for the same anaphoric expressions. Moreover, it permits anaphoric pronouns and phrases to be viewed as rigid designators. Unlike the systems of Heim and Kamp, it does not require a possible-world account of propositions.

It is important to distinguish my project from that of linguists. One central task of linguists is to develop precise algorithmic, or "construction," rules for translating parts of natural language into their representation in a formal language. The development of the embedding formal language need not concern linguists. One central task of logicians is to present formal systems and a formal semantics for such systems. The development of algorithms for embedding parts of natural language into such formal systems need not concern logicians. My project is that of a logician.

A word of caution is in order. First, when I say that we want to assign a truth value to individual sentences of a discourse, I do not mean that if a sentence, say,

(1)   Some woman will land on Mars in the year 2051,

is false, we can nevertheless assign an independent truth value to any sentence containing an expression anaphoric upon some expression in (1), such as

(2)   *She* will be an American.

If the A-B sentence is false, then sentences anaphoric upon expressions in this sentence cannot be true. In fact, it is my view that the truth of the A-B sentence is a presupposition for sentences anaphoric upon expressions in it to have a truth value. Thus sentences containing anaphoric expressions will not have a truth value independently of the truth value of its A-B sentence and the like, as we see and specify in section 8.1. But these constraints, unlike those of Kamp, Heim, and Groenendijk and Stokhoff, are basically limited only by the A-B sentence of the anaphoric expression of the discourse, not by every sentence in the discourse, as their systems require. Second, when I say that my project is to present a model-theoretic semantics for plural quantification and intersentential binding, I am not making the additional claim that meaning is to be identified with truth conditions. My project is independent of any particular philosphical views on what a theory of meaning for natural language should be like.

8.1   Some Examples of Formalization in the Extended Language

We now indicate, through examples, how our extended first-order language, L_A, may be used to formalize anaphoric discourse, that is, discourse that contains one or more occurrences of expressions, such as pronouns, used anaphorically. Our first example is as follows:

Example 1:
Some students are passing the course.
Some of them (i.e., some of those students who are passing) are intelligent.
Some of *those* (i.e., students who are passing who are intelligent) will go to graduate school.

We now show how this chain of sentences can be formalized in our language.

The first sentence is normally formalized, in first-order logic, as

(3) $(\exists x(Sx \,\&\, Px))$,

where 'Sx' is interpreted as 'x is a student' and 'Px' as 'x is passing'. This sentence serves as an A-B sentence for the pronouns 'those' and 'them' occurring in the last two sentences of the chain. In order to formalize such sentences as these, which contain an anaphoric expression, we introduce *superscripted* variables. Whereas unsuperscripted variables range over the entire domain, superscripted variables have their range restricted to a given subset of the entire domain and may be further restricted as the formalization of the discourse progresses. We specify the initial range of a superscripted variable at this initial stage by indicating some (usually open) sentence that each member of the range of the variable must satisfy. We call the range of the superscripted variable "the pronominal satisfier class" (hereafter, the *PSC*), which is determined at this initial stage by that open sentence.

Accordingly, in order to formalize the second sentence, which contains the expression 'some of them' used anaphorically, we first introduce a superscripted variable, x^1, and we let its range, or PSC, be determined by the open sentence '$Sx^1 \,\&\, Px^1$'. Thus in example 1, the PSC for the superscripted variable x^1 at this initial stage is the class of students who are passing. Since the range of the superscripted variable x^1, is *restricted* to the members of its PSC, what we are saying in the second sentence is that some of *them* (i.e., some passing students) are intelligent. That is, we are pronominalizing on the PSC of x^1 as determined at this stage. Accordingly, we write

(4) $(\exists x^1 Ix^1)\,[(Sx^1 \,\&\, Px^1)]$,

where '$(\exists x^1 Ix^1)$' is the *formalization* of the second sentence and the *bracketed expression* '$[(Sx^1 \,\&\, Px^1)]$' specifies the range, or PSC of x^1, (and indeed of any variable with superscript '1' at this stage). Thus we could have used, for example, the variable y^1 instead of x^1 in (4).

Intuitively, an existential quantifier binding a superscripted variable is taken to mean the same as "some (at least one) of them" or "he," "she," or "it." A universal quantifier binding a superscripted variable in a sentence is taken to mean the same as "all of them" or "they." In each case, the occurrence of the superscripted variable that represents the anaphoric pronoun refers back to a member or members of the PSC determined at that stage of the anaphoric chain or, as we will see, sometimes at earlier stages in the anaphoric chain.

In order to formalize the third sentence of our example, we need to *restrict further* the PSC of x^1 to those passing students that are intelligent. We represent this further restriction of x^1 as follows: $[Ix^1]$. We then write the formalization of the third sentence and the additional restriction on the PSC as follows:

(5) $(\exists x^1 Gx^1) [Ix^1]$,

where the PSC for the superscripted variable x^1 at this stage is restricted to objects satisfying all the open sentences determining the PSC for x^1 at prior stages, that is, from the lines above, and is further restricted to objects satisfying the bracketed open sentence, $[Ix^1]$. Thus the range of the variable x^1 as it occurs in (5) is now the class of passing students who are intelligent. (We note that we could have used any variable with superscript '1', e.g., y^1.) Where a variable with a given superscript occurs at a line in which there is no bracketed well-formed formula (henceforth wff) containing a free occurrence of a variable with that superscript, the stage of a variable with that superscript at that line is to be the stage of the PSC for a variable with that superscript as determined at the last stage prior to that line.

Intuitively, if there is a sentence of an anaphoric discourse formalized as '$(\exists x(Ax \ \& \ Bx))$', and later a sentence as '$(\exists x^s Cx^s) [(Ax^s \ \& \ Bx^s)]$', where 's' is a superscript, then the sentences of the chain mean the same as "Some As are Bs; some of them (those As that are Bs) are Cs." Any further occurrence of a variable with the same superscript s, intended to refer back to (some or all) As that are Bs that are Cs, will require that we restrict further the PSC for a variable with the superscript 's' by specifying in brackets 'Cx^s'. For example, if we go on to say "some of those (As that are Bs that are Cs) are (also) Ds," we would express the form of this sentence as '$(\exists x^s Dx^s) [Cx^s]$'. If we wish, instead, to say "they (all of them) are (also) Ds" (i.e., those As that are Bs that are also Cs are also Ds), we would then express the form of this sentence as '$(\forall x^s Dx^s) [Cx^s]$'.

Let us consider next, the anaphoric discourse:

Example 2:
There is a boy.
There is a girl.

He loves her.
She loves him.

The first two sentences are formalized as

(6) $(\exists x Bx)$

(7) $(\exists y Gy)$

Here the first two sentences serve as A-B sentences for the pronouns 'he', 'she', 'her', and 'him', which occur in the last two sentences of the chain. In the third sentence, the singular pronoun 'he' refers back to a member of the class of boys, and the singular pronoun 'her' refers back to a member of the class of girls. In order to pronominalize on members of the two classes, boys and girls, respectively, we introduce two superscripted variables, 'x^1' and 'y^2'. The PSC for 'x^1' is the satisfier class for the open sentence 'Bx^1', obtained from (1) by removing the quantifier. Similarly, the PSC for 'y^2' is the satisfier class for the open sentence 'Gy^2', obtained from (2) by removing the quantifier. Then in our extended language, we may formalize the third sentence of example 2 and indicate the PSCs as follows:

(8) $(\exists x^1 (\exists y^2 Lx^1 y^2))$ $[Bx^1]$ $[Gy^2]$.

Notice that the pronouns 'she' and 'him' in the fourth sentence of example 2 refer, respectively, to the same objects as the pronouns 'her' and 'he' in the third sentence. We thus need to represent coreference in our extended language. Accordingly, the fourth sentence may be formalized as

(9) $Ly\,^2x^1$.

The occurrences of the superscripted variables 'x^1' and 'y^2' in the wff in (9) do not have quantifiers binding these occurrences, respectively, in the wff in which these occurrences appear. Nevertheless, there are quantifiers binding variables with the same superscript, respectively, in the prior (8). The occurrences of a superscripted variable in (9) are *covarying occurrences of a superscripted variable;* the values they are assigned covary with the values assigned to the occurrences of the variable with the same respective superscript that lies within the matrix of the wff on line (8). Consequently, if we are to satisfy the wff in (9) containing these covarying occurrences, they must be assigned the same value as that assigned to occurrences of variables with the same respective superscript that occur in (8) after removing the respective quantifiers that have these variables bound.

In our semantics, the respective values assigned to the covarying occurrences of the superscripted variables that lie within the matrix of the wff appearing in (8) (after removing the quantifier binding these occurrences) must be assigned to the variables with the same superscript in the wff in (9) in order for that wff to be satisfied. We may thus think of these respective values assigned to the covarying occurrences of superscripted variables in (8) as parameters. Accordingly, we call a covarying occurrence of a superscripted variable that lies within the matrix of a wff containing a quantifier binding this occurrence, a *parametric covarying occurrence.* An occurrence of a variable with the same superscript in a wff occurring at a later line and lacking within the wff a quantifier binding the variable we shall call a *dependent covarying occurrence of a variable with that superscript.* All dependent covarying occurrences of superscripted variables have parametric covarying occurrences and are to preserve coreference (under an assignment) with their parametric covarying occurrences.

This semantics applied to (9) assigns the dependent covarying occurrences of superscripted variables in (9) the same value as that assigned to their respective parametric covarying occurrences at line (8). Thus (9) may be interpreted as saying of a girl who is loved by some boy that she (i.e., *that girl* who is loved by *that boy*) loves that boy.

A given wff containing a dependent covarying occurrence of a variable in the chain that appears after a line containing a wff with the parametric covarying occurrence of the variable is to be satisfied if (i) the value assigned to its dependent occurrence of the variable will be (a) the same value as that assigned to the parametric covarying occurrence of the variable after removing the quantifier expression to the wff containing the parametric occurrence and (b) that value assigned will be a member of the PSC for a variable with that superscript at the stage of the PSC at the line in which the given wff containing the dependent covarying occurrences of a variable appear (in this case, the PSC at that stage for x^1 and x^2 is the class of boys and the class of girls, respectively); (ii) the wff containing the parametric occurrence is satisfied; and (iii) the value assigned to the dependent occurrence of the given wff is in the extension of this open wff, that is, satisfies the given open wff in the chain containing the dependent occurrence of the variable. The given wff need not require other wffs of the chain that contain dependent occurrences of a variable with that superscript to be satisfied in order for this given wff to be satisfied, however, as we see in our next example.

The next example illustrates how to formalize an anaphoric chain in which some sentences containing an S-type term do *not* further restrict the range of values of the PSC. Thus, some later wffs in the chain (perhaps said by another speaker) may be true, while earlier wffs may be false. Of course, as we have previously noted, the A-B sentence (or sentences) must be true in order for the other sentences containing the S-type term to have a truth value.

Example 3:
Consider again the conversation:
Some woman will land on Mars in the year 2051.
She will be an American.
She won't be American; she will be Russian.

The conversation of example 3 will be rendered as follows:

(10) $(\exists x(Wx^1 \& Lx^1))[(Wx^1 \& Lx^1)]$,

where the predicates 'Wx^1' and 'Lx^1' are interpreted as 'x^1 is a woman' and 'x^1 lands on Mars in the year 2051', respectively.

(11) Ax^1

(12) $\sim Ax^1$

(13) Rx^1

In (12), the range of the superscripted variable 'x^1' is *not* further restricted from the class of people who satisfy both being a woman and being someone who lands on Mars in the year 2051 to those women who are also Americans. Thus (11) can be false while (12) or (13) can be true.

There are cases in which we may formalize an anaphoric chain without explicitly specifying the PSC. Where this occurs, the PSC is the entire domain. Accordingly, we may formalize the above anaphoric chain of sentences as follows:

(10′) $(\exists x^1(Wx^1 \& Lx^1))$

(11′) Ax^1

1. In not further restricting the range of the variable in (12) to the class of Americans, we are, in effect, assuming that (11) is *not* taken as part of the anaphoric background. Given the right context, however, it would be just as plausible to suppose that (11) is part of the anaphoric background, and thus the range in (12) would be further restricted.

(12')   ~Ax^1

(13')   Rx^1

Notice, first, that in (10') we make use of a superscripted variable, but we do not specify the range of its PSC. Where this is the case, the PSC for the superscripted variable is the entire domain. Second, (10') contains parametric covarying occurrences of a variable for a given superscript, and all the other links in the chain contain dependent covarying occurrences of a variable with that superscript. Thus the occurrence of variable, x^1, in lines (11'), (12'), and (13') must be assigned the same value as that assigned to the parametric covarying occurrence of x^1 in line (10'). There are no further restrictions to the occurrences of dependent covarying variables on these lines.

Neither Kamp's nor Heim's systems, nor their variant DPL, can give correct truth conditions for the above discourse. On their approach, such a discourse must always express a false proposition. Their analysis renders the truth conditions of the discourse in example 3 as

($\exists$x(Wx & Lx & Ax & ~Ax & Rx),

which contains contradictory conjuncts. That our semantics assigns truth values to each sentence of a discourse and allows for some of them to have a truth value independently of the truth value of others is one of the central differences between our semantics and DRT or DPL and one major advantage of our system over theirs.

Our next example, from Strawson, illustrates a case where, unlike in example 3, it is coherent for someone in the dialogue to renege even on the very first sentence of the dialogue.

Example 4:

A man was leaning against a window and fell out.
He didn't fall; he was pushed.

The dialogue will be rendered as follows:

(14)   ($\exists$x(Mx & Lx & Fx)),

where the predicates 'Mx', 'Lx,' and 'Fx' are interpreted, respectively, as 'x is a man', 'x is leaning against a window,' and 'x fell out the window'.

(15)   ~Fc,

where the constant 'c' denotes the unique individual to whom the discussants are referring.

(16) Pc,

where 'Px' is interpreted as 'x is pushed'.

Unlike in example 3, in example 4 the dialogue presupposes some (shared) anaphoric background not mentioned in the dialogue, such as "the man discussed in the newspapers." This anaphoric background establishes a reference to a unique individual referred to in the dialogue by the pronoun 'he', which we represent by the constant c. Thus sentence (14) is not the A-B sentence for the dialogue. It is for this reason that, unlike in example 3, it is coherent for a speaker of the dialogue to renege even on sentence (14), and for sentence (14) to be assigned the truth value false while the rest of the sentences in the discourse may be assigned the truth value true. The anaphoric referential connection between sentence (14) and the rest of the dialogue is based upon speaker's reference, rather than semantic reference, that is shared by both speakers and that goes back to some presupposed A-B sentence not mentioned in the dialogue.

Here again, DRT and DPL cannot give correct truth conditions for a discourse that involves such pronominalization. Again, according to these systems, such a discourse must express a false proposition. The truth condition that these systems assign to this discourse is

$(\exists x(Mx \ \& \ Lx \ \& \ Fx \ \& \ {\sim}Fx \ \& \ Px),$

which, once again, contains contradictory conjuncts.

Our next three examples (along with example 1) illustrate how we restrict the range of values of a variable representing a pronoun the A-B statement of which carries existential force. We say that a sentence carries existential force if in order for a sentence to be true certain kinds of things have to exist. A sentence carries existential force if and only if its subject phrase includes an existential expression such as 'there are', 'many', 'some', or 'not all'. We present rules for specifying the PSC for pronouns the A-B sentences of which carry existential force below. Consider:

Example 5:
Some students who are passing are learning a lot.
They will go to college.

(17) $(\exists x((Sx \ \& \ Px) \ \& \ Lx))$

(18) $(\forall x^1 Cx^1) \ [(Sx^1 \ \& \ Px^1) \ \& \ Lx^1]$

Let us consider next:

Example 6:
Not all students are passing, but they are learning something anyway.

(19) $(\sim(\forall x(Sx \to Px)))$ & $(\forall x^1 Lx^1)$ $[Sx^1 \ \& \sim Px^1]$

Example 7:
Tom owns some sheep and Harry vaccinated them.

(20) $(\exists x(Sx \ \& \ Otx))$ & $(\forall x^1 Vhx^1)$ $[Sx^1 \ \& \ Otx^1]$

Our next three examples illustrate how we restrict the range of values of a variable used in representing a pronoun the A-B statement of which is a universal statement. We present rules for specifying the PSC for pronouns the A-B statements of which are the universal statements that follow.

Example 8:
All apples are fruit.
They (all of them) are edible.

We may formalize the previous two sentences as follows:

(21) $(\forall x(Ax \to Fx))$

(22) $(\forall x^1 Ex^1)$ $[Ax^1]$

In (22) we restricted the range of values of the variable, x^1, to members of the class of apples.

Our next example involves an existential expression containing a pronoun the A-B statement of which is a universal statement.

Example 9:
All apples are fruit.
Some of them are tasty.

(23) $(\forall x(Ax \to Fx))$

(24) $(\exists x^1 Tx^1)$ $[Ax^1]$

We now illustrate how we restrict the range of values of a variable representing a pronoun whose A-B statement is a universal statement of the form 'no A's are B's'.

Example 10:
No MPs came to the party.
They had a good time anyway.

(25) $(\forall x(Mx \to (\sim Px)))$

(26) $(\forall x^1 G x^1) [M x^1]$

Intuitively, when we pronominalize on a term that appears after a universal quantifier expression ('all', 'each', 'every', 'no', and so on), we restrict the PSC for the variable representing the pronoun to the denotation class of the pronominalized term.

The next two examples illustrate various kinds of restrictions of the PSC.

Example 11:
There are boys.
There are girls.
Some boys love some girls.
Some of them (girls who are loved by some boy) love some boys (but not necessarily the boys who love or who love them).

(27) $(\exists x B x)$

(28) $(\exists y G y)$

(29) $(\exists x^1 (\exists y^2 \, L x^1 y^2)) [B x^1][G y^2]$

(30) $(\exists x^1 (\exists y^2 L y^2 x^1)) [(\exists x (B x \;\&\; L x y^2))]$

Here the range of values of y^2 is restricted to girls loved by some boys, and the range of values of x^1 is restricted to boys.

Example 12:
There are boys.
There are girls.
Some boys love some girls.
Some of them (girls who are loved by some boys) love some of those boys (i.e., boys who love girls, but not necessarily the boys who love *them*).

(31) $(\exists x B x)$

(32) $(\exists y G y)$

(33) $(\exists x^1 (\exists y^2 L x^1 y^2)) [B x^1] [G y^2]$

(34) $(\exists x^1 (\exists y^2 L y^2 x^1)) [(\exists y^2 L x^1 y^2)] [(\exists x^1 L x^1 y^2)]$

Here the range of values of x^1 is restricted to boys who love girls, and the range of values of y^2 is restricted to girls who are loved by boys.

Example 13:
There are boys.

There are girls.
Some boys love every girl.
They (all the girls) love some boy (or other).

(35) $(\exists xBx)$

(36) $(\exists yGy)$

(37) $(\exists x^1(\forall y^2Lx^1y^2))\,[Bx^1]\,[Gy^2]$

(38) $(\exists x^1Ly^2x^1)$

The next example shows how we may iterate the operation of superscription, that is, apply it to a variable that is already superscripted.

Example 14:
Some A's are B's.
Some of them are C's.
Certain of those C's are D's.
Some others are E's.

Here the pronominal phrases are 'some of them', 'certain of those' and 'some others'.

The first two sentences are formalized as follows:

(39) $(\exists x(Ax \,\&\, Bx))$

(40) $(\exists x^1Cx^1)\,[(Ax^1 \,\&\, Bx^1)]$

In order to formalize the remaining two sentences, we introduce a multiply superscripted variable, $x^{1,2}$. A superscript 'j' applied to a superscripted variable 'v^i', forms a superscripted variable '$v^{i,j}$', the range of which is a certain subset of the PSC of the initial superscripted variable v^i. A universal quantifier binding a multiply superscripted variable can be read as "all of some of them," that is, all the members of that subset. An existential quantifier binding a multiply superscripted variable can be read as "some of some of them," that is, at least one member of the subset. In practice, we will not bother with an existential quantifier, since "some of some of them" is equivalent to "some of them."

Accordingly, we may then write:

(41) $(\forall x^{1,2}Dx^{1,2})\,[Cx^1]$ (i.e., all members of a certain subset of the class of things that are A's and B's that are C's are D's).

We come now to the fourth line where the pronominal phrase 'some others' appears. Here we need to introduce another multiply superscripted variable, $x^{1,3}$, the range of which must have no members in common with that of $x^{1,2}$. Then to formalize the fourth line,

Some others are E's,

we use a combination of two formal expressions. The first formal expression

(42) $(\forall x^{1,3} E x^{1,3})\,[C x^1]$

tells us that all members of a certain subset of the class of things that are As and Bs that are Cs are Es. The second one tells us that no member of the range of $x^{1,2}$ is identical with a member of the range of $x^{1,3}$ (i.e., *some other* things that are A's and B's that are C's are E's).

(43) $(\forall x^{1,2}(\forall y^{1,3}(x^{1,2} \neq y^{1,3})))$

The next example utilizes several of the above-mentioned devices.

Example 15:
Some critics admire only one another.

(44) $(\exists x^{1,2} C x^{1,2})\,[C x^1]$

(45) $(\forall x^{1,2}(\sim\! A x^{1,2}, x^{1,2}))$ (every member, $x^{1,2}$, of a subset of critics, that is, every one of some of these critics, $x^{1,2}$, does not admire $x^{1,2}$, that is, is not a self-admirer).

(46) $(\forall x[(\forall z^{1,2}(z^{1,2} \neq x)) \rightarrow (y^{1,2}(\sim\! A y^{1,2}, x))])$ (if any x is not identical with any one of them, each one of them does not admire x).

Note that in this example involving plural quantification, this approach avoids quantifying over second-order entities since the plural pronouns ('all of some of these', 'any one of them', and 'each one of them') are represented by variables that range over first-order individuals. (See the formal semantics in section 8.2 for details.)

8.2   Rules of English for Determining the PSC

We next summarize and present some rules for determining the reference of anaphorically used expressions, given the logical form of their anaphoric background sentences.[2] These rules may be used to help to determine the PSC of the variable representing the pronoun in our formalization.

---

2. Much of this section has been influenced by various proposals suggested to me by Fred Sommers. Formulations and details remain my own. See also his book, *The Logic of Natural Language* (New York: Oxford University Press, 1982).

Our first rule, suggested by examples 1, 6, and 7, involves A-B sentences that carry existential force.[3] When an A-B sentence is of the form 'some A's are B's' or any other variant formalizable as '$(\exists x(Ax\ \&\ Bx))$', and the second sentence is of the form 'they are C's' or 'some/all of them are C's', then, if the pronominal expression is used distributively, it refers back to A's that are B's. Thus the PSC for the superscripted variables of which the occurrences are bound by the existential or universal quantifier in the second sentence is simply the class of things that are As and Bs. We call the class denoted by 'A' the *pronominal subject class* and the class denoted by 'B' the *pronominal predicate class*.

Sometimes a sentence does not appear to have existential force because its surface structure, and perhaps even its deep structure, is not strictly of the form '$(\exists x(Ax\ \&\ Bx))$'. For example, the sentence 'Tom owns some sheep' in example 7 is formalized as '$(\exists x(Sx\ \&\ Otx))$', even though the surface structure subject of this sentence is not of the form 'some A'. Often we pronominalize on a noun phrase that is not the subject of the sentence, and this noun phrase serves as an existential expression even if the sentence in which the noun phrase appears does not carry existential force. For example, consider the sentences 'Every child loves a toy. Some of them are too expensive to buy.' Here 'some of them' refers to toys loved by *some* child. As in example 7, the noun phrase pronominalized on, 'some toy', is not the surface structure subject of the sentence in which it appears. We call the terms pronominalized on ('sheep' and 'toy', respectively) the *pronominal subject terms,* and we treat the noun phrases containing them as the subjects of the sentences.

Here, however, we must be careful. When we transform a sentence by taking as its subject a noun phrase containing a quantifier that is an existential expression, and the sentence in which this noun phrase appears

---

3. The notion of existential force was first suggested to me by Fred Sommers (and see p. 211). He has also suggested that a test for whether a sentence carries existential force is to consider the equivalence of any given sentence formed by "driving in" any negation sign as far as possible within the sentence in a manner that preserves logical equivalence. If the resulting equivalent sentence begins with an existential quantifier (or "there are many"), then the sentence carries existential force. For example, applying this method to a sentence of the form 'Not all A's are B's' would result in the sentence of the form 'Some A's are not B's', and thus the original sentence carries existential force.

does not carry existential force, then usually this transformation fails to preserve truth conditions. For example, a sentence expressed in the active voice is generally not equivalent to its passive transformation. "Every child loves a toy" is not equivalent to its passive transformation "Some toy is loved by every child." The latter requires for its truth that there be at least one toy that every child loves. The former merely requires for its truth that every child love some toy or other, but not necessarily the *same* toy. Thus we cannot treat the expression 'some of them' as if its A-B sentence is "some toy is loved by every child." Instead, when we have a pronominal expression pronominalizing on a noun phrase carrying existential force and the sentence in which it occurs does not carry existential force, we nevertheless treat the sentence as if it has existential force. Our rule above applied to such a case then yields as the PSC for the pronominal phrase 'some of them' the class of toys loved by some child, that is,

$$[(\exists x(Ty^1 \ \& \ Cx \ \& \ Lxy^1))].$$

Consider now an A-B sentence of the form 'Not all As are B's', as in example 6. Such a sentence makes an existential claim. Its truth requires that there exist an A that is not B. Let the second sentence be of the form 'They are C's', or 'Some/all of them are C's.'

The pronominal phrase of this second sentence refers back to A's that are not B's. Thus the PSC for the superscripted variables whose occurrences are bound by the existential or universal quantifier in the second sentence is the class of things that are A's but not B's.

Our second rule, suggested by examples 8, 9, and 10, involves A-B sentences that contain as part of their subject phrase universal quantifier expressions, such as 'all', 'every', 'each', and 'no'. Sentences containing such expressions do not require the existence of certain kinds of things in order for them to be true. When an A-B sentence is of the form 'Every (all) A(s) is (are) B(s)' or any variant formalizable as '$(\forall x(Ax \rightarrow Bx))$', and the second sentence is of the form 'they are C's' or 'some/all of them are Cs', then, if the pronominal expression is used distributively, it refers back to As. Thus the PSC for the superscripted variables the occurrences of which are bound by the existential or universal quantifier in the second sentence is the class of A things.

An A-B sentence of the form 'No A's are B's', as in example 10, also makes a universal claim. Its truth requires simply that all A's are non-B's.

Once again, the second sentence of the form stated just above refers back to A's. Hence the PSC for the superscripted variables the occurrences of which are bound by the existential or universal quantifier in the second sentence is the class of A things.

Our third rule involves A-B sentences that contain relative clauses. A relative clause that modifies a noun occurring in a noun phrase restricts the reference of any expression that pronominalizes on that noun phrase. In example 5,

Some students who are passing are learning a lot.
They will go to college.

the simple pronominal subject term (i.e., the noun part of the subject expression) of the pronoun 'they' is 'students', and the relative clause 'who are passing' modifies 'students'. Here, the relative clause combines with the simple pronominal subject to form a complex pronominal subject term. The relative clause determines the denotation of this complex subject term by restricting the class denoted by the simple pronominal subject term (i.e., the class of students) to those who are passing. The existential force of the first sentence restricts the PSC of the pronoun 'they' to the class of A's that are B's, where 'A' is the (complex) pronominal subject, and 'B' is the pronominal predicate (i.e., the class denoted by the predicate of the sentence when A is placed in subject position). Accordingly, the PSC for the pronoun 'they' is determined by two restrictions: (1) the relative clause restricts the PSC from the simple pronominal subject class to the (complex) pronominal subject class (namely, A), and (2) our first rule (i.e., the rule for "Some A's are B's. They are C's.") then restricts the PSC from the pronominal subject class to members in the extension of the pronominal predicate. The resulting PSC for the pronoun 'they' in our example is the class of students who are passing who are learning a lot.

Our fourth rule involves sentences in which a noun phrase consisting of an existential expression and a pronominal subject term is embedded within the antecedent of a truth-functional conditional expression. The rule states that in such a case, we first drop the conditional. Next, as in the previous rules, we transform the sentence by taking as its subject the noun phrase consisting of the existentially quantified expression containing the pronominal subject term. We then treat the existential quantifier expression as if it were a universal quantifier expression and nominalize on the resulting antecedent of the conditional. Finally, we preface what was the consequent of the original sentence with the phrase "is such that."

A familiar example is the donkey sentence

If Pedro owns a donkey, he beats it.

After dropping the conditional from this sentence we obtain the two sentences:

Pedro owns a donkey. He beats it.

We first treat the noun phrase containing the pronominal subject term, 'donkey', as the subject of the sentence. We apply the passive transformation of the first sentence to obtain:

A donkey is owned by Pedro.

Next, we change the existential quantifier expression 'a' to the universal quantifier expression 'every' and nominalize on the resulting expression to obtain:

Every donkey owned by Pedro.

Finally, we preface the consequent of the original sentence, "he beats it," with the phrase "is such that" to obtain:

Every donkey owned by Pedro is such that he beats it.

This sentence we may formalize as

$(\forall x((Dx \mathbin{\&} Opx) \rightarrow Bpx))$,

which is the standard formalization of the original conditional donkey sentence. The PSC for the pronoun 'it' (treating the phrase "owned by Pedro" as the relative clause "that is owned by Pedro") is the class of donkeys owned by Pedro, and the pronoun 'it' refers to every member of this class.

Last, we consider the donkey sentence

Pedro owns a donkey and he beats it.

This sentence becomes

A donkey is owned by Pedro and he beats it.

We apply rule (1) directly to the first conjunct of this sentence to obtain the PSC for the pronoun 'it' in the second conjunct. The result is the class of donkeys owned by Pedro, and the pronoun 'it' refers to a member of this class.

8.3   The Formal Language L_A

We assume a standard first-order language with identity supplemented in the following way.

We introduce as new terms a set of variables, called *superscripted variables*. A superscript is a finite sequence of distinct integers (i.e., no integer occurs more than once in a given sequence.) If s is a superscript and v is a nonsuperscripted variable, then v^s is a superscripted variable.

We next specify the language and its formation rules.

8.3.1   Vocabulary of L_A

1. (,),[,] (punctuation)
2. An infinite set of superscripted and nonsuperscripted variables: V
3. The infinite set of every finite sequence of distinct integers: S
4. An infinite number of individual constants
5. An infinite number of n-place predicates
6. An infinite number of function symbols
7. The truth-functional sentential connectives and quantifiers: ~, &, v, →, ↔, ∀, ∃
8. Identity: =
9. Modal operators: □, ◊
10. The sentential operator: A (it is actually the case that)

8.3.2 Formation Rules of L_A

The well-formed expressions are of three kinds: variables, terms, and formulas.

1. If s ε S and v ε V and v is nonsuperscripted, then v^s ε V.
2. (a) All variables and individual constants are terms.

(b) If **f** is an n-place function symbol and $\alpha_1, \ldots, \alpha_n$ are terms, then $f(\alpha_1, \ldots, \alpha_n)$ is a term.

(c) An expression is a term only if it can be shown to be a term on the basis of clauses (a) and (b).

3. If **P** is an n-place predicate and $\alpha_1, \ldots, \alpha_n$ are terms, then $P(\alpha_1, \ldots, \alpha_n)$ is a wff. (These are the atomic wffs.)

4. If Φ and Ψ are wffs, then $(\sim\Phi)$, $(\Phi \;\&\; \Psi)$, $(\Phi \;v\; \Psi)$, $(\Phi \rightarrow \Psi)$, and $(\Phi \leftrightarrow \Psi)$ are wffs.

5. If Φ is a wff and α ε V, then $(\forall\alpha\Phi)$ and $(\exists\alpha\Phi)$ are wffs.

6. If both α and β are terms, then $(\alpha = \beta)$ is a wff.
7. If Φ is a wff, then $(\Box\Phi)$ and $(\Diamond\Phi)$ are wffs.
8. If Φ is a wff, then $(\mathbf{A}\Phi)$ is a wff.

This completes the formation rules for L_A.[4]

Any open wff may be contained within brackets, where we assume any standard definition of an open wff for wffs within brackets. We also assume any standard definition of "scope," "free," and "bound" occurrences of a nonsuperscripted variable. Any standard definition of these notions for occurrences of a superscripted variable not contained in brackets, and thus any standard definition of an "open" and "closed" nonbracketed wff, must, however, as we will soon see, be modified.

8.4 Anaphoric Chains, Covarying and Free Occurrences of Variables

We define an *anaphoric chain* (hereafter, a-chain) as an ordered set of wffs such that: (i) there is at least one wff in the a-chain that contains an occurrence of a superscripted variable v^s, where s is a single integer; (ii) if s is a superscript consisting of a sequence of distinct integers of length $k > 1$, and there is an occurrence of v^s in the a-chain, then there is an occurrence of a superscripted variable, $v^{s'}$, prior to any occurrence of v^s in the chain, where s' is a sequence of distinct integers of length $k-1$ and is an initial segment of s; (iii) if a wff in the a-chain contains a superscripted variable, v^s, where s is a sequence of integers of length k, that is, the k-tuple $\langle n_1, \ldots, n_k \rangle$, then for each n_i, n_i appears only with those superscripted variables in the chain the superscript s' of which contains the initial segment $\langle n_1, \ldots, n_i \rangle$ of s.

To illustrate condition (ii), assume that a certain wff in an a-chain contains the superscripted variable $x^{3,5}$. Then the chain must contain a prior occurrence of some superscripted variable having as its superscript the number 3 (for example, x^3 or y^3 or z^3, and so on). To illustrate condition

4. We also need further syntactic machinery to deal with truth relative to a context. But the notion of the truth of a sentence in a discourse does not require anything beyond the standard analysis due to Kaplan of truth relative to a context. For the sake of simplicity, we omit any such required syntactic machinery. For details of this account, see David Kaplan, "Demonstratives," in Joseph Almog, John Perry, and Howard Wettstein, eds., *Themes from Kaplan* (New York: Oxford University Press, 1989), 481–563.

(iii), the same chain (i.e., one containing an occurrence of $x^{3,5}$) may contain the superscripted variables $x^{3,5,4}$ and $y^{3,5,4,6}$ (occurring in the chain after the occurrence of $x^{3,5}$) but the chain cannot contain, say, $x^{3,4,5}$, x^5, or $y^{5,3}$, since for any of these superscripts, either the number 3 does not occur as the first member of the sequence or, where the sequence is greater than of length one, the number 5 does not occur as the second member.

Anaphoric chains may be represented symbolically as a column of wffs. On certain lines we add a bracketed open wff representing the class of satisfiers of that bracketed open wff in order to indicate successive restrictions of the PSC for variables with the same superscript as the free superscripted variable appearing in that wff.

Under certain circumstances, our extended language treats occurrences of superscripted variables not bound by a quantifier within the (non-bracketed) wff in which these occurrences appear as bound nevertheless. Consider on line k an occurrence of a superscripted variable v_i in a wff that does not have a quantifier binding the occurrence in this wff. Further, let a wff containing a quantifier binding v_i occur on a line j preceding line k. (Hereafter, "line j preceding line k" will be "j < k".) We call an occurrence of v_i in the wff appearing on line j but not in a quantifier of that wff a *parametric covarying occurrence* of the superscripted variable v_i. We call an occurrence of v_i in a wff on line k, where the wff does not contain a quantifier binding this occurrence, a *dependent covarying occurrence* of the superscripted variable v_i.

We extend the notion of scope for quantifiers containing superscripted variables. As is standard, 'Φ' is the scope of a quantifier within the wff '$(\exists v_i \Phi)$'. *The scope of a quantifier containing a superscripted variable* '$\exists v_i$' *or* '$\forall v_i$' *is*, in addition to 'Φ', to include all and only wffs containing dependent covarying occurrences of the superscripted variable v_i—even though the quantifier is in a different wff on a preceding line of the a-chain. (We do not permit any free occurrences of 'v_i' in a wff containing dependent covarying occurrences of this variable.) Accordingly, we say that *an occurrence of a variable v_i is bound if and only if* either it appears with the quantifier expression '$\exists v_i$' or '$\forall v_i$' or it lies within the scope of such a quantifier. Otherwise, the occurrence is said to be *free*. Given a wff that lies within the scope of quantifiers Q_i and Q_j, Q_i appearing on line k has a wider scope in the given wff than a quantifier Q_j appearing on line l if and only if k < l. A dependent covarying occurrence of a superscripted variable is bound by the same quantifier binding its parametric covarying occurrence and thus covaries with it.

A wff is *closed* or is a *sentence* if and only if it contains no free occurrences of any variable. A wff is *open* if and only if it is not closed. If the only occurrences of variables not bound by a quantifier within the wff in which they occur are dependent covarying occurrences, the wff is thus nevertheless closed.

8.5   The Formal Semantics for L_A: Truth and Satisfaction for Sentences in Anaphoric Chains

In standard model theory, we are given a model, $I = \langle D, I \rangle$, consisting of a domain D of individuals and an interpretation function I that maps individual constants of a given language L into D, n-place predicate symbols P^n into ordered n-tuples $\varepsilon\ D^n$, and n-place function symbols f^n into functions with domain D^n and range D.

We also introduce the notion of a sequence, $s = \langle d_1, d_2, \ldots \rangle$ of elements in D, that is, $d_i\ \varepsilon\ D$ for each i. We can think of s as an assignment of an element in D, that is, d_i, to each variable v_i. Given this sequence, we can then define the semantic notion of truth of a wff Φ in an interpretation I, via the notion of satisfaction with respect to an assignment s.

In our model theory, however, in order to define the notion of satisfaction for a sentence containing an anaphoric expression, the range of values of superscripted variables in a given formula at a given line of an a-chain will be restricted to members of *subsets* of D. These subsets, members of which are assigned to these variables, we call *pronominal satisfier classes*. In this section, we present precise definitions of *pronominal satisfier class*, *satisfaction*, and *truth* for expressions involving anaphora.

In order to define pronominal satisfier classes, we first define the *stage of a given superscript, s, for any variable with that superscript at a given line, k, (st(s) at k) of an anaphoric chain*. Given an a-chain, let $\vec{x}$ be the sequence of free variables $x_1, \ldots, x_n$ occurring in that order in a bracketed wff on a given line. Let v^s be any variable with a given superscript s. If v^s occurs at a line k prior to any line in which there is a bracketed wff, [. . . $\vec{x}$ . . .], containing a variable with the same superscript s that occurs in $\vec{x}$, then st(s) at k = 0. (All nonsuperscripted variables may also be thought of as having stage 0.) Next, enumerate all bracketed wffs [. . . $\vec{x}$ . . .] (in the order of their occurrence in the given a-chain) in which a variable with the same superscript s occurs in $\vec{x}$. Consider a line k containing a bracketed wff in this enumeration. Then st(s) at k = n, where n is the number assigned to the bracketed wff in the above enumeration ($[\ldots \vec{x} \ldots]_{s,n}$). At a line k in which there is no bracketed wff in this enumeration, st(s) at k = the last stage for s determined prior to line k.

The *PSC for any variable with superscript s at a given stage m* ($PSC_{s,m}$) may now be defined inductively on the stage of s. This notion gives the range of values of a variable with a superscript s at a given stage in an a-chain.

When st(s) = 0, the range of any superscripted variable v_i with superscript s is the entire domain. That is, the $PSC_{s,0}$ is the entire domain. Next, let the st(s) = m, at a given line k, and let a variable with superscript s be the i-th variable x_i in $\vec{x}$ for $[\ldots \vec{x} \ldots]_{s,m}$, where $[\ldots \vec{x} \ldots]_{s,m}$, is assigned the number m in the enumeration of all bracketed wffs containing a free variable with superscript s. Then the $PSC_{s,m} = \{u : \exists n (n$ is an n-tuple that satisfies $[\ldots \vec{x} \ldots]_{s,m}$ & u = the i-th component of n} and $u \in PSC_{s,m-1}$. (Note that for a variable $x_i \in \vec{x}$ with superscript s in $[\ldots \vec{x} \ldots]_{s,1}$, the $PSC_{s,1} = \{u : \exists n (n$ is an n-tuple that satisfies $[\ldots \vec{x} \ldots]_{s,1}$ & u = i-th component of n}.)[5]

By an interpretation, *I*, for an arbitrary wff in an arbitrary a-chain, we mean an ordered triple, $I = <D, PSC, I>_{c,k}$, where $c \in$ **AC**, k is the k-th line of c, and where

i.   D is a nonempty set of objects,

ii. PSC is a class of subsets of D,

iii. AC is a class of a-chains,

iv. I assigns to each individual constant a_i an object $I(a_i) \in D$,

v.   I assigns to each n-place predicate symbol P^n a set of n-tuples from D^n,

vi. I assigns to each n-place function symbol f^n a function from D^n into D.

vii. I assigns to each bracketed open wff ($[\ldots \vec{x} \ldots]$) the class of n-tuples that satisfy the open wff in standard first-order model theory (i.e., not the notion of satisfaction relative to a line and a-chain defined later).[6]

5. In defining $PSC_{s,m}$, we have appealed to the notion of satisfaction. Here we are referring to the standard first-order notion of satisfaction according to which an n-tuple satisfies a bracketed open wff if and only if the n-tuple is in the extension assigned to the open wff according to the interpretation function I.

6. See footnote 5. Also, we need further semantic machinery to deal with truth relative to a context. For example, we also include a class of contexts, possible worlds, agents, positions and times in order to relativize the sentences in an anaphoric chain to contexts, as we do when we use the actuality operator. See also footnote 4.

We are now ready to present the satisfaction and truth definitions for an arbitrary wff in an a-chain at a given line, k. We consider an interpretation, $I = <D,PSC,I>_{c,k}$ (where $c \in AC$ and k is the k-th line of c) of our language L_A and a sequence, $s = <d_1,d_2, \ldots >$, where for each i, $d_i \in D$. As is standard, we can think of s as an assignment of an element in D to each variable v_i by extending s to a function s^* that assigns an element of D to each term t. The function, s^*, is defined inductively on the length of t as follows:

i. $s^*(x_i) = d_i$
ii. $s^*(a_j) = I(a_j)$
iii. $s^*[f^m(t_1, \ldots ,t_m)] = I(f^m)(<s^*(t_1), \ldots ,s^*(t_m)>)$

Using the new function s^*, we can give the required definitions of *satisfaction* and *truth for a wff Φ at a given line k of a given a-chain in Interpretation I* as follows (For simplicity, we define these notions for wffs in prenex normal form):

1. if t_i is a free occurrence of a variable (i.e., either a free nonsuperscripted variable or a free noncovarying occurrence of a superscripted or multiply superscripted variable) or t_i is an individual constant and Φ is an atomic wff $P^m(t_1, \ldots ,t_m)$, then s satisfies Φ at line k iff $<s^*(t_1), \ldots ,s^*(t_m)> \in I(P^m)$, and (a) if t_i is a free (noncovarying) occurrence of a superscripted variable with superscript r and $st(r) = p$ at k, then $s^*(t_i) \in PSC_{r,p}$, and (b) if t_i is of the form $v^{r,h}$, where r is a non-empty n-tuple of integers $<r_1, \ldots ,r_n>$ and the superscript 'r,h' denotes $<r_1, \ldots ,r_n,h>$ (i.e., a multiply superscripted variable) and $st(r) = p$ at k, then there is a subset S of $PSC_{r,p}$ such that $s^*(t_i) \in S$.[7]

2. s satisfies (~Φ) iff s does not satisfy Φ.

3. s satisfies (Φ & Ψ) iff s satisfies Φ and s satisfies Ψ.

4. s satisfies ($\exists v_i \Phi$), where Φ does not contain a dependent covarying variable, iff there is at least one sequence s′ differing from s in at most its i-th component, such that s′ satisfies Φ, and if v_i is a superscripted variable with superscript, r, such that $st(r) = p$ at k, then $s′^*(v_i) \in PSC_{r,p}$.

7. Our formulation of the semantics for multiply superscripted variables commits us to second-order semantics, but we do not quantify over sets. The range of the second-order variable, that is, the multiply superscripted variable, consists of individuals of a subset. This is all that is required for second-order pronominal sentences, since we are talking about all or some individuals of a subset of a given class of objects.

Remark: We note in clause (4) that if v_i is a superscripted variable, after removing the relevant quantifier $\exists v_i$ that binds occurrences of v_i in Φ, we *do not* treat those occurrences that were bound by the quantifier $\exists v_i$ *as dependent covarying occurrences of the variable* in evaluating whether s' satisfies Φ even if there is another quantifier '$\exists v_i$'appearing in a wff on line j < k in the a-chain that has the resulting wff Φ within its scope. Instead we are to treat these occurrences as free (i.e., nondependent covarying) occurrences of v_i in Φ.

5. s satisfies Φ, where Φ is a wff containing any dependent covarying variables, iff s satisfies χ at line k, where χ is the result of conjoining the wff Φ to the wff Ψ on line j, containing a quantifier binding a (dependent covarying) variable in Φ and $j \geq i$, where i is a line containing a wff with a quantifier binding a (dependent covarying) variable in Φ as follows:
Let the rightmost (innermost) quantifier in Ψ that binds a dependent covarying variable in Φ be the n-th rightmost quantifier in Ψ. Then, replace Ψ's n rightmost parentheses with the concatenation of the conjunction sign '&', the wff Φ, and n right parentheses.

6. s satisfies Φ with respect to a context c, world w, and time t iff for all worlds w' accessible to w, s satisfies Φ in w' with respect to c, w, and t.

7. s satisfies $A\Phi$ with respect to a context c, world w, and time t, iff s satisfies Φ with respect to c, t, and w_c, where w_c is the world of that context.

To illustrate clause (5), we consider again example 13.

There are boys.

There are girls.

Some boys love every girl.

They (all the girls) love some boy (or other).

The formalization of this discourse is the following:

(35) $(\exists x Bx)$

(36) $(\exists y Gy)$

(37) $(\exists x^1 (\forall y^2 L x^1 y^2))\,[Bx^1]\,[Gy^2]$

(38) $(\exists x^1 L y^2 x^1)$

The wffs on lines (35), (36), and (37) are standard applications of clause (4). We now apply clause (5) to the wff on line (38).

S satisfies $(\exists x^1 Ly^2 x^1)$ at line (38) iff $\forall s'(s'$ is a sequence $\&$ s' satisfies $(\exists x^1 Ly^2 x^1)$ $\&$ $s'^*(y^2)$ ε $PSC_{2,1} = \{girls\}$ $\&$ $\forall v(v$ is a variable $\&$ $v \neq y^2) \rightarrow s^*(v) = s'^*(v))$.

S' satisfies $(\exists x^1 Ly^2 x^1)$ iff $\exists s''(s''$ is a sequence $\&$ s'' satisfies $Ly^2 x^1$ $\&$ $s''^*(x^1)$ ε $PSC_{1,1} = \{boys\}$ $\&$ $\forall v(v$ is a variable $\&$ $v \neq x^1) \rightarrow s'^*(v) = s''^*(v))$, and

$<s''^*(y^2), s''^*(x^1)>$ ε $I(L^2)$.

Truth is defined in the standard way as follows:

A wff Φ is *true under* I, with respect to an a-chain at a given line k, context, time, and world iff Φ is satisfied by all sequences s from D.

A wff Φ is *false under* I, with respect to an a-chain at a given line k, context, time, and world iff no sequence from D satisfies Φ.

An interpretation *I* is said to be a *model* for the sequences of wffs constituting an a-chain iff every wff in the a-chain is true under the interpretation.

An a-chain c is *satisfiable* iff there is an interpretation $I = <D, PSC, I>_{c,k}$ and a sequence, s, from D such that every wff in the a-chain is satisfied by s relative to *I*.

A wff Φ is *logically valid* with respect to c and k iff Φ is true in every interpretation. We write $\models_{c,k} \Phi$.

A wff Φ is a *logical consequence* of an a-chain iff for every interpretation $I = <D, PSC, I>_{c,k}$ and every sequence s from D, if every wff in c is satisfied by s, then Φ is satisfied by s. We write $\models \Phi$.

Finally, we note that other semantical notions are extended in the obvious way to wffs with respect to an a-chain c, and a line k.

Index